Crown, Covenant and Cromwell

Crown, Covenant and Cromwell

The Civil Wars in Scotland, 1639–1651

Stuart Reid

Frontline Books, London

Crown, Covenant and Cromwell: The Civil Wars in Scotland, 1639–1651

This edition published in 2012 by Frontline Books,
an imprint of Pen & Sword Books Ltd,
47 Church Street, Barnsley, S. Yorkshire, S70 2AS
www.frontline-books.com

ISBN: 978–1–84832–687–3

CIP data records for this title are available from the British Library

For more information on our books, please visit
www.frontline-books.com, email info@frontline-books.com
or write to us at the above address.

Printed and bound by CPI Group (UK) Ltd, Croydon, CR0 4YY
Designed and typeset in 11/14 point Bembo by Wordsense Ltd, Edinburgh

Contents

List of Illustrations   vii

Chronology   ix

Introduction   xiii

1   Scotland, the Scots and the Art of War   1

2   Treason Never Doth Prosper: The Bishops' Wars   17

3   Blue Bonnets Over the Border: The Campaign in Northumberland
    and the Battle of Marston Moor   34

4   With Brode Swordis but Mercy or Remeid: Rebellion in Scotland,
    Tibbermore and Aberdeen   51

5   Bitter Winter: The Fall of Newcastle and the Ravaging of Argyll   70

6   We Gat Fechtin' Oor Fill: Auldearn and Alford   89

7   High Noon: Kilsyth and Philiphaugh   109

8   An End and a New Beginning   127

9   The King in the North   143

10 Curs'd Dunbar   159

11 The Last Hurrah: Inverkeithing and Worcester   177

Appendices

1   The Irish Brigade Under Montrose 1644–1645   197

2   News from His Majesty's Army in Scotland, by an Irish Officer
    in Alexander MacDonnel's Forces   201

3   The Scots Army at Dunbar 1650   204

Notes   209
Bibliography   231
Index   235

Illustrations

Plates

(all from the author's own collection)

1 King Charles I
2 Archibald Campbell, Marquess of Argyle
3 James Graham, Marquis of Montrose
4 Gentleman reviewing his somewhat motley levies
5 Alexander Leslie, first Earl of Leven
6 Contemporary cavalry trooper
7 Montrose wearing 'a coit and trewis as the Irishis were clad'.
8 Huntly Castle
9 Strathbogie Regiment colours 1644
10 Irish brigade colour
11 Another Irish brigade colour
12 George Keith's Regiment colours 1648
13 Fraser's Firelocks colours 1648
14 Bronze cannon 1642
15 Tin and iron core of leather gun
16 Double-barrelled leather gun
17 Soldier with Lochaber axe
18 Highland bowman
19 Scottish musketeer
20 Musket drill
21 Auldearn – Boath Doo-Cot on Castle Hill
22 Alford – the ford at Mountgarrie where Baillie crossed in 1645
23 Oliver Cromwell

24   Highland piper
25   A splendidly romantic but far from accurate depiction of a struggle
      between a Highland soldier and some of Cromwell's men
26   Forbes' Regiment colours 1650 or 1651
27   Balfour of Burleigh's Regiment colours 1650
28   Colonel John Innes' Regiment colours 1650
29   Another of Forbes' colours
30   Montrose's foot colours 1650
31   Archibald Johnston of Wariston
32   The Scots holding their young king's head to the grindstone
33   Major-General John Lambert
34   Colonel George Monck
35   Panoramic view of the battlefield of Dunbar
36   Colonel William Stewart's Regiment colours
37   Preston of Valleyfield's Regiment colours 1650
38   The Dunbar medal, struck for the officers of the victorious English army
39   King Charles II

Maps

1	Northeast Scotland	xv
2	Perth and Forfarshire	54
3	Aberdeen 1644: The Craibstane Rout	66
4	Fyvie 1644	75
5	Inverlochy 1645: 'Over the hills the nearest way'	79
6	Auldearn 1645: Early morning	93
7	Auldearn 1645: The crisis	97
8	Auldearn 1645: Counter-attack	99
9	Alford 1645	106
10	Kilsyth 1645	114
11	Dunbar 1650: Early morning	167
12	Dunbar 1650: The crisis	171
13	Inverkeithing 1651	187

Chronology

1638

28 Feb   Scots begin signing National Covenant
13 Mar   Royalist forces muster in north but are disbanded almost immediately
21 Mar   Edinburgh Castle stormed by Covenanters
26 Mar   Dumbarton Castle seized by Covenanters
15 May   Royalist victory at Turriff
20 May   Main Scots army confronts king's forces at Duns on Anglo-Scots
          border
15 Jun   Royalists defeated at Megray Hill
18 Jun   Pacification of Berwick
          First day of battle for Bridge of Dee outside Aberdeen
19 Jun   Covenanters' victory at Aberdeen

1640

20 Aug   Scots army under Alexander Leslie invades England
28 Aug   Scots victory at Newburn
30 Aug   Scots capture Newcastle upon Tyne
26 Oct   Treaty of Ripon

1641

25 Aug   Scots army disbanded and Alexander Leslie created Earl of Leven
23 Oct   Rebellion in Ireland

1642

3 Feb   Scots regiments authorised to be raised for service in Ireland

| 3 Apr | First Scots regiments land in Ulster |
| 22 Aug | King Charles I raises standard at Nottingham, formally opening English Civil War |

1643

| 18 Aug | Mobilisation of Scots army begins |
| 25 Sep | Solemn League and Covenant signed, committing Scots to intervene in England |

1644

19 Jan	Leven leads Scots army across the border at Berwick
3 Feb	Scots arrive outside Newcastle upon Tyne
19 Feb	Indecisive battle at Corbridge near Newcastle upon Tyne
28 Feb	Scots shift base to Sunderland
7/8 Mar	Royalist probe towards Sunderland halted at Humbledon Hill
19 Mar	Royalist uprising in Scotland; Marquis of Huntly occupies Aberdeen
20 Mar	In England, Scots take South Shields, closing off mouth of Tyne
25 Mar	Scots victory at Boldon Hill near Sunderland
13 Apr	Royalists under Marquis of Montrose occupy Dumfries
20 Apr	Royalists chased out of Dumfries
24 Apr	Royalists storm burgh of Montrose
29 Apr	Huntly evacuates Aberdeen and disbands forces
2 Jul	Scots and Parliamentarians win English Civil War at Marston Moor
27 Jul	Scots siege of Newcastle upon Tyne begins
29 Aug	Marquis of Montrose raises king's standard at Blair Atholl
1 Sep	Royalist victory at Tibbermore outside Perth
13 Sep	Royalist victory at Aberdeen; the Craibstane Rout
19 Oct	Newcastle upon Tyne stormed by Scots
28 Oct	Indecisive battle at Fyvie
13 Dec	Royalists seize Inveraray

1645

2 Feb	Royalist victory at Inverlochy
9 Feb	Royalists occupy Elgin
15 Mar	Royalists surprised at Aberdeen
4 Apr	Royalist assault on Dundee ends in disaster

9 May	Royalist victory at Auldearn
28 Jun	Carlisle surrenders to Scots army under David Leslie
2 Jul	Royalist victory at Alford
15 Aug	Royalist victory at Kilsyth
13 Sep	Royalists badly beaten at Philiphaugh outside Selkirk

1646

29 Apr	Royalists under Montrose lay siege to Inverness
5 May	Charles I surrenders to Scots army outside Newark and forces disband
8 May	Siege of Inverness raised
14 May	Royalists under Huntly storm Aberdeen
5 Jun	Scots army in Ireland badly defeated at Benburb
30 Jul	Montrose disbands forces at Rattray near Blairgowrie

1647

Feb	Scots army 'new modelled'
24 May	Alasdair MacColla flees to Ireland
5 Jul	Dunveg Castle surrenders, ending war in Scotland
26 Dec	Scots change sides, signing Engagement to assist Charles I regain throne

1648

23 Mar	Second Civil War begins with Royalist uprisings in England and Wales
4 May	Mobilisation of Scots army begins
12 Jun	Scots dissidents defeated by Earl of Callendar at Mauchline Moor
8 Jul	Scots army led by Marquis of Hamilton crosses border at Carlisle
17 Aug	Hamilton defeated by Cromwell at Preston
19 Aug	Scots surrender at Warrington
25 Aug	Hamilton surrenders at Uttoxeter
5 Sep	Covenanters seize Edinburgh in Whiggamore Raid
12 Sep	Royalists seize Stirling
1 Oct	Both sides agree ceasefire

1649

30 Jan	King Charles I executed by Parliament
8 May	Royalist uprising under Mackenzie of Pluscardine defeated at Balvenie

1650

27 Apr	Royalist invasion force under Montrose destroyed at Carbisdale
21 May	Marquis of Montrose executed in Edinburgh
24 Jun	King Charles II signs Covenant and lands in Scotland
25 Jun	Mobilisation of Scots army begins
22 Jul	English army under Cromwell crosses border near Berwick
26 Jul	English halted by fortified line between Edinburgh and Leith
28 Aug	English retreat to Dunbar
3 Sep	English victory at Dunbar
7 Sep	Edinburgh surrenders
18 Sep	English advance halted at Stirling
4 Oct	Attempted Royalist coup at Perth
21 Oct	Royalist victory at Newtyle
1 Dec	Scots win and then contrive to lose battle at Hamilton
13 Dec	Augustine's raid on Edinburgh
23 Dec	Edinburgh Castle surrenders

1651

1 Jan	King Charles II crowned at Scone, outside Perth
14 Apr	Scots victory at Linlithgow
19 May	Scots victory at Paisley
20 Jul	English victory at Inverkeithing
26 Jul	Cromwell marches on Perth
31 Jul	Scots army marches south for England
2 Aug	Perth surrenders
6 Aug	Scots army crosses border near Carlisle
	Stirling surrenders
1 Sep	English storm Dundee
3 Sep	Cromwell defeats Scots at Worcester
21 Nov	Marquis of Huntly surrenders
3 Dec	Earl of Balcarres surrenders last Scots field army

1652

26 May	Dunottar Castle surrenders

Introduction

This is a military history of the Great Civil War as it was fought in Scotland and by Scottish armies in England between 1639 and 1651, and while political matters are necessarily touched on from time to time in order to understand why armies were raised in the first place and sometimes despatched in particular directions, it is really about what those armies and the men who marched in them actually did to each other on the battlefield.

Historians sometimes seem to regard battles as rather too exciting to be a respectable field of study, but this remains an important but frequently neglected aspect of the story. While it might appear perfectly possible to examine the religious, political and economic issues surrounding those tumultuous times without direct reference to anything but the outcome of a particular battle, determining just how that battle was won or lost is often just as important as unravelling the underlying reasons why it came to be fought in the first place or the consequences that followed.

This is of course true of almost any conflict, but the question is particularly accented in Scotland due to the apparent unequal nature of many of the battles. The Justice Mills fight outside Aberdeen in September 1644 provides a typical example. The outcome was at first uncertain in that the Royalists were probably better soldiers but were outnumbered and faced with carrying out a frontal assault on a naturally strong position. It is therefore important to establish just how they then won their fight, for unlike the battle of Tibbermore two weeks earlier this one spilled into the streets of the burgh and resulted in widely broadcast atrocities with far-reaching political consequences.

Similarly at Dunbar in 1650 the Scots army faced the English with a number of apparent material advantages, yet were very heavily defeated, so again it is just as important to understand exactly why that unexpected result happened, as it is to understand what flowed from it.

Beyond such worthy issues battles are still worth reading about in their own right, for while the generals get the credit or blame for the outcome they were all of them fought by ordinary people who sometimes reacted to the experience in extraordinary ways. Some turned out of course to be heroes, while on the other hand as an officer named August Kaust sagely observed during the American Civil War: 'in battle men are apt to lose their heads and do very absurd things'. Therefore this story is not just about politics, strategy and tactics, but also about very human individuals such as the Royalist soldiers determined to give one of their comrades a proper burial, who fired a volley inside the kirk of Turriff, forgetting they had loaded with ball ammunition and blissfully oblivious to the fact that one of their opponents was hiding in the loft above, disguised in women's clothing!

This is, in short, a very extraordinary story of courage, adversity and absurdity too, and it should never be forgotten that it was acted out by our own ancestors, great and small, and in that sense is our story too.

As always the telling of that story has been accomplished with the help of a surprising number of others, not least David Ryan of Partisan Press and Caliver Books. He set me on the road many years ago with an innocent request to write a straightforward piece on the battle of Kilsyth, which turned out to be anything but when William Baillie's detailed report contradicted what was then the accepted version of events as postulated by the late great Samuel Rawston Gardiner. It has been a long road with many windings and side paths. I must also thank Michael Leventhal for bringing me back to my initial task, as well as the others who have contributed their assistance wittingly or otherwise, including as ever the staff of the library of the Literary and Philosophical Society of Newcastle upon Tyne.

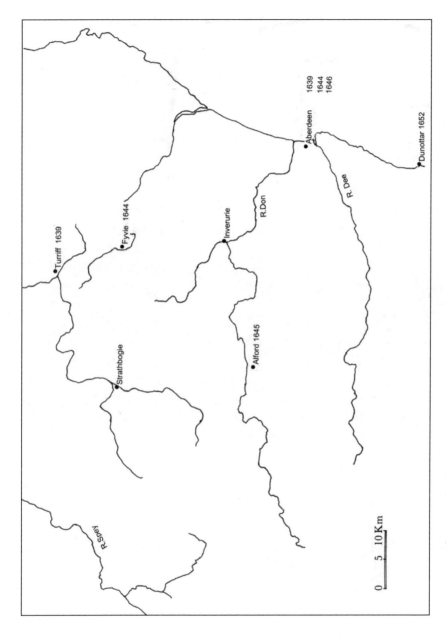

MAP I: *Northeast Scotland.*

Chapter 1

Scotland, the Scots
and the Art of War

When James VI of Scotland found himself become King James I of England in 1603 he undoubtedly regarded it as a happy event long anticipated if not entirely welcomed on both sides of the border. Half a century earlier England had gone to war with the aim of forcing the Scots to agree to a marriage between their then infant Queen Mary and her cousin, the marginally less infant King Edward, but despite inflicting a crushing defeat at Pinkie Cleugh, just outside Musselburgh, on 10 September 1547, the attempted coercion ended in failure. The Scots refused to surrender.[1] Instead Mary married first a French prince and then her cousin, Henry Stewart, Lord Darnley. As the son and heir of the Earl of Lennox, Darnley had a fair claim to the Scottish throne in his own right, but it was the fact that both he and Mary were also grandchildren of King Henry VIII's sister, Margaret Tudor, that eventually brought their son James, the Scottish king, to the English throne in succession to the childless Queen Elizabeth.

Hurrying south to take up his eagerly awaited inheritance before a native-born English candidate might emerge James was also making a fortunate escape from the seemingly endless round of rebellions, kidnappings, assassination attempts and coups, which passed for court life in sixteenth-century Scotland. The sad fact of the matter was that traditionally the Scots took a far more robust view of kingship than might be supposed from the later cult of romantic Jacobitism. Instead while the authority of the Crown was outwardly unquestioned, the man (or woman) who wore it was often a different matter entirely. All too often regime change in Scotland was effected by securing physical possession of the king and thenceforth acting in his name. After that austere and often exciting experience an opulent English court schooled in the cult of *Gloriana* must have seemed to James like something akin to paradise. While the king's new courtiers might be just as disposed to intrigue and treachery as his old ones, they at least stopped well short of open warfare in the precincts of the palace and he could at last retire to his bed without too much fear of awakening to a ring of armed men intent on securing his person dead or alive.

Instead, as he boasted from Westminster in 1607: 'Here I sit and govern it with my pen: I write and it is done: and by a Clerk of the Council I govern Scotland, which others could not do by the Sword.'[2] It was perfectly true, but Scotland had not become England. James was king of both countries but they were not yet politically united – as they might have been had Edward married the young Mary. James' Scottish kingdom remained an entirely separate realm in law, language and custom and, as he himself recognised only too well, this new-found complaisance was going to be enjoyed only for so long as he gave his Scottish subjects no cause to set aside old rivalries and combine against his distant authority. Consequently he stepped carefully with his proposed reforms and innovations, such as the reintroduction of bishops, but unfortunately his son and successor, King Charles I, had no such inhibitions. Having been brought south of the border at the tender age of three, Charles never fully appreciated the all-important political and cultural differences between his two kingdoms, and moreover utterly lacked the pragmatism that underpinned his father's governance. King James, memorably lampooned as the 'Wisest Fool in Christendom', might have hopefully espoused the doctrine of the divine right of kings, but he still had the great good sense not to push his luck by actually trying to govern his kingdoms accordingly. Charles on the other hand really did appear to believe that as God's anointed he could do no wrong, and so he embraced Absolutism long before Louis XIV of France made it respectable. As a result his belated Edinburgh coronation in 1633, fully eight years after James had shuffled off his mortal coil, was the prelude to disaster – to the National Covenant and to two decades of war.[3]

Covenant and Country

The widespread signing of the Covenant in 1638 – outwardly no more than an affirmation of Scottish adherence to the reformed church – unquestionably signalled the beginning of what one chronicler of the time aptly termed the 'Trubles'. While it is easy to view the struggle simply as a religious war, it has rightly been remarked that in seventeenth-century Scotland 'ecclesiastical issues alone, and ministers alone, could never bring about a revolution'.[4] Instead the

Covenant was also a response to a wide-ranging set of secular as well as religious grievances, which came about and grew over a long number of years. It is a measure of Charles' political ineptitude that he encompassed his own downfall by initiating what was intended to be a revolution in both church and state – while simultaneously alienating all four of the country's 'Estates'.

Unlike Charles' moribund English Parliament, the Scots legislature comprised not two discrete houses but four collegiate 'Estates'. Traditionally there had been three, although the tenants in chief – that is those holding lands directly from the Crown – were themselves divided between the nobility, sitting in their own right as lords of Parliament, and the lesser tenants, who elected only a proportion of their number to serve as representatives for each shire, thus creating in effect another Estate. The others were the representatives of the royal burghs; and the representatives of the church or Kirk. It was the latter who proved controversial. Before the Protestant Reformation it was the bishops as lords spiritual who sat in Parliament, just as they did in England, but ousting the bishops in favour of Calvinist presbyteries gave this Estate into the hands not only of ministers of religion who owed no allegiance but to their God and their presbytery, but also opened it to the lesser lairds, burgesses and tradesmen serving as lay elders of the Kirk.

Almost by default John Calvin's religious teaching had also brought about a far greater degree of democratic accountability in secular government, little dented by King James' reintroduction of bishops as presidents of their presbyteries in 1610. Outwardly this particular measure might appear to have restored the political status quo, but in reality it was a compromise under which the new bishops found themselves to a degree accountable to their presbyteries on both temporal and spiritual matters.

Charles on the other hand had an altogether different notion of the power and the authority of the bishops, whom he regarded from the outset of his reign principally as an executive arm of his own personal authority. Simply put, his view was that since he was the head of the church, its officials were therefore his to command.

However another important cause of what was to follow can also be traced back to Charles' accession to the Scottish throne in 1625 and to the Act of Revocation which accompanied it. The frequency with which Scotland was ruled by regents, acting in the name of infant monarchs, led to the convention that between the ages of twenty-one and twenty-five the king could revoke all gifts of land and property made during his minority, because he may have been unduly influenced by whoever was acting as regent at the time. There was no justification for such a Revocation in Charles' case because he was already of age and indeed almost out of time when he succeeded his father. However not only did he go ahead and proclaim one in 1626, but against all precedent he also extended it backwards to encompass all disposals of both royal and ecclesiastical lands that had been made since 1540!

The significance of this distant and seeming arbitrary point in time was that it predated the death of King James V in 1542 and the Rough Wooing which followed as first England and then France sought to gain control of Scotland. It was a period of near anarchy, complicated by the Protestant Reformation and by power struggles between the various factions intent on securing the regency, which would later be dramatised by William Shakespeare as the central theme of *Macbeth*.[5] In the end Scotland's independence was maintained but it was a ruinously expensive business which saw the old Catholic Kirk shorn of its vast landholdings; taxed, mortgaged and otherwise secularised first to help pay for the war against England and latterly to the benefit of the Protestant Lords of the Congregation, who then fought to secure the Reformation and expel their soi-disant French allies. Now although most of those lost lands were to remain in the actual possession of their present occupiers, all the feus and other taxes attaching to them were to revert directly to the Crown. While the analogy is not an exact one, Charles was in effect proposing to convert the tenure of the lost lands from freehold to leasehold. By way of softening the blow, compensation for their revenues valued at ten years' purchase was promised to the present owners, but the Exchequer was all but bankrupt and this was sagely regarded as unlikely to materialise. More importantly in a culture where the number of a man's tenants and followers was still generally accounted of rather greater importance than more material indicators of wealth, the potential loss of those tenants and followers was a very serious matter indeed.

Outwardly Charles' belated return to Scotland in 1633 might have begun promisingly enough with all the pomp and splendour a coronation demanded, and the Edinburgh militia even tricked themselves out in new white satin doublets, black velvet breeches, silk stockings and feathered hats especially for the occasion.[6] No sooner had the necessary ceremonies been observed and the king departed southwards again than the real trouble began, for by then, in addition to the still festering matter of the Revocation, a number of other serious grievances had arisen.

Insofar as he ever deigned to explain himself at all, Charles' ostensible justification for the dubious recovery of those former ecclesiastical lands was to enable him to employ their revenues to provide proper stipends for ministers of the church and also to finance radical changes in religious practice in parallel with Archbishop Laud's concurrent remodelling of the Church of England. Such changes would see the return of full Episcopal government of the church untrammelled by presbyteries, together with a prescribed book of common prayer and Anglican forms of worship which appeared little altered from those of the Catholic Church.

Unfortunately for the king's ambition, this enforced counter-reformation, suspected by many as heralding a complete return to Catholicism, alienated the Protestant population at large and deepened the resentment of those whose revenues were ostensibly to be diverted to the purpose. By November 1637 opposition to the king's policies was nearly universal. Instructions to use the prayer book had generally been ignored and the few attempts to read it only provoked rioting. Royal authority evaporated and in the absence of a formally constituted parliament the ordinary running of the country was soon being conducted by noblemen, lairds, burgesses and ministers serving together on a variety of *ad hoc* boards or 'Tables'.

Finally, in flat defiance of the law forbidding the signing of private bands or agreements binding men to support each other either personally or in pursuit of a common object, on 28 February 1638 the first signatures were being applied to a general band[7] known as the National Covenant, pledging the Scots nation to the defence of the Protestant religion. The king was not explicitly challenged by the text of this Covenant, but as the perceived threat to the reformed Kirk came from him alone there was no mistaking the significance of what was being signed.

Throughout that year negotiations aimed at averting the impending crisis were conducted between the Tables and the king's commissioner, James, Marquis of Hamilton. In fairness to the much criticised Hamilton, he was in an impossible position with nothing but the empty authority of the Crown to back him up against men whose ancestors had once declared at Arbroath that the king of Scots ruled only by the consent of his people and that he could be deposed if he misused the powers entrusted to him. Moreover Hamilton was not unsympathetic to their cause and consequently the role he played was an equivocal one – on the one hand publicly acting for the king in the council chamber and yet at the same time secretly encouraging the Covenanters, as the dissidents were now known, to stick by their demands.

The result was inevitable. Charles, finding his servants unwilling or unable to uphold his authority, resolved to crush the Covenanters by force, while they for their part equally stoutly resolved to resist him. And so before embarking on the campaigns of Leslie, Montrose and Cromwell, a brief look at Scotland's strategic geography and the art of war as it was to be practised in the mid-seventeenth century is in order.

Going to the Wars

Other than a few garrison soldiers and ceremonial bodyguards, there were no standing armies on either side at the outset of what eventually grew to become the War of the Three Kingdoms. It is a commonplace to preface histories of the time with comments as to the lack of military knowledge or experience to be found in countries that had been at peace for generations. In a broad sense this was true, but there were always soldiers in Ireland and an expeditionary force had been mustered for a half-hearted war with France in the 1620s. Far more importantly, in addition to countless individuals who had tried their luck in the seemingly never-ending wars in the Netherlands, or Germany, or even farther afield in Poland and Muscovy, military contractors (including the Marquis of Hamilton) had recruited whole regiments for the Swedish service in the 1630s. There was therefore a deep pool of professional expertise available to raise, mould and train armies according to the very latest doctrines, and as war became inevitable both sides scrambled to secure the services of these veterans.

Most of them as it happens were Scots, and, while many having no doubt left their country for their country's good never returned home again, more than enough of them responded to the Covenanters' invitation and 'cam in gryte numberis vpone hope of bloodie war, thinking (as thay war all Scottis soldiouris that cam) to mak wp thair fortunes vpone the rwin of our kingdome.'[8] There were sufficient in fact to permit the Covenanters the luxury of interlarding every regiment with professional soldiers who knew their business. If a nobleman was placed at the head of a regiment then his second-in-command would be a veteran of the German wars, and if each company within that regiment was led by a bonnet laird, then he too would have an old soldier for his ensign and one or two others as sergeants. South of the border the process was never as formalised, but Charles too did his best to ensure that in 1639 his infantry regiments at the very least were led by experienced soldiers.

The rank and file of course were a different matter. In England the king's regiments were at first intended to be drawn from the county Trained Bands – a militia supposedly drawn from the propertied classes who had a proper stake in defending the country and maintaining the peace: 'none of the meaner sort, nor servants; but only such as be of the Gentrie, Freeholders, and good Farmers, or their sonnes, that are like to be resident'. Each of those respectable country gentlemen was assessed according to his means as being capable of providing arms for himself, either as a cavalryman or a foot soldier, and if wealthy enough for his sons and tenants too. Inevitably, although the law required personal service, all too often those who actually appeared were Oliver Cromwell's infamous 'decayed serving men and tapsters', or as a professional soldier named William Barriffe grumbled: 'Porters, Colliars, Water-bearers, & Broom men, are thrust into the rooms of men of better quality, as though they themselves were too good to do the King and their Country service.'[9] They behaved dismally during the first encounters with the Scots in 1639 and 1640, and therefore when the civil wars got under way in earnest in the 1640s King Charles settled for taking their weapons and equipment and instead left it to his officers to recruit the men they needed by whatever means they chose. His rebellious English Parliament did likewise, and initially filled the ranks of its regiments with enthusiastic volunteers. In the fullness of time, as that early enthusiasm waned, both parties eventually resorted to an *ad hoc* form of conscription, simply demanding that the local authorities turn over the men required without troubling themselves overmuch as to how they were to be found.

In Scotland, although in some areas the very first regiments were through necessity levied directly by local noblemen and lairds from among their tenants and dependants, most soldiers were raised under the old fencible system. By custom and law, and irrespective of status, all those men aged between the traditional ages of sixteen and sixty were liable to turn out as required for up to forty days' service. In January 1639 as the crisis deepened instructions were circulated by the Tables for the forming of local committees of war. They were charged with managing the process by first carrying out a series of preliminary musters or Wapenschaws (weapon-showings) to establish the extent of the available manpower, whittle them down to a manageable pool of young and unmarried men who were actually fit for service, and then as directed by the government to levy out one man in four or occasionally one in eight from the rolls and form them into regiments.

The local committees of war were also responsible for clothing, equipping, feeding and even paying them for those forty days. John Spalding recorded of a contingent raised in Aberdeen in 1644 that each soldier was provided with two shirts, coat, breeches, stockings and bonnet, bands and shoes . . . each was to have six shillings (Scots) a day, and each twelve a baggage horse and cooking utensils.[10] It sounded impressive, but if their services were required beyond that forty-day period responsibility then passed to the central government, often with indifferent results.

With some few exceptions, this system was to operate throughout the wars. As a result Scottish regiments always had a strong regional identity, albeit if insufficient men for a regiment could be levied from one sherrifdom, then the government would instruct that two contingents might be combined. Thus in 1644 for example the Master of Yester would find himself commanding a regiment composed of quite separate contingents from Linlithgowshire and Tweeddale, while a proportion of the Aberdeenshire levies were traditionally allocated to the regiments raised by the Keith family in order to cover the shortfall from their own Mearns.[11] This was particularly true of cavalry units as it was difficult for the individual committees to assemble and equip large numbers, and very typically the Earl of Balcarres' Regiment was allocated four troops from Fife, four more from the Mearns and part of Aberdeenshire, just twenty men from Forfar, and two other troops whose origins are unknown.

The exceptions were a number of regiments raised for what could be described as general service, outwith the restrictions of the fencible system. In 1640 and 1643 a small number of units were raised as a security force ahead of the general mustering to ensure that it proceeded smoothly, and in 1642 seven regiments were recruited by voluntary enlistment for indefinite service in Ireland.

On both sides of the border the infantry regiments into which most of these levies were gathered were theoretically supposed to comprise ten companies mustering as many as 1,500 men in total.[12] In actual practice such numbers were rarely seen after the initial mustering, if at all. On all sides there was a pernicious tendency to form any fresh levies into completely new regiments, commanded by newly appointed officers, rather than forwarding the recruits to reinforce existing regiments.[13] Consequently, without those reinforcements, wastage in veteran units could be quite dramatic. On campaign a strength of anything between 200 and 500 men was common, with the latter being considered a large regiment, and instead of forming two wings of battalions as recommended in the drill books of the day, most regiments could muster just a single battalion, or were even joined together in a composite one formed of detachments or remnants of more than one regiment.

New regiments of course inevitably went through the same process of decay, often accelerated by the fact that the best officers had already found billets in the early levies, leaving the newer ones to be commanded by men whose political connections counted for more than their ability. Moreover the emphasis on raising fresh regiments meant that the numbers of officers rose in quite inverse proportion to the falling off in numbers of rank and file. Eventually the only solution was to reorganise or 'new model' the armies, a process that achieved near mythical status in the English Parliamentarian army, but which was primarily an accounting process that saw the wholesale disbandment of unviable units and the transfer of their personnel to bring others back up to their proper establishment. While the wage bill of the rank and file was unchanged, the reduction in the number of regiments in which they were serving inevitably led to mass redundancies among the surplus officers. Inevitably this once again introduced a political element, as each faction strove to ensure that its own candidates were appointed to the remaining posts.[14]

Weapons of War

At the time all infantrymen were equipped or at least expected to be equipped either as pikemen or as musketeers. The former, armed with 5-metre-long weapons and sometimes still wearing body armour, were held to be the more prestigious arm, and if a gentleman was to serve as an ordinary volunteer on foot he would strike a classical pose with a pike rather than fumble with a grimy musket. The length of the pike was calculated to outreach a cavalryman's lance. In addition to that defensive role, pikemen still supposedly performed an important offensive role as shock-troops. In battle they were drawn out of their parent companies and grouped together in a single body or 'stand' in the centre of the battalion and were intended to roll forward irresistibly at the decisive moment and engage the enemy at 'push of pike'. Such an encounter was graphically described in an account of the battle of Langside, near Glasgow, in 1568 where: 'They met with equal courage, and encountered with levelled lances, striving, like contending bulls, which should bear the other down.'[15] Surprisingly enough the intention was not that the opposing front ranks should mutually impale each other (something that was physically quite difficult as well as morally improbable), but that they would quite literally push the enemy backwards and so burst the opposing formation apart by main force, putting them 'on thair backis'. Seemingly only then did the blood-letting begin as the victorious party dropped their pikes to set about their hapless losers with their swords.

Nevertheless, just as the lethal qualities of the bayonet were to be overestimated in the following centuries, the storied 'push of pike' between two resolute bodies of pikemen was becoming an increasingly infrequent occurrence in the 1640s. Successful attacks normally depended on the accompanying musketeers first winning the firefight, with the result that when the pikemen were finally ordered forward the battle was already decided and their already shaken opponents would like as not drop their pikes and run before any contact was made. Inevitably this near redundancy meant that those soldiers who could not find an excuse to carry muskets took to more or less unilaterally lopping a metre or so off their long pikes in order to lighten them and make them more manageable. This was a 'damned thing to be suffered' in the opinion of one officer who fought at Benburb in Northern Ireland in 1646. He bitterly attributed the defeat there both to the Scots' pikes being broad-headed, 'which are the worst in the world', and far more importantly to the fact that the Irish, recently re-equipped with brand-new Spanish weapons, had supposedly *not* yet shortened their own pikes and so enjoyed a crucial advantage when the two sides met.

However such accidents were rare, and instead infantry combat was almost always decided through firepower rather the lethal application of cold steel. Consequently, although contemporary doctrine throughout the war and afterwards still called for one-third of the rank and file in each regiment to be armed with pikes, in reality by the mid 1640s only dire necessity compelled the large-scale issue of the weapons – as in 1645 when the Earl of Seaforth was sent equal numbers of muskets and pikes to arm his northern levies. Conversely in that same year the 7,500 infantry of the English 'new model' army were completely re-equipped from scratch with 5,650 muskets but only 2,000 pikes – a ratio of nearly 3:1 rather than 2:1 – and there seems to have been nothing unusual in this. Indeed after the first campaigns it was becoming increasingly common to find regiments entirely composed of musketeers, with no pikemen in their ranks at all, notwithstanding the alleged shortcomings of the matchlock musket.

It is rather too easy to overemphasise those shortcomings, especially on viewing the elaborately illustrated drill books of the time. A single-shot weapon discharged by a simple firing mechanism which brought the burning end of a hempen fuse, known as slow-match,[16] into contact with an open pan filled with a priming charge of gunpowder. This, in flashing through a small 'touch-hole', ignited the main charge earlier tipped down the barrel and tamped down with the weapon's scouring stick or rammer. One major problem was that in poor weather the matchlock was very susceptible to misfiring through wet match failing to burn or wet powder forming an inert black mush. Even in moderately damp conditions the slow-match will often not burn hotly enough to ignite dry gunpowder. In windy weather it was also said to be possible for the priming powder to be blown out of the pan. In less extreme conditions another drawback was that it consumed formidable quantities of slow-match, particularly if it was kept waiting in readiness for any length of time. For that reason it was common to extinguish the match if action was not considered imminent, which of course meant that, should a body of musketeers be attacked unexpectedly at night or on the march, their weapons would be useless until their slow-match could be lighted again.

On the other hand, beyond these frequently trumpeted drawbacks, the matchlock was comparatively cheap, robust, soldier-proof and in reasonable weather surprisingly reliable. Notwithstanding the elaborate step-by-step explanations in those drill books, after a couple of hours' training it could also be loaded relatively quickly and, if the soldier was dextrous and not overly scrupulous, fired about twice in the space of a minute rather than the several minutes carelessly offered in many secondary sources.[17] Moreover it was actually reasonably accurate out to about fifty metres, and its one ounce soft lead ball was a very effective man-stopper indeed.

At the outset the prevailing tactical doctrines required infantry regiments to form up in six ranks deep, partly for the sake of solidity in the case of the pikemen and partly as we shall see to accommodate the reloading of matchlock muskets. However as units became progressively weaker on campaign it was common not only to combine them but to find them instead forming five deep, or in some cases only four or even three deep, in order to preserve a reasonably broad front. As a general rule of thumb and allowing for intervals between sub-units, one metre should be allowed for each soldier in the front rank and ordinarily a regiment or battalion of 500 men would therefore have occupied a frontage of about a hundred metres.

In the early days all musketeers were trained to fire by a process called *extraduction*, whereby the men in the first rank fired a volley then dropped to the rear to reload while the second rank shuffled forward to do the same, in the pious expectation that by the time the sixth rank had moved up to the front and fired, the original first rank would be standing behind them ready to carry on the cycle. If carried out correctly a steady succession of volleys could be fired with some regularity, but while it no doubt looked very clever on the exercise ground, in battle it was usually a rather different matter and increasing use was made of massed volleys or salvees, by three or even four ranks firing together or at least firing in very quick succession. This experiment was initially compelled by the fact that, if the number of ranks had to be reduced to four or even three deep in order to maintain a broad front, it was quite impractical to fire by extraduction, but it was soon realised that if delivered in this manner their fire could have a much more decisive effect.[18]

Instead of reloading after delivering their salvee, if all was well they would then launch an immediate assault through their own smoke, sometimes moving steadily and holding their ranks in good order, but at other times simply falling on 'happy go lucky' at a run. Attacks of this kind were to be particularly associated first with the Irish troops serving under the Marquis of Montrose in the days when he fought for the king, and also with the Highland levies who came to join him. Indeed this has been held to be the forerunner of the celebrated Highland charge, but it was a common tactic just as frequently used on the continent and south of the border as well. At the battle of Naseby in June 1645 for example the English Royalist infantry, who largely comprised musketeers, with very few pikemen among them, launched just such an attack on their Parliamentarian counterparts – marching up close, firing a single volley and then charging straight in.

As to those Highlanders, they were certainly a familiar sight in Scots armies but ordinarily they served only as lightly equipped auxiliaries with a well-deserved reputation for unreliability, as would be illustrated by their prompt departure from the battlefield at Megray Hill. Their supposed predilection for charging straight at their foes sword in hand was in fact simply a reflection of the fact that they were neither trained nor equipped to fight in any other way and were quite incapable of standing off and engaging in a firefight. Individually Highland soldiers were just as brave and just as amenable to training and military discipline as any others if mustered into the ranks of 'standing' or regular regiments. There were however practical difficulties in mustering, organising and training clansmen from the west Highlands, as they were both remote from the centres of administration and socially and geographically fragmented. In time of dire necessity it was possible to summon forth clan levies from those areas, but generally speaking they lacked everything except raw courage to be effective soldiers.

This may at first appear a sweeping contradiction in the light of the Marquis of Montrose's victories in the mid 1640s, but as will become apparent in due course it is an assessment justified by the facts. Strikingly a detailed survey carried out in five Perthshire parishes in 1638 minutely lists the weapons held by each armed man: out of the 451 men only eleven lacked swords, but as only 124 of them also boasted targes or shields to accompany them it may safely be concluded that the remainder were actually armed with dirks or daggers rather than broadswords. Similarly only a quarter of them (and they for the most part the same men possessing both sword and targe) had muskets, although a fair few had bows. Most were a poorly armed rabble of ghillies – the forerunners of the old men and 'perfect herd-boys' unwillingly dragged on to the field of Culloden a century later.

Before leaving the subject of the infantry, Highland or otherwise, it is perhaps worth noting that each of the companies within a regiment had its own flag or colour. In the Scots service that colour carried by the colonel's company was white (like a German *leibfahne*) and often as not bore his own arms or crest, but otherwise they generally followed a common pattern with various marks to distinguish between the different companies. Then as now these colours were regarded as the spiritual embodiment of the company and were fiercely defended. Therefore the capture of colours was significant in that each one taken was not merely a trophy but represented an enemy company so badly cut up or demoralised that it was no longer capable of defending its flag and by implication was to all intents and purposes destroyed. The number of colours captured in a battle was therefore often a clearer indication of the scale of a victory than mere casualties alone, and moreover one which could be triumphantly displayed before all.

Those victories were rarely attributable to the use of artillery, and contemporary accounts telling of men such as John Seton of Pitmeddan being cut in two by a cannon shot tend to be couched in terms of astonishment rather than horror. It is in fact rather difficult to find instances of many casualties being inflicted by cannon – on Scottish battlefields at any rate. Heavy guns were of course indispensable for siege work but of little importance on the battlefield, being quite immobile once emplaced and far from effective.

By and large the only way to transport them any distance was to carry them by sea, as Leven did in 1644 and Cromwell did in the opposite direction during the campaigns of 1650 and 1651. This was largely because most cannon were literally too heavy to drag around the countryside, particularly in Scotland where the majority of roads south of the Forth and all of them north of it were only capable of being traversed by pack-horses. For that reason the Scots artillery expert Sandie Hamilton introduced a class of light 3-pounders carried on pack *fframes*, and his successor James Wemyss a series of twin- and quad-barrelled leather guns. Both were designed for infantry support, but seem to have been too light to be effective, and those captured at Dunbar in 1650 seem to have been regarded simply as curiosities.

Cavalrymen on the other hand were unquestionably useful, being organised in troops of up to seventy officers and men with anything from three to eight troops forming a regiment. In England as in Germany there were in theory two classes of horse soldier; cuirassiers or heavy cavalry, armoured from head to foot and carrying sword and pistols; and harquebusiers or light cavalry, wearing protective buff leather coats with just a corselet or breastplate and helmet, but armed with a carbine in addition to the obligatory sword and pistols. The cuirassiers were the supposedly more important of the two, with the harquebusiers intended to provide fire support and cover their flanks. Although there were a few individual troops of cuirassiers raised in the early days, the harquebusiers as exemplified by Cromwell's Ironsides soon took on the heavy cavalry role.

North of the border it was a very similar story, but with an interesting twist. Once again the overwhelming majority of cavalry was raised as harquebusiers[19] wearing buff coats and armed with carbine and pistols – and often an excessive number of firearms at that. In 1639 John Spalding saw some troopers laden down with 'fyve schot at the leist', including carbines, two pistols by their sides (presumably thrust into their boot tops) and two more in holsters at the front of their saddles.[20] However, according to the mustering instructions issued by Edinburgh in 1643, troopers were to muster with only a single pair of pistols 'of ane lairge boare', broadswords and steel caps, just as they were in England.

While there was no real difference between Scots and English infantry other than the fact that the former were almost invariably dressed in hodden grey and wearing blue bonnets on their heads, there was a significant difference between their respective cavalry, or rather their horses. English troopers were mounted on large strong horses and in battle they locked their formation up tightly, riding knee to knee and advancing at no more than a steady trot. If the opposition did not obligingly run away before contact was made they would then try to push back the enemy formation in order to burst it apart – very much in fact as pikemen did.[21] Being generally mounted on smaller horses – 'light but weak nags' as Lord Saye and Sele commented after Marston Moor – and often less well armoured, the Scots were at a considerable disadvantage in such a deliberate fight against heavy cavalry in which weight quite literally counted for everything.

For that reason at Marston Moor, where the Scots cavalry were posted in reserve, their commander General David Leslie deliberately avoided committing his troopers directly into the scrum in favour of throwing them against the flanks instead – which he did to great effect. After their service in England during the First Civil War the Scots cavalry sought to improve on this lesson. While it had originally been hoped to equip all of them with pistols and carbines, in practice each of Leslie's regiments had been mustered into two squadrons (each formed by pairing off the individual troops), one of which comprised harquebusiers with carbines, while the other was equipped as light horse lancers.[22] Subsequently, in order to compensate for the disparity in weight, *all* Scots cavalrymen were equipped with lances. As they then proved at Preston in 1648, the faster-moving lancers often had a good chance of beating their heavy opponents in the first rush, particularly if the unit being attacked was caught while not properly 'locked up' or had already been disordered by an earlier fight. Equally obviously however if that initial onset was successfully withstood, and it came back down to a matter of pushing, the greater weight of the English troopers would still inevitably triumph in the end, particularly as the later Scots cavalry regiments were very weak, with those raised in 1648 mustering just three troops apiece.

With the harquebusiers taking on the heavy cavalry role, their original supporting and scouting role was soon taken on by another variant of cavalry designated as dragoons. At the start of the wars dragooners were actually mounted infantry rather than proper cavalry, and ammunition warrants recorded in the various ordnance papers reveal that most were originally equipped with matchlock muskets like infantrymen. In the absence of any information to the contrary it may also safely be assumed that they were dressed as infantry and lacked helmets and body armour. Initially they were very popular as they could be raised and mounted more easily and cheaply than conventional cavalry, but the mounted infantry role soon fell out of favour, partly because large regimental-sized formations were found by experience to be unwieldy and partly through the age-old reluctance of any soldier to get off a horse. Otherwise the practice grew up on both sides of the border of attaching just a single troop of dragoons to heavy cavalry regiments in order to act as light cavalry and perform the scouting and skirmishing duties once performed by harquebusiers, which would otherwise wear out heavy cavalry and their horses before they ever got near the battlefield. If they sometimes still dismounted that was only because the situation might occasionally demand it, rather than it was expected of them as a matter of course.

The process of evolution is usefully illustrated by the history of Colonel Hugh Fraser's Dragoons. It was the only full regiment to be raised in Scotland in 1644, and as Fraser and his men came from the Inverness area it is hard to avoid the suspicion that they were only designated as dragooners in the first place because it was impossible to find sufficient good horses there to mount a proper cavalry regiment. Be that as it may, they did good service as mounted infantry at Marston Moor and are credited with shooting down enough of the Royalist Whitecoats to let Leslie's Horse get in among them. However as the campaign progressed they followed the usual pattern of gradually assimilating themselves into the cavalry proper. A muster report of January 1646, less than four months after the battle of Philiphaugh, notes that they 'were lately Dragoones and not yet armed as troopers; more than that there's some have pistols by ther sides nor have they horses fit for troopers'. Unfortunately the ordnance papers do not reveal when they turned in their matchlock muskets and nor do they record when or indeed where they acquired all those pistols thrust into their boot tops. It is likely however that the process was a gradual one and that their formal redesignation as a regiment of horse was more in the nature of recognising the inevitable rather than a signal promotion.

And so, with the armies assembled – horse, foot, dragoons and the occasional gun – it is time to look at the campaigns in which they fought.

Chapter 2
Treason Never Doth Prosper
The Bishops' Wars

It was a complicated plan which had ambitions to be a cunning plan. The king himself proposed to come north with an army in the spring of 1639 to reimpose his royal authority on those he regarded as rebels, but even he recognised the danger of turning the dispute into a national conflict between his two kingdoms. There was to be no outright invasion of Scotland by an English army, but rather a counter-revolution from within. On the one hand political and religious concessions were promised to woo the uncertain and to split moderates from extremists, while the carrot of reasonableness was to be seconded by a stick in the form of not one army but three. An Irish army, led by his viceroy Thomas Wentworth, was to land at Dumbarton in the Clyde in order to provide a disciplined force around which the MacDonalds and other supposedly loyal western clans might rally. At the same time, the Marquis of Hamilton was to sail north to Aberdeen with 5,000 English soldiers and join with an army to be levied there in the king's name by George Gordon, Marquis of Huntly. Only then, with his loyal forces already on the march in Scotland and his enemies in confusion, would the king himself cross the border to finish the business.

Instead, like many of Charles' complex intrigues, it fell apart at the first touch and very largely thanks to an 'old little crooked souldier' named Alexander Leslie. An illegitimate son of George Leslie of Drummuir[1] born in Aberdeenshire in about 1582, he went for a soldier in Holland in 1605 and three years later was in the Swedish service. He remained there for the next thirty years, serving with some considerable distinction before retiring with the rank of field marshal and a fair fortune. In 1636 a daughter had married the Earl of Rothes, one of the more prominent Covenanting leaders, and thus, while personally indifferent to religion, Leslie was drawn into their service. At first he acted merely in an advisory capacity, and it was he who put the word out to those other veterans, inviting them to come home to train and lead the county levies, but that background role changed dramatically on 21 March 1639.

Edinburgh is dominated by its castle and still had the king's garrison in it when a number of the more prominent Covenanters went up in a body that morning and politely invited the governor, Captain Archibald Haldane, to render it up to the Tables. There is some suggestion they thought him likely to do so, or at least open to fair persuasion, but if so they were disappointed when he peremptorily refused. Not so Leslie. While the great and the good were parlaying he had quietly brought up some companies of infantry and concealed them in the narrow wynds or passages at the head of the High Street. Then he and two other mercenaries, Alexander Hamilton and Robert Monro, having mingled with the party, quietly attached a petard or shaped charge to the outer gate,[2] and as everyone else drifted off back down the hill Leslie casually lit the fuse. The gate blew in; an inner gate quickly succumbed to axes, hammers and battering rams, and within moments Leslie and his men were receiving the astonished surrender of the governor.

As a propaganda coup it took quite some beating, and the feat has never been repeated, but an equally bloodless and scarcely less significant capture took place five days later. As was his habit, on Sunday 26 March a pious gentleman named Steuart, who happened to be the governor of Dumbarton Castle, peaceably went out to attend divine service at a nearby church. His enemies, being rather more worldly than they are generally credited, were waiting, and as soon as Steuart was out of sight of the castle he was seized, stripped and forced 'to divulge the password'. His clothes were then donned by another gentleman 'of his schape and quantetie'. Once it was dark enough to hide his face this bold spark called out for admittance, and as soon as the gate was opened to receive him in rushed the Covenanters as successfully as at Edinburgh.[3] To all intents and purposes the castle changed hands as smoothly as if it were changing its guard, and Wentworth's Irish army was deprived of its bridgehead.

That just left the Marquis of Huntly in the north, but he too had also contrived to get himself arrested! In retrospect his lacklustre behaviour and seeming lack of decisiveness form a sorry contrast to that of his great rival, Montrose, but from the beginning he suffered from a number of crippling disadvantages. While Aberdeen and its university were held to be a stronghold of Episcopalianism, and he could count on a wide circle of relatives and dependants to obey any summons, these advantages were balanced on the one hand by an equally large number of families who were traditionally at odds with the house of Gordon, and on the other by the plain if unpalatable fact that, if there was no great enthusiasm for the Covenant in the countryside, there was even less popular support for the king.

Nevertheless at first Huntly tried his best. When the local Covenanters convened a meeting at Turriff on 14 February and packed the place with some 800 heavily armed men under the Earls of Montrose and Kinghorn, no one was particularly surprised when Huntly also turned up. The question was what was he going to do? According to that invaluable chronicler John Spalding, Huntly had been innocently attending a funeral in Aberdeen the previous day with his two eldest sons and a number of other Gordon lairds. Turriff lay on his direct route home and so he took the opportunity to summon their followers to put on a show of strength of his own. Packing a town with rival sets of supporters, each intent on staking out their territory and intimidating all and sundry, was a very traditional technique in Scottish politics, as dramatically witnessed by the infamous 'Cleanse the Causway' fight between the Hamiltons and the Douglases a century before. Ordinarily there was a great deal more snarling at each other and brawling in back wynds than actual bloodshed, and on this occasion Huntly's followers were accordingly instructed to muster only with muskets and swords rather than more serious hardware. Unfortunately Turriff was neither Edinburgh nor Stirling, and nor was it Aberdeen for that matter. Getting themselves in there first gave the Covenanters a crucial advantage, for they had secured all of the available accommodation (and taken over all the ale houses) long before the Gordons turned up. Huntly was very politely offered the use of the young Earl of Erroll's house to 'refresh himself', but there was no way he was going to be able to bring his supporters into the already packed town. Instead he had to content himself by leading them 'hard under the dyckes of the churchyarde, westward within two picke lenth to Montrose company without salutatione or worde speaking on either side'.[4]

The first round, clearly, had gone to the Covenanters. Then on 9 March Sir Alexander Gordon of Cluny arrived at Aberdeen on board one of the king's yachts, escorting a collier laden with 1,000 pikes and 2,000 muskets and other warlike supplies, which might have been sufficient to alter the local balance of power decisively in Huntly's favour, if only some of the promised troops had accompanied it. Instead as Patrick Gordon of Ruthven observed: 'He was constrained to make the best of an evill day; raising such forces as he could upon the sudden, and many of them but coldlie affected and all of them, through a long continued peace, ignorant of all militarye discipline.'[5]

There was also, still, at this stage a very natural reluctance to disturb that 'long continued peace'. No one needed any reminding that a brutal war had been raging in Germany for the past twenty years, with hundreds of thousands killed, towns burned and whole states devastated to no good purpose. Perhaps not surprisingly, after debating the matter, they rather sensibly decided that they knew their duty, but it was no time for pointless gestures and so agreed to go home again. A number of the keener loyalists, including sixty volunteers from Aberdeen itself, 'weill armed with suord, musket and bandolier' took ship for the south.[6] Otherwise Huntly's forces had seemingly evaporated by the time the Earl of Montrose and Alexander Leslie arrived at the burgh on 30 March at the head of two or three thousand men, marching under five flags bearing the inscription *For Christs Croun and Couenant* and wearing blue ribbons hung about their necks and under their left arms as a pointed distinction from the 'reid flesche cullour' ribbons earlier worn by Huntly's people. They then proceeded to busy themselves agreeably enough in living at free quarter, seizing arms and indulging in a little discreet plundering. All the while Huntly did his best to reach an accommodation, frequently conferring with the Covenanting leaders under safe conduct, and as he plainly no longer represented a threat Leslie took himself back off south with all the infantry and guns on 12 April, to rejoin the army assembling at Edinburgh. Montrose and the Earl of Kinghorn on the other hand were intended to be left behind with just a few hundred cavalry to keep an eye on the area, but Montrose had no intention of acting as a policeman when glory beckoned on the border and next day Huntly was arrested and packed off to Edinburgh Castle.

Notwithstanding his noisy protestations of outrage at this treatment, and the animus he subsequently displayed towards Montrose, the marquis probably regarded his genteel incarceration with a degree of equanimity for it safely extricated him from what was seemingly turning into an impossible position. On the other hand the move backfired spectacularly for the Covenanters, for no sooner was Huntly safely out of the way and Montrose down at Dundee busy recruiting men for the expedition to the border, than the wilder spirits among the Gordons decided to fight after all.

The insurrection however got off to an inauspicious start when a man named David Prat earned the dubious distinction of being the very first man to be killed in the wars during a failed attack on Towie Barclay Castle on 10 May. In response, the local Covenanters assembled some 1,200 men at nearby Turriff under Lord Fraser and a number of the Forbes lairds – all of them traditional rivals of the Gordons – whereupon the insurgents equally promptly resolved to attack them. At this stage with just 800 men they were badly outnumbered, but they had a trump card in the form of the Strathbogie Regiment. Although most of them were indeed 'ignorant of all militarye discipline', a professional soldier – Colonel William Johnston – had equipped six companies of infantry with the king's muskets and pikes and was now whipping them into shape.

Rather optimistically the Gordons' first impulse was to sally forth there and then from their base in the burgh of Strathbogie[7] and attack the Covenanters under cover of darkness. However just as they were on the point of setting out it suddenly occurred to them that it might be a sensible idea to appoint a commander to take charge of the expedition. As the only one who really knew what he was doing, Colonel Johnston might have seemed the obvious choice, but he was seemingly regarded as no more than the hired help and instead one of the first candidates to be proposed was Huntly's brother, Lord Adam Gordon. Unfortunately, while he may have had the breeding, his brains were 'craicted'. Because Huntly's only available son, Lord Lewis Gordon, was just a twelve-year-old schoolboy, Sir George Ogilvy of Banff was acclaimed instead. As the loudest advocate of fighting (and the architect of the Towie Barclay business) he won ready acceptance, but, since he was not actually a Gordon, Sir John of Haddo was also appointed to command with him jointly.

The Trot of Turriff

By the time the leadership question had been debated and settled and the even weightier question of their authority for taking up arms in the first place briskly dismissed, it was about ten o'clock at night. After a 'troublesome' march, they eventually got the length of Turriff by the 'piep of day' on 14 May 1639. At that point the carriage of one of their four small cannon broke and inevitably instead of leaving it by the roadside the two leaders called a halt while it was fixed again 'as weall at the time wold permitte'. Fortunately most the Covenanters were still asleep, while others were drinking and smoking or even excitedly walking up and down, and no one noticed the army hanging about on their doorstep until a sudden peal of trumpets and the loud rattle of the Strathbogie drums greeted the dawn's early light.

Naturally enough wild confusion erupted within the town, but unlike the Gordons they had not yet gotten around to appointing any leaders so that 'as it befalls in such cases, all commanded, and no bodye obeyed'. In the meantime the insurgents realised to their dismay they were in the wrong place to launch an assault, for Turriff stood 'upon highe and steepe ground upon the north side of the valleye. They could not enter it in aeqwalle termes upon any side but either on the north or upon the easte, but best upon the east side, though it wer the ende of the village farrest removed from them, who wer come from the west that night.'[8]

There was no alternative therefore but for a thoroughly exasperated Colonel Johnston to march his Strathbogie Regiment right around to the far (eastern) side of the town, which allowed the Covenanters to form a hasty battle line in the broad main street of the village and start throwing up a quick barricade. Two musket shots fired at the insurgents from the Earl of Erroll's house were promptly answered by two cannon shots, and the battle was on. Johnston's half-trained soldiers immediately charged forward, tore down the barricade and sent a volley crashing down the street accompanied by a third cannon shot. Two of the Covenanters' leaders, Hay of Delgaty and Keith of Ludquharn, did their best to rally their men 'first by faire persuasione, and then by threttings, but all in vaine'. Instead, a fourth and final cannon shot and the appearance of the two small troops of Gordon cavalry finished the business as the Covenanters incontinently fled in all directions.

Predictably enough there were very few casualties in the affair, which was soon dubbed the 'Trot of Turriff'. Just two of the Covenanters were killed, while Spalding cattily added that Lord Fraser was reported to have filled his breeches as he fled.[9] On the winning side only one casualty was reported, and he, poor fellow, was supposedly killed 'by the unskillfullnesse of his owne comerades fyring ther musketts'. The speed of the victory seems to have taken everyone by surprise and finding themselves at something of a loose end after their swift victory the Gordons accorded the unfortunate a full military funeral, culminating in two volleys being fired in salute over his grave. However not only were those volleys fired *inside* the tiny church, but the soldiers had unthinkingly loaded with ball ammunition rather than blanks and the bullets ripped up through the ceiling to the understandable terror of the minister, Mr Thomas Michell, 'who all the whyle with his sonne, disgwised in a woman's habite had gott upp and was lurkinge above the syling'.[10]

After that there was nothing to do but thoroughly plunder the place, more or less as a matter of course, and then march on Aberdeen, where they were joined by Huntly's rather delinquent youngest son, Lord Lewis Gordon, and several hundred Highland clansmen under Donald Farquharson of Monaltrie. Unfortunately that seemingly marked the limit of their ambition. They might have quite literally beaten the king's enemies before breakfast, but beyond that they still had no clear idea of what they were actually supposed to achieve and so very soon afterwards they dispersed again.

No sooner had they gone when the Covenanters, led this time by another local magnate, William Keith, the Earl Marischal, reoccupied the burgh in the name of the government and were soon joined by Montrose and Kinghorn with an army optimistically estimated as 4,000 strong with thirteen guns. The good citizens of Aberdeen were thoroughly unimpressed and according to Spalding tied blue ribbons around their dogs' necks 'in despyte and derisioun'. Montrose, alas, thereupon suffered a major sense of humour failure, and, after his men had killed all the unfortunate animals they could find, he imposed a swingeing fine and allowed his dog catchers to plunder those known or suspected to be anti-Covenanters.[11] Once that was done, but no longer sporting blue ribbons, they marched north in search of the Gordons and their friends.

Hardly had Montrose set off than word came that another of Huntly's sons, Lord Aboyne,[12] had appeared off the coast in one of the king's ships. Jumping to the entirely natural conclusion that this foretold the landing of Hamilton's 5,000 English troops, Montrose immediately abandoned his punitive expedition and hurried back south to round up more men in the Mearns and his native Forfarshire.

Hamilton however was already out of the game. Mustering the three Trained Band regiments levied from Kent, Suffolk and Cambridgeshire which had been assigned to him took longer than anticipated, and reduced their professional commanders to near despair. Sir Simon Harcourt complained that his regiment's arms were defective and old fashioned, the muskets too heavy and the pikes rotten. Edward Rossingham similarly reported that, when the Kent Trained Bands were inspected at Gravesend, their ranks were filled with substitutes hired at £8, £10 or £12 a head and equipped with totally unserviceable weapons: 'many of their muskets having no touch-holes, and some others having them so large as one might turn ones thumb in them, and the pikes were so rotten as they were shaken many of them all in pieces'.[13]

This sorry crowd did not begin embarking until 18 April, which was already two weeks after Huntly was arrested. Learning of the fact, Hamilton instead dropped anchor off Leith on 1 May. Ostensibly his purpose was to issue a proclamation in Edinburgh calling on all to submit to the king's authority or face the customary consequences. Far from being overawed, the Covenanters not only refused to allow Hamilton to land, but also numbered among their ranks his own mother, who was reported riding 'with her pistollis and carbine' and expressing a unmaternal willingness to blow her son's brains out.[14]

Whether or not he was intimidated by his mother's theatrical display, Hamilton was certainly alive to the political consequences of being seen to invade his country at the head of an English army. Accordingly he took the hint and stayed where he was, riding at anchor while two of his regiments were recalled to join the king, and Aboyne sailed north alone except for a few Scottish professional officers and the bold volunteers, who had fled Aberdeen back in March. It was hardly an army, but it was a start. The Gordon lairds dutifully mustered their men to join him, and by mid June Aberdeen was yet again under military occupation in the king's name. This time they were serious.

Megray Hill

Whether he actually contemplated marching all the way to Edinburgh or as is more likely simply wanted to make his presence felt is unclear, but probably rather late on Friday 14 June 1639 Aboyne marched south out of Aberdeen at the head of some 2,500 horse and foot, including 500 Highlanders under Farquharson of Monaltrie. The Earl Marischal, barring their advance in the small fishing village of Stonehaven, for his part could muster only half that number, even after Montrose hurried up with a few reinforcements, and a brisk assault should have been sufficient to clear them out. Indeed the Marischal left word that the gates of his nearby castle at Dunottar were to be left open in anticipation of a hasty retreat. Instead next morning the king's men came no closer than Megray Hill, a little to the north, drew up in order of battle and then waited while their leaders went off to find some breakfast!

Afterwards the pro-Gordon chroniclers were rather too quick to attribute this odd behaviour to the malign influence of Colonel William Gunn, a professional soldier from Sutherland who had come north with Aboyne to act as his military adviser. However it is equally likely that finding the enemy waiting for them they simply stopped to take stock of the situation. Thus far none of the fighting had been serious: a few musket shots fired from a castle and the near comic affair at Turriff, which between them had seen a total of only four men killed, hardly counted for much. A deliberate battle such as they were now shaping up for was going to be a very different matter, and Aboyne can be forgiven for pausing to think first, and to work out a suitably cunning plan.

In the meantime some skirmishing broke out between small parties of cavalry, but as ever both sides were still careful not to engage too closely and contented themselves with exchanging ineffectual pistol shots at long range. However, over the breakfast table, Colonel Johnston proposed that the skirmishing should be maintained to fix the Covenanters' attention while the infantry slid around to the west and attacked the village from the flank rather than head on. So when a second party came out from Stonehaven, and this time forced the 'Anti-Covenanter' horsemen to retire, he was quick to send in a reinforcement of his own – probably the troop of 'volunteer gentlemen cuirassiers' who had taken the van with a handkerchief tied to a lance by way of a standard. Once again the Covenanters fell back, this time drawing their opponents into an ambush. As soon as they came within range of the Stonehaven position Montrose let fly with both artillery and musket fire. Once again it was harmless enough but noisy and exciting; and the Gordons very promptly retired in a disorderly fashion with only the loss of their dignity and a few individuals unseated by the 'restlessness' of their horses.

However, having successfully extricated his horsemen, Johnston was dismayed on looking round to see that, instead of briskly marching around to the flank, the infantry were still standing on Megray Hill, cheering his men on but otherwise not stirring. This was doubly unfortunate for now the Covenanters' artillery started shooting at them as well.

While no formal order of battle has survived we know that the 220 musketeers of the Aberdeen Militia stood on the right of the front line with the Strathbogie Regiment on the left and the rest of the low country foot between them.[15] The 500-odd Highlanders, far from being employed as shock-troops, were tucked away in the rear, and any doubts as to their steadiness were dramatically vindicated when the whole lot responded to the cannonade by running away as fast as their legs would carry them. They were eventually brought to bay in a bog, a kilometre to the rear, but all of Aboyne's entreaties and threats proved unavailing and there they stayed until mid-afternoon, when they 'beganne to dropp awaye and marche off in whole companies'. According to Rothiemay only two or three of the low country foot were killed or maimed by the artillery fire, but the flight of the Highlanders 'made the rest of the foote for to reele'. Colonel Gunn was forced to draw them out of range, back as far as a farm at Logie, and there they too soon began to drop away.

It is hard to blame them. Troops will usually accept casualties when advancing or at least waiting for the order to advance, and they will likewise accept casualties if ordered to hold their ground against an attack; but if their leaders were not going to fight, then getting themselves killed or maimed to no purpose was pretty pointless. Recognising that the army was liable to dissolve at any moment, Aboyne gave the order to retreat and a disorderly one it was too, albeit most of the cavalry were persuaded to hold together as a rearguard while they all straggled back to Aberdeen.

The Brig o' Dee

For their part the Covenanters were understandably nonplussed by this easy victory and at first seemingly unaware that the Gordons had actually gone. As a result it was not until two days later, on 17 June, that Montrose got moving again and by then Aboyne was starting to pull his forces together. The Highlanders were gone beyond recall, straggling back up Deeside and plundering as they went, but some 4,000 foot were said to be mustered at Leggatsden, a traditional rendezvous to the northwest of Aberdeen. Unfortunately when the news came in of the Covenanters' advance all that were immediately available in the burgh itself were what remained of the cavalry, some 400 men of the Strathbogie Regiment, now under a Captain Nathaniel Gordon, and an independent company under a Captain Grant.

Until now, although Aberdeen had been occupied and reoccupied by every army and armed gang that passed, no one had yet fought for the place as the burgh was unfortified and to all intents and purposes indefensible. Its only real protection from an army moving up from the south was the river Dee, and as the Covenanters approached Aboyne rounded up every man he could find and marched them out three kilometres along the road known as the Hardgate to Bishop Elphinstone's seven-arched, brown sandstone bridge. There were at least two fords nearby, but as the river was in spate at the time it was the only practicable crossing point and an easily defended one at that. The bridge itself was typically narrow with a fortified gateway at the south end and passing bays or 'ravelins' over every buttress, all of them stuffed with musketeers drawn from the Aberdeen Militia, while the north bank of the river was lined with the Strathbogie Regiment and Captain Grant's men, and the cavalry standing well back in reserve. The position's only weaknesses were that it was overlooked by high ground on both sides of the river and that Aboyne had too few men to hold it properly.

Nevertheless throughout 18 June a succession of hasty assaults by the Covenanters got nowhere, and Rothiemay gleefully recounted how the Aberdeen men, now under the immediate command of Colonel Johnston, took particular pleasure in shooting up a company of their hated rivals from Dundee.[16]

There was even something of a holiday atmosphere to the affair, especially after the wives and servants of the militia brought supplies of food, drink and other refreshments, but shortly afterwards it turned sour when a burgess named John Forbes was shot through the head by the Covenanting Laird of Dunsmill. Incensed by the fact that Dunsmill had taken deliberate aim at Forbes, one of the Strathbogie men retaliated by equally deliberately shooting dead a Captain James Ramsay on the Covenanters' side of the river. There it ended, but Forbes' death was to have further repercussions, for early next morning half of the militia returned to Aberdeen intending to give him a proper funeral, leaving just fifty men on the bridge itself.

Disappointed by the ineffectiveness of his poorly placed artillery, Montrose had it shifted during the night and, taking advantage of the fact that it never gets properly dark at that latitude in summer, he had it repositioned to fire directly at the bridge. On the previous day all it had achieved was to demolish one of the two stone watch towers flanking the entrance, but now almost as soon as the cannonade was resumed the gate was blown in and thereafter the heavy cannonballs 'scoured the bridge all along'. It must have been an interesting experience for the musketeers crouching in the ravelins, but as long as they remained packed into them they were safe enough. Aboyne however recognised that a renewed assault on the bridge was now imminent and so moved his cavalry forward to reinforce the Strathbogie men.

Montrose for his part responded by ordering his own cavalry to move upstream as though making for a nearby ford at Banchory Devenick, and Colonel Gunn in turn insisted on shadowing them with the Gordon Horse. Hardly had they started when an unlucky cannon shot cut John Seton of Pitmeddan in two, and the whole lot then scattered, crying out that Gunn had betrayed them. Encouraged by this, one of Montrose's professional officers, Colonel John Middleton, assembled a storming party and with splendid timing the artillery demolished the remaining gate-tower, burying Colonel Johnston in the rubble. He was quickly dug out by his men, but finding one of his legs broken they flung him over a horse. As Johnston was hastened away he called out: 'Gallantis do for your selffis, and haist yow to the toune.'[17] Unsurprisingly they obeyed with some alacrity and ran from the bridge even as Middleton approached. The Strathbogie men ran with them and when the Gordon cavalry, having pulled themselves together, proposed to counter-attack as the Covenanters debouched from the bridge, Gunn instead ordered them back to the town. This produced an unseemly row, with Gordon of Arradoul yelling that he was a traitor and Gunn employing what Rothiemay called his old trick of threatening to complain to the king if his orders were not obeyed.

In the end they went north, abandoning Aberdeen to the Covenanters. Spalding recorded that three more of the militia were killed that day, with some others wounded and forty-eight taken prisoner (presumably most of those who had not taken themselves off to Forbes' funeral), while Gordon of Sallagh reckoned fourteen of the Strathbogie men killed over the two days. The Covenanters' losses are unknown, but may have been heavier as the Rev. Robert Baillie spoke of 'some slaughter on both sides', and a contemporary newsbook mentions 'divers killed whom they buried in the mosses'.[18] Unlike the anticlimactic victory at Megray Hill this had been a real battle with just enough killed and wounded to make it respectable without dampening any of the excitement. Montrose's soldiers could now claim to be veterans and entitled to their just rewards. Nothing loath he readily agreed but then primly insisted that the plundering of the burgh should be delayed until the following morning when it could all be done in broad daylight and under proper supervision. Alas for their ambitions; at two o'clock in the morning a ship arrived from Berwick bearing the happy news that a ceasefire had been agreed, even before the battle was fought.

Finding his royal authority somewhat weaker than he supposed, the king had succeeded in mustering only some 8,000 men of the Trained Bands at Berwick, albeit another 5,000 were daily expected out of Yorkshire and two of Hamilton's regiments under Harcourt and Morton were recalled to reinforce them. Against them Alexander Leslie, who had at last been formally commissioned as 'generall off all the Scotis forces, armies, troupes, regimentis and companies, alsweill foot as hors and alsweill natives as foreigners, who sall serue or assist vs',[19] reckoned to have 12,000 men, largely mustered on Duns Law, just above the border and well placed to block an advance up the coast or fall on any attempt to take the Soutra road.

Inevitably there was some bickering between patrols and detachments, but as in the northeast at this stage both sides were extremely anxious to avoid an all-out fight and, while a small detachment was pushed across the border to observe the Scots mustering on Duns Law, Charles still hesitated to bring the army into Scotland uninvited. The trouble was of course that the invitation never came, and a minor skirmish near Kelso on 3 June, when a 3,000 strong detachment under the Earl of Holland fled after being fired on by less than half their number of Scots musketeers, only confirmed the futility of the king's position.

Negotiation it had to be, and, while the talks were spun out for two weeks, the outcome was never in doubt. In the so-called Pacification of Berwick, signed on 18 June, Charles apparently conceded that ecclesiastical matters should be settled by assemblies of the Kirk and secular matters by Parliament, but it soon became clear that too much rested on his verbal assurances. Parliament was duly convened in Edinburgh on 31 August, but Charles himself declined to attend in person lest he be forced to make substantive concessions. Instead he substituted John Stewart, Earl of Traquair, a commissioner whose actions could be repudiated if he conceded too much. Predictably enough the Parliament promptly insisted on ratifying the acts of the general assembly – asserting the primacy of the presbyteries and repudiating the bishops. Unable or unwilling to sanction this clear contradiction of the king's wishes, Traquair thereupon prorogued the Parliament. However, instead of meekly dispersing until the following August as directed, the members reconstituted themselves as a less formal Committee of Estates, which served as a continuation of the earlier Tables. It was just as well that they did, for the king had resolved on another war in order to reimpose his tattered authority.

To War Again: Newburn Ford

By January 1640 a Council of War in Whitehall had sketched out a fresh plan of campaign and estimated that an army of some 20,000 foot and 2,500 horse was going to be required to deal with the Scots. Edinburgh Castle, having been duly handed back to the king immediately after the treaty, was reprovisioned and repaired and provided with a professional soldier named Patrick Ruthven as its new governor. Ennobled for the purpose as Lord Ettrick, Ruthven was an altogether tougher proposition than the hapless Captain Haldane, and in early February 1640 ships arrived in Leith carrying a hundred English soldiers, ammunition and other supplies. Fearing that Ruthven might bombard Edinburgh the surprised Covenanters allowed these reinforcements to proceed up to the castle, but they had already begun to make their own preparations for a fight. By Leslie's advice, food and lodgings were provided for the professional soldiers over the winter, and now they were instructed to once again take their levies in hand. He himself was reappointed as general, and in April the raising of troops began in earnest.

This time there was no real opposition to the new regime within Scotland itself. A regiment was sent north to Aberdeenshire, and the Earl of Argyle's clansmen to Perthshire and the Angus glens, where some of the king's more prominent supporters had their lands plundered, but it was literally no more than a series of sporadic police actions, for the anti-Covenanters were effectively leaderless.

Instead the real focus of attention was the army despatched to the border, where Leslie soon assembled some 15,000 men. Essentially the moral victory over the king's forces at Berwick in the previous year had been a colossal bluff and had Charles not accepted their offer to negotiate there would have been no alternative but to fight or withdraw for lack of sufficient supplies. This time around the Covenanters faced exactly the same problem in subsisting their army. While the greater number were again quartered at Duns, other regiments were scattered all across the East March, with Lord Ker's Regiment at Kelso, Lothian's at Jedburgh and at least four others as far back as Haddington and Dunbar.[20] With nothing much facing him, other than the all too formidable fortress of Berwick, Leslie took the bold step of invading England. Ironically, while the king had waited in vain for his Scottish supporters to justify his crossing the border, the Scots were first careful to obtain the tacit if not altogether open endorsement of the king's English opponents.

On 20 August, the same day Charles himself set out from London, Leslie crossed the Tweed at three points. The Earl of Montrose, having diced for the honour, took the first regiment across at Cornhill, while other units did so at Wark and Carham. Once on English soil they moved swiftly. According to intelligence reports Newcastle upon Tyne was virtually undefended, and Leslie correctly reckoned that a direct threat to the city would bring about a swift confrontation. No one however could have anticipated what actually happened. The local commander, Viscount Conway, steadily fell back before him, and within the week Leslie was standing on the north bank of the Tyne at Newburn, just a few kilometres upstream from Newcastle.

Inside the city Sir Jacob Astley was hard at work throwing up a ring of earthwork forts to protect the mediaeval walls, and strengthening the castle, but while he was confident of its security he and Conway were keenly aware of the likelihood that the Scots would simply bypass them. Cavalry watched the fords between Newcastle and Hexham, and some 3,500 men under Viscount Conway covered the tidal ones at Ryton Willows below Newburn. Conway apparently had just two regiments of cavalry; his own and Lord Wilmot's, and two of infantry commanded by Colonel Thomas Lunsford and Sir Thomas Glemham. He was also promised a further 2,000 men under Astley, but rightly judging himself hopelessly outnumbered he soon resolved to abandon the position and fall back into Newcastle. In the circumstances this was probably the only realistic option, but instead just at that moment the future historian, John Rushworth, arrived with orders from the Earl of Strafford (safely back in York with the king) positively instructing Conway to stand and fight.

Strafford was under the erroneous impression that Leslie was intending to cross at Hexham, and as Rushworth readily admitted:

> The Scots, having the advantage of the rising ground above Newbourne, easily discerned the posture and motion of the English Army below in the Valley on the Southside [of] the River, but the posture of the Scots Army the English could not discern, by reason of the Houses, Hedges, and Inclosures in and about Newbourne. The Scots brought some Cannon into Newbourne Town, and planted some in the Church Steeple a small distance from the River Tyne, their Musqueteers were placed in the Church, Houses, Lanes and Hedges in and about Newbourne.[21]

With the tide running too high for the Scots to cross there was still a last chance for Conway to disengage, but instead time was wasted in a council of war until eventually a Scots officer with a black plume in his hat was seen taking a rather too keen interest in the depth of the water. He was promptly shot and then everyone else joined in as a body of Scots cavalry made a tentative attempt to force their way across before coming under an enthusiastic musket fire. Concluding the water was still too deep for infantry, Leslie unmasked his big guns:

> The Scots played with their Cannon upon the English Breast-works and Sconce . . . the King's Army played with their Cannon to beat the Scots out of the Church-steeple; thus they continued firing on both sides, till it grew to be near low water, and by that time the Scots with their Cannon had made a breach in the greater Sconce which Colonel Lunsford commanded, wherein many of his men were killed and began to retire, yet the Colonel prevailed with them to stand to their Armes, but presently after, a Captain, a Lieutenant, and some other officers more were slain at that work. Then the Souldiers took occasion to complain that they put upon double duty, and had stood there all night and that day to that time, and that no souldiers were sent from the Army at Newcastle to relieve them; but Colonel Lunsford again prevailed with them not to desert their Works, but another Cannon-shot hitting in the Works amongst the souldiers, and killing some more of them, they threw down their Armes and would abide in the Fort no longer.[22]

Someone blew the powder magazine as it was being evacuated, and Leslie then turned his guns on the remaining sconce, which soon crumbled under the weight of fire directed on it. By now it was about four in the afternoon and the tide had fallen sufficiently to allow infantry as well as horsemen to cross the ford, so Leslie judged it time to order an advance, headed by his own regiment of horse, and his lifeguard, commanded by Sir Thomas Hope, supported by a third regiment of horse under Sir James Ramsay.[23] Quite coincidentally one of Conway's two cavalry regiments, commanded by Lord Wilmot, had been ordered forward to try and recover the cannon abandoned in the larger fort, and instead charged the lifeguard as they emerged from the ford, driving them back. Wilmot afterwards claimed to have cut down two of the Scots with his own hand, but Leslie was already pushing infantry across under the Earls of Lindsay and Loudoun, and a second charge apparently broke up without even making contact with the Scots.[24]

That signalled the beginning of the end of the battle for they tried to rally on the higher ground above, only to be charged and broken a second time by the Scots Horse. Wilmot and at least two of his senior officers were captured, and this time the fugitives also carried away Conway's own regiment of horse as well as riding over their already retreating infantry. All in all Conway seems to have lost about sixty killed and thirty or forty captured in the battle.[25] It could easily have turned into a massacre, but, sensitive to the political need to avoid spilling too much English blood, Leslie restrained the pursuit. While the cavalry fled all the way to Durham, Conway was allowed to disengage and get the remnants of his infantry and two guns back to Newcastle.

Much good it did him. The inevitable council of war quickly concluded that the place was untenable for while Astley had done some useful work to the walls the fact that most of the city was built on the north side of a gorge meant that it was wide open to any bombardment from the southern side. Immediate evacuation was decided on, and so back they tumbled all the way to Durham and beyond while a pleasantly surprised Leslie sent Sir William Douglas to demand the city's surrender. For form's sake the mayor and corporation at first demurred, protesting their loyalty to the king's majesty, while Douglas equally politely regretted the circumstances of their disagreement and artlessly alluded to the destructive power of artillery. The decencies having thus been observed, on Sunday 30 August 1640 a Scots army entered Newcastle in triumph for the first time in many centuries of cross-border conflict.

In the days that followed, Scots detachments also took possession of Tynemouth Castle, Durham and Sunderland. All manner of public monies and stores were seized, but it was scrupulously done by the book, with none of the private enterprise practised on the king's Scottish subjects. In short they were all on their very best behaviour and anxious to demonstrate that they were engaged in a dispute with the king rather than with the Kingdom of England. Charles for once took the hint and conceded that the river Tees should mark the boundary between the Scots army and his own and that they might subsist themselves in the counties of Northumberland and Durham at the rate of £850 per day until a treaty, addressing the Scots demands and acknowledging the independence of the Kirk, could be signed and ratified, a protracted process that took almost a year until 10 August 1641.

Despite having so signally failed to defeat the Scots in battle, Charles could still not admit himself beaten and no sooner was the Treaty of Ripon ratified than he set off for Scotland, met with Leslie at Newcastle and then accompanied the army home to Edinburgh. His purpose soon became clear; although the army was disbanded on 27 August (almost exactly a year to the day since its triumph at Newburn) three regiments were retained in service.[26] On 11 October Leslie learned that the commander of one of them, a mercenary named Colonel John Cochrane, was planning to kill or seize a number of the Covenanters' leaders, including astonishingly enough Hamilton and his brother Lanark. Exactly what was really going on has never been adequately explained, but the upshot of the 'Incident' was that Cochrane was arrested, Hamilton and Lanark fled, and Leslie was ennobled by the king as Earl of Leven! What might have happened next is an interesting question which must remain unanswered, for on 28 October the king's early morning round of golf was interrupted by news that the Irish Catholics, encouraged by the Scots' successful defiance, had launched an altogether much bloodier and more dangerous rebellion of their own.

Chapter 3

Blue Bonnets Over the Border

The Campaign in Northumberland
and the Battle of Marston Moor

The immediate reaction to the outbreak of rebellion in Ireland was one of horror, for while the dispute between the king and the Covenanters was a relatively civilised affair concerned with exploring the limits of secular and ecclesiastical power within a Protestant kingdom, the Irish business was seen as a true religious war accompanied by all manner of horrors and ethnic cleansing. The true scale of the massacres and the numbers of Protestant refugees harried out into the snow that winter was certainly exaggerated, but there is no doubting that there was a factual basis for the often lurid atrocity stories. Consequently, although mistaken, a great many influential people in Scotland and England came to honestly believe that Ireland was become Germany – that tens of thousands of Protestants were barbarously murdered by their Catholic neighbours – and they reacted accordingly.

The three regiments of the Scots army that escaped disbanding in August were immediately despatched to Ulster, while a further seven fresh regiments were ordered to be raised under Leven himself. England too was to provide an army for Ireland, but the raising of that one led directly to an even greater war. In order to pay off the victorious Scots and ratify the Treaty of Ripon, Charles had been constrained to call another Parliament, which promptly insisted in asserting its own rights in the face of a visibly weakened Crown. The king considered that all military forces should come under his royal authority, but Parliament, while willing to pay for an army for the specific purpose of succouring the beleaguered Irish Protestants, was uncomfortably alive to the possibility that once the current crisis was settled Charles might be tempted to turn that army on his political opponents at home. The signs were ominous enough; when the Covenanters discharged their county levies as required by the treaty, those three 'standing' regiments had been retained and their general, Alexander Leslie, much caressed and shown every sign of royal favour, being translated at a single bound from commoner to earl. The result – an attempted coup! Likewise in England there was an equally abortive 'Army Plot' involving officers of the king's disbanded regiments and supposedly aimed at cutting off some of the leading lights in Parliament.

Then, in the first week of January 1642 Charles finally over-reached himself by attempting to have five leading MPs arrested. Denied legal sanction for doing so he attempted to seize them by invading Parliament at the head of an armed gang, once again largely made up of his erstwhile soldiers. Success might have justified his action, but all five members escaped. With Parliament and the mob united against him, the king fled from London on 10 January, and the English Civil War was begun.

In reality it took several months of furious bluster for both sides to muster sufficient forces to begin actually fighting each other, and it was at first a horribly mismanaged affair which reached a certain stalemate in the summer of 1643. Neither king nor Parliament was strong enough to defeat the other decisively without outside assistance, and so both looked elsewhere – the king to Ireland and Parliament to Scotland.

Notwithstanding the public rapprochement between king and Covenanters in 1641, the Scots and the English Parliamentarians were still natural political allies with a common purpose, and as early as 27 June 1643 formal approaches were made to the Committee of Estates in Edinburgh. This eventually led to the signing of the famous Solemn League and Covenant on 25 September and to a more definitive treaty of assistance on 29 November committing Scotland to provide an army of 18,000 foot, 2,000 horse, 1,000 dragoons and a competent train of artillery. In anticipation of this treaty, mobilisation of the army actually began as early as 28 July, when the Estates ordered the raising of five companies of foot and three troops of horse.[1] Ostensibly they were intended to serve as a police force, but no sooner was the Solemn League and Covenant signed than Leven, who had himself been reappointed as general on 26 August, marched them into Berwick upon Tweed. The Treaty of Ripon had stipulated that the town be left ungarrisoned, and this bloodless coup infuriated the local Royalist commander, Colonel Edward Grey. However there was nothing he could do about it other than step up his patrols along the border.

In the meantime the first mustering of the fencibles was ordered on 18 August. For once there was time to make a proper job of it and to ensure that all of the troops were properly organised, trained and equipped for the adventure ahead. It is all the more surprising therefore that when the Earl of Leven took his troops across the border on 19 January 1644 the army was still far from complete.

It is in fact difficult to establish just how strong it actually was. Most historians have rather uncritically accepted Rushworth's statement that it numbered 18,000 foot, 3,000 horse and 500 or 600 dragoons[2] as contracted in the treaty of assistance; however a close analysis suggests that this is rather too high. There were in total fifty-two troops of horse, which allowing an average of fifty men apiece produces a total of 2,600 troopers; this is not too far adrift from Rushworth's figure. Colonel Hugh Fraser's solitary regiment of dragoons on the other hand mustered just four companies[3] and will have been lucky to parade half the number of men cited by Rushworth. The greatest discrepancy however lies in the number of infantry. There were twenty-two regiments in all, but while most presented the required ten companies apiece others had rather fewer. Most notable was the Earl Marischal's Regiment, which was still in process of being organised when the invasion began and only had three companies on hand. In total Leven would actually appear to have had some 198 'colours' or companies, which would imply a total of as few as 9,900 infantry at an average of fifty men to each company. While it might be argued that this was rather too low for newly raised units the fact remains that when three more companies of the Earl Marischal's Regiment marched out of Aberdeen on 16 February they amounted in total to just 130 officers and men, which equates to only forty men per company.[4] Consequently an English Royalist intelligence report estimating the whole of Leven's army crossing the border at 14,000 men may be a lot closer than Rushworth's figure of over 22,000 men[5] and is not entirely inconsistent with Sir Thomas Fairfax's estimate of 14,000 foot and 2,000 horse on 20 April.[6] It would also help to explain what happened next.

Leven had two strategic objectives. Thus far the north of England had been firmly held by Royalist forces and throughout 1643 the Marquis of Newcastle had battled two quite separate Parliamentarian armies: one under Lord Fairfax and his son Sir Thomas in Yorkshire; and another under the Earl of Manchester in Lincolnshire. On the whole he had been successful, and indeed in the summer had all but destroyed Fairfax's army at Adwalton Moor near Bradford, but the end of the year found him distracted from pushing south by the growing threat of Scottish intervention in his rear. Leven's primary objective therefore was to turn that threat into reality by engaging and defeating Newcastle's army, and so assist Fairfax and Manchester in securing the north for Parliament, but his immediate objective was once again Newcastle upon Tyne.

The city was something of an anomaly in that it was an outward-looking mercantile community with strong links to London and a substantial Puritan party, which had largely welcomed the Scots in 1640. It would have been natural for the city to side with Parliament, but it also lay deep inside Royalist territory and a coup had secured it for the king early in 1642. Ever since, the Tyne had been blockaded by the pro-Parliamentarian navy, and the coal industry, almost wholly dependent on seaborne exports, was to all intents and purposes shut down. On the other hand from the Royalist point of view, the out-of-work colliers provided a ready source of recruits for the king's regiments and the blockade was porous enough for the river to become the centre of Royalist gun-running operations from the continent. The city was therefore both an important military objective in itself, and an economic one. Politically there was also an urgent need to reopen the vital 'sea coal' trade between the Tyne and London as soon as possible, for finding alternative sources of supply for the capital was seriously dislocating an already strained logistics network.

Leven therefore had to launch his invasion at the earliest opportunity, even if that meant an otherwise unthinkable winter campaign, and on 19 January the Scots army crossed Berwick bridge and closed up that night at Haggerston.[7] At first it looked as though he might be unstoppable for all that opposed him were at best some 5,000 men under Sir Thomas Glenham. Glenham, poor man, had been relieved of his charge as governor of York in November and ordered to muster an army at Newcastle upon Tyne. In the circumstances he probably did pretty well to get so many, but only half of them were armed and very few were infantry, reluctantly scraped up from the local Trained Bands. All he could realistically do was call for help and fall back slowly towards the Tyne, while his little army melted away from him. That help could only come from York, a hundred kilometres to the south, where the Marquis of Newcastle was himself complaining that he could muster only 5,000 foot ready to march. That was on 28 January, and at that point Leven's advance guard was at Morpeth, just twenty-four kilometres north of Newcastle upon Tyne. The city was wide open, but the next few days were to prove critical.

The problem for both sides was the weather. When the invasion began, the frost-hardened roads were passable enough, but on the night of 24 January a thaw had set in, swelling the rivers with rain and meltwater and turning the roads to mud. Consequently Leven was forced to wait three days at Morpeth for the last of his men to close up before resuming his march on the morning of 1 February. His intention was still to get within three kilometres of the city by the next day, but once again mud and flooded fields defeated him and night found him no farther than Stannington. All the while, the Marquis of Newcastle was struggling northwards along equally bad roads, eventually leaving his infantry behind to throw himself with his cavalry into the city literally hours ahead of Leven. The mayor, Sir John Marley, was heartily glad to see him for all he had to defend the place were the 500 men of the city Trained Band[8] and, although his own loyalty was not in question, he must have had a shrewd suspicion that his militia were ready to open the gates to whichever army arrived first.

As yet unaware of the marquis' arrival, at about noon on 3 February two of the army's political advisers, Argyle and the English Parliamentarian commissioner Sir William Armyne, addressed a kindly invitation for Marley to surrender the city, while Leven simultaneously set about providing a demonstration of the consequences of refusal. As noted in the previous chapter, Newcastle upon Tyne occupied a rather irregular position on the north bank of the deep Tyne Gorge. The greater part still lay along the quayside, but behind that area it stretched uphill to the castle, situated on a bluff overlooking the bridge and then fanned out in a semicircle, facing the flat moors to the north. For the most part it was encircled by mediaeval stone walls, but these were partially overlooked not only from the south bank of the Tyne but also on the east by some high ground on the other side of the Pandon Dene. Recognising this weakness, a detached earthwork fort or sconce had been built at the Shieldfield. Without waiting for a response to the summons, Leven had it attacked out of hand.

Records of the ammunition replenishments made next day show that detachments of musketeers were told off for the purpose from the Earl of Lindsay's Regiment, Colonel James Rae's Edinburgh Regiment, Hepburn of Waughton's and Lord Gordon's regiments, and an anonymous Scots account related how:

> Some of our men were drawn up to a stone Bridge a quarter of a mile from the town, at the entrance to the Shield-field to beat out some men of theirs out of a little Sconce that lay near it, and did it presently without losse, but they retiring to a sharper work near the Windmill, where the controversie was more hot . . . in six houres assault or thereabouts wee lost onlie fourteen men. The enemie having lost seven or eight fled to the Town, and we possessed the Fort, which is within halfe musket shot of the walls. After that they sent forth eight Troopes of Horse which the Major General of the Horse [David Leslie]

charged with five, though they could not charge three abreast together in respect of the
Coal-pits; notwithstanding which, the charge was so hard upon the Enemie, that they
presentlie retired into the Town, there was none killed on either side, only we took two
prisoners, whereof one was a Lievtenant who cursed and railed for halfe an hour together.[9]

Another Scots account admitted to the loss of only nine men, naming one of
them as Captain-Lieutenant Patrick English of Lindsay's Regiment, but while
it was a useful little victory it failed in its object of intimidating the garrison.
Sir John Marley and his deputy Sir Nicholas Cole returned a polite refusal to
Argyle's summons. And by interrogating that angry cavalry officer Leven will
have learned why. The Marquis of Newcastle had forestalled him and unless
Leven moved fast a siege was inevitable.

That night the outlying suburbs were burned as the Royalists withdrew
within the walls, but frustratingly there was little Leven could do until his guns
arrived. Sensibly enough no attempt had been made to drag them over the
wintry roads, and instead they were shipped by sea to the Northumberland port
of Blyth, just a few kilometres north of the Tyne. Even so they did not arrive
until 7 February, and by then Leven had decided to try throwing a bridge of
boats across the river just downstream from Newcastle, in order to bombard it
from the Gateshead side and so bring about a swift surrender as in 1640. Next
day a number of keel boats (barges normally used to carry coal) were found, and
that night Colonel William Stewart was assigned the job of splicing them into a
bridge. Unfortunately, despite bright moonlight, the attempt miscarried for they
were stuck fast in the mud by the glassworks, and with a neap tide there was little
prospect of refloating them in hurry. What was more, a number of diversionary
attacks, intended to discourage any sortie by the defenders, got totally out of
hand, and Stewart, convinced that he was actually about to be attacked himself,
quickly gave up the attempt and hurried back to the camp. Needless to say the
fiasco took some living down, but, with the Marquis of Newcastle's weary
infantry closing up, the time for such adventures was already past.

Stymied for the moment, Leven then set about gaining some elbow room
by pushing detachments downstream towards Tynemouth, where there was a
skirmish with some of the castle's garrison.[10] The real focus of attention however
shifted upstream, as he sought to find a crossing point for the whole army. Over
the next two weeks both sides gradually pushed their outposts farther along the
river, until at last Newcastle was persuaded that the Scots were overextended and
open to a counter-attack.

The first move was made by Sir Marmaduke Langdale, who was then occupying the town of Hexham, on the south bank of the Tyne some thirty-two kilometres west of Newcastle. At dawn on 19 February he moved out at the head of his own and Sir John Fenwick's regiments of horse and 300 musketeers. His objective was a Scots cavalry brigade understood to be quartered in nearby Corbridge, and the intention was to launch a surprise attack on the village while a third regiment, commanded by Colonel Robert Brandling, swung around to the south to catch the Scots in the rear. Instead, as he approached Corbridge, Langdale discovered to his dismay that the Scots, commanded by Leven's son, Lord Balgonie, were wide awake and waiting for him. Two regiments – the Lord General's and Lord Kirkcudbright's, commanded by Lieutenant-Colonel James Ballantyne and Lieutenant-Colonel James Mercer respectively – were already drawn up on the flat Red House Haugh. There was nothing for it but to press on, but in three successive engagements Langdale was defeated and driven back on his supporting musketeers. By this time however the Scots were themselves somewhat disorganised, and a volley was sufficient to send them reeling back in turn.

Langdale may have been forgiven for thinking himself given a respite, but as the Scots fell back on Corbridge they ran straight into Brandling and his regiment. For their part the Cavaliers had been expecting to attack the Scots from behind and were understandably taken aback to meet them coming head on. Not surprisingly they pulled up, and in an effort to get them going again Brandling himself spurred forward to challenge one of the Scots officers to a single combat. This also turned out to be a mistake, for a Lieutenant Elliot of the Lord General's Regiment promptly accepted his challenge, and in the first exchange of pistol shots must have wounded Brandling's mount, for it stumbled as they were wheeling about to draw their swords. Elliot thereupon dragged him off it, and at that point his men started to run and were chased through the streets of Corbridge and back across the Tyne.

The day was not yet over, for farther downstream another Royalist detachment based in Prudhoe Castle had been rather more successful in beating up the quarters of Fraser's Dragoons directly across the river in Ovingham. However the English commander, Sir Gamaliel Dudley, then tarried too long and was still on the north side of the river when Balgonie turned up and unceremoniously chased him into it. Afterwards the usual inflated claims of casualties were published abroad, but all in all round about sixty seem to have been killed or wounded in the two fights, most of them English.

Of itself it was a fairly inconclusive affair, although one correspondent rightly predicted 'it was like to grow into a great victory before it come at Oxford',[11] but it alerted Leven to the weakness of the Royalist forces above Newcastle. Apart from those few musketeers in Hexham, there were no infantry or guns to contest a crossing and so two days later Leven got his army moving again.

The Forgotten Battle: Boldon Hill

Besides the five companies of Sinclair's Regiment in Morpeth, five other regiments – the Earl Marischal's, Lord Coupar's, Oliphant of Gask's, Home of Wedderburn's and Douglas of Kilhead's – together with a few troops of horse were left behind under Sir James Lumsden to mask Newcastle and Tynemouth, while everyone else moved six kilometres westwards to Heddon on the Wall.[12] This was where they had encamped before the battle of Newburn in 1640, but this time the ford was properly fortified, and instead on Wednesday 28 February they crossed the river farther up by three smaller fords around Ovingham. They were in the nick of time for the river, already swollen by meltwater, was rising fast and any further delay would have compelled Leven to cross at Hexham, dangerously far away from Lumsden's detachment and his already tenuous supply line.

All too often military strategy during these wars consisted of finding where the enemy was and then marching straight at him, but the crossing of the Tyne initiated an unusual period of manoeuvre. At first neither side was keen to engage the other. Leven's main priority, particularly as snow was setting in again, was to establish a new base, and so once across the river he turned east and marched hard for the port of Sunderland. For his part the marquis scrambled to avoid his army being trapped in Newcastle. Langdale had already evacuated Hexham and, although the movement was glossed over somewhat in his report to the king, the Marquis of Newcastle fell back towards Durham as soon as the Scots crossed the river. Their paths briefly crossed near Chester-le-Street on 3 March, where Leven's army got across a bridge over the river Wear, undisturbed by Newcastle's army drawn up on a hill just three kilometres distant. Once the Scots were safely past, entering Sunderland the next day, the Royalists pressed on to Durham, where they were joined by reinforcements in the shape of a cavalry brigade under Sir Charles Lucas. Thus emboldened, or perhaps prodded, the marquis cautiously advanced towards Sunderland.

On 6 March he got his army over the Wear by the same bridge Leven had used below Lumley Castle and soon came in sight of a Scots cavalry outpost on Penshaw Hill. After a little skirmishing the Scots fell back, but uncertain what was in front of him Newcastle halted and next morning found himself facing the whole Scots army, drawn up in order of battle on Humbledon Hill, just a little to the southwest of Sunderland, while the Royalists took post on Hastings Hill, just to the east of Penshaw.[13] Heavy snowfalls discouraged any movement during the morning, and when Newcastle tried to probe forward in the afternoon he found the Scots strongly posted behind banks and hedges with their front well covered by the Barnes Burn, which ran through a deep dene. At nightfall the marquis fell back to Penshaw Hill, and next morning Leven decided to press forward in turn, whereupon the Royalists set fire to the houses where they had been sheltering and began a general retreat, covered by the smoke and by their cavalry.

For their part the Scots followed up with their own horse and some parties of musketeers, but after a little bickering and the usual claims on both sides of a famous victory Newcastle broke contact and retired to Durham, with nothing to show for his efforts but the loss of a considerable number of horses due to the bad weather and shortage of fodder.[14] Leven then tried to follow up his advantage by moving towards the marquis, but as he declined to come out and fight Leven in turn fell back on 13 March.

Supply was also becoming a concern, for although Leven had shifted his main base down from Blyth to Sunderland, bad weather was taking its toll: of five ships sent from Scotland at the beginning of March, three were lost and two driven to take shelter in the mouth of the Tyne. The entrance to the river was dominated on the north side by Tynemouth Castle and its outworks, and on the south by a fort at South Shields. Capturing this fort would finally close the river to Royalist gunrunners and privateers, and perhaps provide shelter for any other storm-driven supply boats. Accordingly an unsuccessful attempt was made to storm it on 15 March before a second attack on 20 March accomplished it as related by one Scot:

> Col [William] Stewart, Colonel [William] Lyell, Lieutenant Col. [Andrew] Bruce, and Lieutenant Col. Johnson, with some inferiour officers, led on the party, the Fort was very strong, the Graffe without being esteemed 12 foot broad, and 11 deep, the work above ground three yards high, and within it five iron peece of Ordnance, some nine pound ball, some more, an hundred souldiers, seventy musquetiers, and thirty Pike-men: It was situated with great advantage, being defended on the one side by the Ordnance of Tinemouth Castle, and on the other by a Dunkirk Frigot with ten peeces of Ordnance; notwithstanding 140 of our souldiers, without any other Armes but their swords, carried bundles of straw and sticks, wherewith they filled the ditch, set up scaling ladders

(whereof some did not reach the top of the Fort, the ditch not being well filled) and with their swords gave the first assault, then a party of Musquetiers, and after them a party of Pikes, all marching up till they entred the ditch, where they disputed the matter above ane houre, in which time the Enemy discharged upon them 28 shot of Cannon, some with Musquet ball, others with cut lead and iron, besides many Musquet shot: our souldiers did resolutely scale the ladders, and some entred in by the gunports: the Defendants behaved themselves gallantly till it came to stroke of sword, and then they fled away by water in boates; sixteen of them were killed, a Lieutenant and five souldiers who stood out to the last, were taken.[15]

With the mouth of the river now closed, the Marquis of Newcastle was once again prodded into action. Heading north from Durham on 23 March, this time he kept the Wear on his right, swinging around on to the north bank to get between Leven and the Tyne in order to attempt the recapture of South Shields. As this effectively meant marching across the front of the Scots army, Leven was soon alerted to what was happening and quickly got the bulk of his men across to the north side as well, forestalling Newcastle by drawing up on a north–south line along a limestone ridge known as Whitburn Lizard, blocking the approach to South Shields.

Discovering the Scots waiting for him the marquis halted on the rather higher Boldon or Down Hill, about five kilometres to the westward. Between the two armies lay a flat, open expanse of moorland in part cut into by the deep valley of a stream called the Don and interspersed with hedged enclosures particularly around the villages of East and West Boldon and Cleadon.[16] The ground is also wet and prone to ponding in bad weather, and consequently there seems to have been general agreement that it was bad ground for cavalry. With the aid of local keelmen, Leven's artillery commander, Sandie Hamilton, got one of his big guns across, but then two others were somehow lost in the river and rather than repeat the experiment Leven contented himself with just a few *fframes*.[17] It was going to be an infantry battle.

Newcastle was clearly at a loss. In fairness to him he was in a most unenviable position. Duty demanded that he attack, for the Scots army stood before him, alone, unsupported and quite literally with its back to the sea. He had the opportunity to win the war in an afternoon, but he might also lose it. He had come north with some 5,000 foot, to which Glenham must at least have added enough to cover the inevitable wastage from a forced march in winter, and in addition of course he had his cavalry. Leven on the other hand had perforce left a substantial detachment on the north bank of the Tyne and garrisons in Morpeth, Blyth and Sunderland besides, albeit Sir James Lumsden rejoined him with most of the cavalry who had been left behind. Be that as it may, while the numbers on both sides are tolerably vague, Newcastle will have struggled to achieve parity and may indeed have been quite badly outnumbered. Were the Scots to be beaten they would be destroyed and the north secured, but that would mean advancing across that wide expanse of broken moorland to launch a frontal assault on an army holding a naturally strong position and in greater in numbers than his own. The risk was simply too great, so the Marquis of Newcastle stayed where he was and it was the Scots who in the end came to him.

To cover his position Newcastle had stuffed the hedges at the foot of the hill around East and West Boldon with musketeers, and at about five o'clock in the afternoon, with the light already failing, Fraser's Dragoons opened the fight. Given the numbers involved and the importance of the outcome, Boldon should rank as one of the more important battles of the civil war, but the fact that it was fought in darkness and ended inconclusively means that it also quite literally ranks as one of the most obscure.

Nevertheless some important clues may be gleaned from the sparse evidence. According to Newcastle's official account, as published in the Royalist newspaper *Mercurius Aulicus*, four of his regiments had been engaged by six Scots ones, and sure enough there were indeed six Scots regiments requiring fresh supplies of ammunition on the morning after the battle: the General of the Artillery's (Alexander Hamilton's); the Lord Chancellor's (Loudoun's); the Earl of Lindsay's; Lord Livingston's; the Earl of Lothian's; and the Master of Yester's. All six moreover needed to draw varying numbers of pikes to replace those lost or broken during the fighting, varying from twenty issued to Yester's Regiment all the way up to forty to Lothian's Regiment, which significantly also had its commanding officer, Lieutenant-Colonel Patrick Leslie, reported as badly wounded.

Some of the fighting must therefore have been determined enough and two of the surviving Scots narratives describe how quantities of powder and match were captured as the English were driven back from hedge to hedge. Other than Colonel Leslie the Scots admitted to few casualties and insisted that the numbers of English dead and wounded found on the ground next morning far exceeded their own, while Newcastle for his part admitted to losing no fewer than 240. Even then his wording is ambiguous, and it would appear that he was talking of his dead and missing alone, exclusive of the seven wagonloads of wounded reported by the parish constable of Boldon.[18]

It was not quite a famous victory – the darkness saw to that – but it was a victory nonetheless. While daylight found the marquis still holding the top of the hill he lingered only long enough to get his guns and wounded away before falling back on Durham. Five days later, having rested and re-equipped his regiments, Leven moved southwards to Easington. There he was able to find sufficient forage for his cavalry and still maintain contact with the Royalists, and by 8 April the weather had sufficiently improved to recommence operations in earnest. Moving southwestwards on to the Quarrington Hills Leven took up another strong position a few kilometres south of Durham. Once again the Marquis of Newcastle found himself in an untenable position and faced with the choice of fighting or falling back he once again opted to retreat.

On the night of 12 April the last Royalist cavalrymen evacuated his most northerly outpost at Lumley Castle, near Chester-le-Street. All contact with the garrison of Newcastle upon Tyne was now lost, and a few hours later Durham was also abandoned as the army moved westward to Bishop Auckland. The intention was to swing clear of the Scots and re-establish a new defensive line along the river Tees, centred on the crossing at Piercebridge. Instead, somewhere along the road the marquis was met by a messenger carrying word of a catastrophic defeat at Selby two days earlier. In his absence those few troops left behind in Yorkshire had been entrusted to Colonel John Belasyse, who formed them into a useful little field army of about 1,500 horse and 1,800 foot. At first Belasyse was successful in fending off the equally scattered Parliamentarian forces in the area, but then they concentrated sufficient reinforcements from Lancashire and Lincolnshire to outnumber him by two to one, and utterly destroyed his little army at Selby on 11 April. Only some of the cavalry escaped, and York itself lay wide open.

The Royalist retreat now turned into a headlong flight as the Marquis of Newcastle raced south to save York. Leven did not learn that Durham had been evacuated until about three in the afternoon on 13 April, but without waiting to strike camp he got his own army on the move at once and by seven the next morning the Scots cavalry caught up with the Royalists' rear near Darlington. There was no effective rearguard and a party of Eglinton's Horse, led by Major John Montgomerie, got in among them and 'tuik fourtie men and many horses and slew many of their straggillars and gat tuo thousand merkis worth of silver plait, and mikell cheis, pork and bread.'[19] By now Leven's infantry were too done up to march farther, so he halted for a few hours at Darlington before crossing the Tees later that night and reaching Northallerton the following day. Leaving behind a pathetic trail of stragglers, deserters and abandoned wagons Newcastle kept just ahead of him and on 16 April, with the Royalists only sixteen kilometres short of York, Leven gave up the pursuit and instead turned aside to rendezvous with a Parliamentarian army under Lord Fairfax at Wetherby two days later.

By any accounting the campaign thus far was a spectacular success. Leven had led the Scots army across the border in January with the relatively limited objective of taking Newcastle upon Tyne. Instead, in a sustained campaign of manoeuvre, he had effectively destroyed the Royalist field army in the north. In the siege of York, which followed, and the battle of Marston Moor, which ended it, the Scots no longer fought as an independent force, but as part of a triple alliance with the Northern Association forces under Lord Fairfax and his son Sir Thomas, and those of the Eastern Association under the Earl of Manchester and Oliver Cromwell. Leven, nevertheless was regarded as the senior partner in the enterprise, and it was he who ordered the grandly titled Army of Both Kingdoms to draw up on Marston Moor on 1 July 1644 to intercept an approaching Royalist relief force led by the king's nephew, Prince Rupert.

They waited in vain, for by means of a long day's march the prince, coming over the Pennines from Lancashire, initially avoided a fight by swinging around by Boroughbridge and thrusting his advance guard into the city from the north. Somewhat chagrined by this failure Leven made no immediate attempt to pin Rupert against the walls, but instead decided to fall back to Selby. With another Parliamentarian army led by Sir John Meldrum closing in from the west by way of Wakefield he thus reasoned he could prevent the city from being reprovisioned and would be ideally situated to intercept any breakout towards the south.

The fact that an early southward move was anticipated suggested he knew Prince Rupert was on borrowed time. Two weeks earlier, having just captured Liverpool, the Royalist commander received an urgent message from the king, summoning him to an urgent rendezvous at Worcester. He still had permission to march to the relief of York if he could: 'But if that be either lost, or have freed themselves from the besiegers, or that, from want of powder, you cannot undertake that work, that you immediately march with your whole strength to Worcester, to assist me and my army; without which, or you having relieved York by beating the Scots, all the successes you can afterwards have must infallibly be useless unto me.'[20] At the time the king, having been forced out of Oxford, was being harried up and down the Midlands by two Parliamentarian armies each stronger than his own and desperately needed the prince's 'punctual compliance'. Rupert could not afford to linger in York. True the siege had been temporarily lifted, but the Scots were still close at hand and unbeaten.

However while Leven anticipated that Rupert would move, he did not anticipate just how quickly, and early on the morning of 2 July 1644 his rearguard on Marston Hill was surprised to see Prince Rupert's army filing on to the moor below. The three senior officers on the ground – David Leslie, Oliver Cromwell and Sir Thomas Fairfax – quickly conferred and sent word to their superiors, urging the necessity of making a fight on the ridge where they stood rather than run the risk of Rupert coming up with them on the march. As the head of the Allied column was already the length of Tadcaster it was going to take some time to turn them around, but happily the Royalists were not yet ready to fight either. The previous day's forced march left Rupert's infantry and guns still stretched out along the road some kilometres short of the city, and now they bypassed it to reach the moor, but it was well after midday by the time the first of Newcastle's cavalry appeared on the field and coming on to evening before his infantry started arriving.

By then all of Leven's army had returned, and his deployment is usefully recorded in a plan sketched out by Sir James Lumsden. On the left in two lines under Lieutenant-General Oliver Cromwell stood the Eastern Association cavalry, some 3,000 strong with 1,000 Scots under David Leslie forming a third line. Then came the infantry, again in three lines. Most of the first comprised English units, but the right under William Baillie comprised four Scots regiments – James Rae's Edinburgh Regiment and Sandie Hamilton's forming one brigade, and Maitland's and Lindsay's forming the other. The second line was entirely composed of Scots units: the Master of Yester's and Lord Livingston's; Lord Coupar's and the Earl of Dunfermline's; Douglas of Kilhead's and the Earl of Cassillis', and the Earl of Buccleugh's and the Lord Chancellor's. The third line was somewhat smaller, comprising just a single brigade from each army, with the Scots being represented by Erskine of Scotscraig's and Viscount Dudhope's regiments. Finally, standing behind the lot was another brigade of Scots infantry, seemingly composed of Hepburn of Waughton's Regiment and Lord Gordon's.[21] The right wing then mirrored that of the left with the Northern Association cavalry under Sir Thomas Fairfax drawn up in two lines, with a brigade of three Scots regiments under the Earl of Eglinton forming a third.

On the other side of the moor, one of Rupert's staff officers, Bernard de Gomme,[22] reveals in his own map that the Royalists completely bungled their deployment. Rupert had intended that his own and Newcastle's armies should draw up side by side, but, as the map shows, his own cavalry were posted on the right wing opposite Cromwell and Leslie, and Newcastle's cavalry on the left opposite Fairfax and Eglinton.[23] However Rupert's infantry had to stretch all the way across his projected front in a single line. Eventually at about five in the afternoon Newcastle's 4,000 foot appeared in their left rear. By now there was a general acceptance that the battle would be fought on the morrow, and with the armies more or less in contact there was no question of their carrying out a relief in place until after dark. Instead Leven saw his opportunity and seized it – supposedly declaring that a summer's evening was as long as a winter's day. The Royalists, already relaxing, were taken completely by surprise, and this was compounded by the speed of the Allied advance, for the two armies were separated by a ditch and hedge and it was imperative that Rupert's outposts strung out along it should be overwhelmed before his infantry came up to defend it.

At the western end of the battlefield Cromwell was over the ditch before his opposite number, Lord Byron, could react. The first Royalist charge, launched in haste, bounced off, but then Byron fell back on his supports and brought Cromwell to a stand. Both sides quickly fed in more men until in the end something in the region of 2,600 Eastern Association cavalry were pressing against something like 2,200 Cavaliers. Cromwell's slight advantage in numbers was counter-balanced to an extent by the fact that some of the Royalists were flanking him and so they 'had a hard pull of it' – tightly locked up knee to knee, spurring their horses forward, and quite literally trying to push each other back. For a time neither side could make any impression, but David Leslie eventually settled the business, for instead of simply adding his inconsiderable weight to the press he flanked the Cavaliers and broke them utterly.

Unfortunately this success was counter-balanced by disaster on the Allied right, where the ground was more uneven and the hedges and brambles thicker. As a result Sir Thomas Fairfax's men were insufficiently closed up after getting through it when Newcastle's cavalry crashed into them and so were peremptorily scattered: '. . . the two squadrons of Balgonie's regiment being divided by the enemy each from the other, one of them being Lanciers charged a regiment of the enemies foot, and put them wholly to the rout, and after joined with the left wing'.[24]

At the same time things were going very badly wrong with the infantry in the centre. At first it had looked promising as Rupert's men gave way, but then Newcastle's infantry, exploiting the success of their cavalry, launched a counter-attack through the crumbling Royalist front line and proceeded to rout Fairfax's little brigade in the centre of the line. Hamilton's Brigade standing next to them also gave way, and the panic then spread to the second line. Several regiments fled without firing a shot, and then some more Royalist cavalry joined in. Not all had joined in the pursuit of Fairfax's Northern Association Horse, and first a brigade or more fell on the exposed right flank of the Allied foot:

Sir Charles Lucas and General Major Porter . . . assaulted the Scottish Foot upon their Flanks, so that they had the Foot upon their front, and the whole Cavalry of the enemies left wing to fight with, whom they encountered with so much courage and resolution, that having enterlined their Musquetiers with Pikemen they made the enemies Horse, notwithstanding for all the assistance they had of their foot, at two severall assaults to give ground; and in this hot dispute with both they continued almost an houre, still maintaining their ground; Lieut. Generall Baily, and Generall Major Lumsdain perceiving the greatest weight of the battell to lye sore upon the Earl of Linsies, and Lord Maitland's regiment, sent up a reserve for their assistance, after which the enemies Horse having made a third assault upon them, had almost put them in some disorder; but the E. of Lindsey, and Lieut. Colonell Pitscottie, Lieut. Col. to the Lord Maitland's Regiment, behaved themselves so gallantly, that they quickly made the enemies Horse to retreat, killed Sir Charles Lucas his Horse, tooke him Prisoner, and gained ground upon the foote.[25]

While this bitter struggle was raging another wave of Royalist cavalry rolled over Eglinton's Horse, who had also survived the initial onslaught, and then scattered more of the Allied infantry including the Chancellor's and Buccleugh's regiments in the second line, and Dudhope's and Scotscraig's in the third before the charge spent itself in the Allied baggage train.[26] At that moment it appeared that all was lost, and after vainly attempting to rally the runaways Leven too joined in the flight.

In fact the battle was far from over. Despite its mauling the Allied right was still holding; Eglinton's Horse 'maintained their ground (most of the enemies going on in the pursuit of the Horse and Foote that fled) but with the losse of four Lieutenants, the Lieut. Colonell [Robin Montgomerie], Major [John Montgomerie] and Eglingtons Sonne being deadly wounded'. More importantly Lindsay's Brigade was still grimly holding on while Lumsden brought up those two brigades to plug the gaps. Otherwise there were no uncommitted reserves, but Cromwell and Leslie were gathering their victorious troopers together when up came Balgonie and his regiment with news of the disaster on the right and it was agreed that the first priority was to pass right across the Royalist rear area and deal with the remaining Cavalier horse. Curiously enough this meant that '. . . they fought upon the same ground, and with the same Front that our right wing had before stood to receive their charge; and wee stood in the same ground, and with the same front which they had when they began the charge'. Unprepared, the Cavaliers broke at the first onset, but with the light failing at last there was no attempt at pursuit. Instead Cromwell and Leslie immediately turned on the remaining Royalist infantry.

In the meantime Laurence Crawford and William Baillie had finally turned the tide in the infantry battle by rolling up what was left of Rupert's right wing, and as Royalist resistance finally collapsed the white-coated northern infantry were formed into a rearguard. At first they held together in good order and successfully disengaged from the Allied infantry, who were probably glad enough to see them go, but their retreat eventually came to an end in the area that would later be laid out as the White Syke Close.[27] There Cromwell and Leslie came in on their rear, but still they would not surrender and so Fraser's Dragoons were brought to shoot them down sufficiently to let the cavalry get in amongst them; and there it ended.

The battle was won, and with it the English Civil War. It did not end at Marston Moor, but it was won there and everyone wanted to claim the credit during the political battles that followed.[28] Individuals aside however there can be no doubting the victory was really down to the Scots, for without their invasion and without Leven's ruthless pursuit from the Tyne to the gates of York the battle would never have been fought in the first place, far less won. Arguably too while Leven fled the field it was Leslie rather than Cromwell who settled the business. Yet they got little or no credit for it in the end. Instead of exploiting the victory they lingered just long enough to see the surrender of York then returned northwards again, first to deal with the unfinished business of Newcastle upon Tyne and then an unexpected crisis in Scotland itself in the shape of a Royalist rebellion led by James Graham, the sometime Earl and now Marquis of Montrose.

Chapter 4

With Brode Swordis but Mercy or Remeid

Rebellion in Scotland, Tibbermore and Aberdeen

When last we encountered Montrose he was probably one of the more prominent of the Covenanters' leaders, but 1644 found him playing the part of the king's general. What had happened in the meantime?

The conventional explanation was first articulated in a document that became known as the Cumbernauld Band and later expanded on by his chaplain and hagiographer, George Wishart. It was that while Montrose's early support for the Covenant had been sincere he had come to recognise that Scotland faced a far greater threat from the growing ambition of Archibald Campbell, Marquess of Argyle.

Born in about 1606 and therefore only slightly older than Montrose, Argyle was at first rather in the background of affairs, ostensibly acting on the king's behalf as one of Hamilton's six councillors or assessors, but the death of his Catholic father in late 1638 freed him to display his true colours. Over the coming months he rapidly established himself as one of the main leaders of the Covenanting movement, and as such it was perhaps inevitable that a political and ultimately personal rivalry should grow up between the flamboyant and impulsive Montrose and the careful and pious Argyle.

It was not just a clash of personality, for while no one doubted his early commitment to the cause, Montrose was rather too impulsive and mercurial for his colleagues' liking, as witnessed by that business of the Aberdeen dogs, and by his high-handed arrest of Huntly, which precipitated the very uprising he was supposed to prevent. Nor for that matter did he display much steadiness in the events that followed. It is little wonder therefore that Montrose found first himself becoming increasingly marginalised from decision-making, and then rationalised this disconnection by focusing his frustrations on Argyle. By 1640 Argyle was not alone in believing that it was no longer a question of addressing particular grievances but of limiting the powers of a hostile monarch and so making explicit what was implied in the Declaration of Arbroath. Montrose however preferred to interpret this shift as the 'particular and indirect practicing of a few' aimed at repudiating royal authority entirely and ultimately paving the way for the exultation of Argyle.

The enemy was therefore no longer the misguided king and his bishops but the seeming would-be dictator, and just as he had helped rally opposition to the king through the medium of the Covenant Montrose now sought to rally it against Argyle with the Cumbernauld Band. A fair number of moderate noblemen signed it, but their opposition to what was self-evidently an illusory threat was equally moderate and consequently ineffective. When inevitably the existence of the band was revealed, Montrose was arrested and confined in Edinburgh Castle until after King Charles had been and gone. Whether he had any involvement, peripheral or otherwise, in the Incident does not appear, but having now been spurned by the Covenanting leadership he now equally enthusiastically espoused the king's cause and thus gained a leading role in the tragedy about to unfold.

It was clear to the king and his advisers as early as the summer of 1643 that Scots intervention in the war was likely to be decisive and to counter it they devised a two-pronged strategy. In the short term the Scots were to be counter-balanced by persuading the Irish rebels to accept a Cessation or ceasefire, which would potentially release thousands of the king's soldiers who could be redeployed back to England. Moreover, although it was at first denied, the Cessation also opened the possibility that former rebel troops might be taken into the king's service. Many Irishmen were already serving in the loyalist forces and recruiting even more of them specifically to go to England had the double bonus of depleting the rebel ranks without unduly weakening the Dublin garrison. The logic was unassailable, albeit at considerable cost to the king's reputation, but in the end, although the Irish reinforcements sustained the Royalist armies for three more bloody years, the difficulty of shipping them across a sea dominated by Parliament's navy meant that they arrived in driblets if at all and never achieved their full potential.

In parallel with this scheme an equally ambitious plan was set in train at Oxford to use some of those Irish troops to knock the Scots back out of the war before their intervention could take effect. Once again just as in 1639 there were three main elements to this plan and this time no need for circumspection. Randal MacDonnell, Earl of Antrim, was pledged to bring a Catholic army across from Ireland by 1 April 1644. From Antrim's point of view this expedition was ultimately intended to re-establish the power of Clan Donald in the western Highlands, and the best and most secure way of doing that was in the king's name. In concert with Antrim's intervention, George Gordon, Marquis of Huntly, despite his earlier failure was again required to declare for the king in the northeast of Scotland, while the Marquis of Montrose was to lead a motley collection of Scots mercenaries and English levies northwards across the border from Carlisle to raise a rebellion in the old Catholic southwest.

As the plan was originally set out, in order to avoid the inevitable jealousies all three were to at least notionally serve under Prince Rupert's younger brother Maurice as captain-general. Whether or not there was ever any realistic prospect of Prince Maurice actually coming north, it was Montrose who contrived to have himself appointed lieutenant-general under him. With that commission safely in his pocket Montrose left the king's wartime capital at Oxford on about 1 March and rode north with 200 cavalry, all or most of them Scots mercenaries who had been serving in a regiment commanded by the Earl of Crawford.[1]

Surprisingly enough however Huntly and his people were the first actually to move. Early on the morning of 19 March 1644 Sir John Gordon of Haddo rode into Aberdeen with sixty men at his back, kidnapped the provost in broad daylight and got back to Strathbogie without a finger lifted against him. Only after he was at a safe distance were the militia called out only to make themselves scarce again when the rebels returned a week later. Huntly himself was equally circumspect. True, he declared for the king, recruited men and sent them out to plunder the arms and everything else they needed. At Banff for example they 'took the town without contradiction, meddled with the keys of the tollbooth, took free quarters, and plundered all the arms they could get, buff coats, pikes, swords, carabines, pistols, yea and money also'.[2] That however was about as far as it went, partly through lack of any direction from Prince Maurice or anyone else and partly because the only notionally hostile troops within reach were commanded by his eldest son, Lord Gordon! After calling a general muster of some 2,100 foot and 400 horse at Inverurie, sixteen kilometres northwest of Aberdeen on 13 April, Huntly moved into the burgh and had some colours made: 'whare upon ilk side was drawn a red rampand Lion, having a crown of gold, above his head C.R. for Carolus Rex, having the motto *For God the King and Against all Triattoris* and beneath *God save the King*'. He and his followers also adopted black taffeta sashes as a sign they would fight to the death, but as Spalding cattily commented: 'it provit vtheruayes'.[3]

Beyond that Huntly seemed reluctant to commit himself to action, other than to authorise Irvine of Drum to carry out a reconnaissance in force down

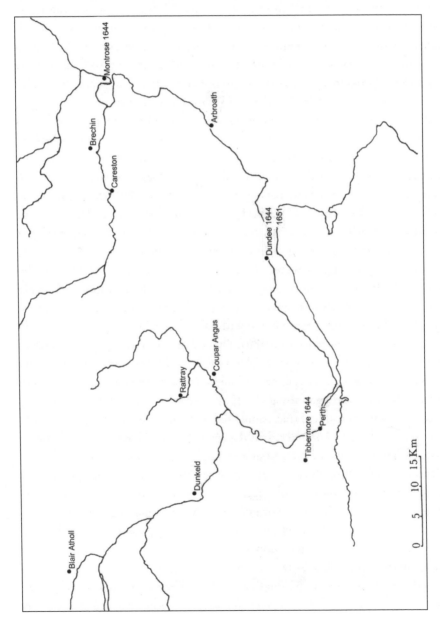

MAP 2: *Perth and Forfarshire.*

into the Braes of Angus, where government troops were assembling under Argyle. Donald Farquharson of Monaltrie had already been ordered south with about 240 foot, most though not all of them Highlanders, and at four in the afternoon of 20 April Drum set out from Aberdeen with seventy-two cavalry. Although he was going to be in overall charge of the expedition, the cavalry were actually commanded by a professional soldier, Major Nathaniel Gordon, which probably accounts for a lot in what followed.[4] So far as their orders were concerned, according to Gordon of Ruthven, all they were supposed to be doing was trying to gain intelligence of the government forces, but instead they ended up storming the burgh of Montrose, ostensibly in order to take possession of two brass 'cartows' or 24-pound cannon. Rendezvousing with Monaltrie somewhere on the North Esk river the rebels moved on the burgh under cover of darkness and at two o'clock on the morning of 24 April found the citizens armed and waiting, the common bell ringing and a beacon blazing to summon troops from nearby Forfar.

Nothing daunted, the rebels pressed on, and while some men ran around the east side of the town and scrambled over the back garden walls Drum himself led a frontal assault on the North Port or gate.[5] With the rebels pouring through the alleyways and into the marketplace behind them the militia abandoned the North Port almost at once, but then took refuge on the forestairs[6] of their houses and continued firing 'desperatlie' until Nathaniel Gordon shot a Baillie named Alexander Pearson, whereupon resistance collapsed and the rebels immediately set to plundering the place.

So far so good, but in order to get those two big cannon home Drum had arranged for an Aberdeen shipmaster named Alexander Burnett to be waiting in the harbour. Unfortunately he had overlooked the fact that Burnett's father was a prominent Covenanter, and it was in fact the younger Burnett who tipped everyone off to the raid and then very considerately offered sanctuary aboard his ship to the burgh's provost, James Scott. In fairness to the provost he also embarked forty musketeers with the intention of assisting in the defence of his burgh, but as it turned out when the rebel attack came in the ship was stuck fast out in the mud of a tidal basin. Unaware that Burnett had betrayed him Drum waited impatiently for the tide to float it only to be disagreeably surprised to be on the receiving end of a volley of musket fire when the boat eventually approached the quayside. Perhaps because the light was still bad only three of the rebels were killed and a few others wounded before Burnett sheered off again. As soon as he did, Drum tipped the two cannon straight into the harbour and then rampaged off intending to burn the whole town in retaliation. Happily Nathaniel Gordon scurried after him, quenching the flames as soon as they were raised, not through any humanitarian feeling but to preserve the spoils. Consequently Spalding waxed quite lyrical about the resulting booty, which included clothing, silks, velvets 'and vther costlie wair', silver and gold, as well as arms and a whole pipe of Spanish wine, which the Highlanders got in among with predictable results.

It was around two in the afternoon before they staggered out of the burgh, reeling drunk, and made their way to the Earl of Airlie's house at Cortachie. Huntly had requested Drum to call in on him with an invitation to declare for the king, but the earl took one look at the drunken rabble on his doorstep and very prudently declined. Next morning they set off again, and by now troops were on their trail, just a few hours behind them. Most of the Highlanders therefore turned straight for home, and Drum, thoroughly disgusted with the whole business, did likewise, leaving Nathaniel Gordon to shepherd the rest back to Aberdeen.[7]

There, faced with the news that Argyle was closing in with more than 2,000 men, Huntly evacuated the burgh on 29 April, intending to take to the hills and await the arrival of Antrim's Irish. Instead, with his men melting away from him or being captured one after the other, Huntly fled north in an open fishing boat to hide in Strathnavar.

For his part the Marquis of Montrose had made an even less auspicious debut as a Royalist commander. He and Crawford's Horse reached Durham in mid March, just in time to witness the battle at Boldon Hill. They had been hoping to pick up more men from the Marquis of Newcastle, who had a fair number of Scots serving in his ranks, but not only did the marquis have his hands full with Leven's invading army, but his own Scots were also deserting in droves to join their countrymen. Consequently it was not until the flight southwards began that Newcastle grudgingly gave Montrose another hundred troopers under Sir William Rollo[8] and sent orders for the authorities in Cumberland and Westmorland to call out the Trained Bands. Surprisingly enough they somehow or other managed to find 800 foot and another three troops of cavalry, and, thus augmented, the marquis crossed the border on 13 April 'in haste not to fail the Earl of Antrim at the time appointed'. This was the very day Huntly was having those banners made in Aberdeen, but of the Irish – already two weeks late – there was no sign.

Notwithstanding, and despite the refusal of most of the Cumberland levies to cross Annan Water, Montrose pressed on and occupied Dumfries in the name of the king. At that point a totally unexpected factor emerged. Earlier, as we have seen, a Scots expeditionary force had been sent to Ireland, where it had been languishing unpaid and poorly supplied for the last two years. In despair three of the regiments had unilaterally returned. One, Argyle's had been sent north to help deal with Huntly's rising, while the other two – Lothian's and Sinclair's – were assigned to hold Stirling Castle. Now, hearing that a Royalist army was over the border, they clandestinely offered to change sides and hand over the key to Scotland – not, as Sir James Turner would afterwards have it, out of loyalty, but rather in hopes of being paid![9] Montrose however was already being menaced by government forces led by the Earl of Callendar and within days evacuated Dumfries and fled back across the border.

He was far from finished though. The commander of his English troops, a Northumberland gentleman named Sir Robert Clavering, decided to return to Tyneside, and so Montrose and Crawford went with him and on or about 10 May launched an attack on the Scots garrison in Morpeth. The little town fell at once, but the garrison, led by Captain Somerville, retired into the castle and refused to surrender. Montrose then sent for some guns from Newcastle upon Tyne and settled down to a proper siege. In the meantime Clavering crossed the river and regained possession of the fort at South Shields, which was 'sold' to him by Captain Thomas Rutherford on 21 May.[10] With that success under his belt, Clavering next essayed an attempt on the supply depot at Sunderland. Unfortunately there does not appear to be an extant account of what happened next, but a good flavour of it may be had from the Scots army's stores ledgers.

The governor, Colonel Allane, had no regular troops at his disposal other than the inevitable rear parties and sick men left behind when the army marched south, and two local militia companies commanded by a Captain Lee and a Captain Knowles. The first hint of trouble came on 21 May when the latter, presumably hearing the Royalists were at South Shields, drew three barrels of powder and some other ammunition for his men. Next day, all hell broke loose. It began quietly enough when one of Knowles' officers, Roger Wouldhave, turned up and drew another three barrels of powder, match and ball and Captain Lee signed for one as well. A fifth barrel of powder and thirty-six rounds of three-pound shot were also sent to an outpost on the other side of the river at Monkwearmouth, and various people drew mattocks and spades. Then came the news that the Royalists were actually on their way, and this precipitated a general rush to the magazine. A further seven barrels of powder, besides match and ball and more than a hundred pikes and other weapons, together with some artillery ammunition were taken by 'several seamen upon compulsion', and worse still the garrison's big gun was afterwards recorded as having been 'Broken at Sunderland by a sea gunner.'[11] Whatever they got up to it was enough to daunt Clavering, who sheered off and returned to Newcastle to await the surrender of Morpeth on 29 May.

For the next month absolutely nothing happened. The detachment left behind by Leven sat tight at Heddon on the Wall, while Montrose and Clavering sat tight in Newcastle. Then at last came word that the Earl of Callendar had crossed the border on 25 June and was coming south with a second Scots army. A siege was inevitable so rather than be shut up within the walls they set off for the south with some 1,300 horse. Whether this was in response to a summons from Prince Rupert, or was simply a breakout, is not apparent. The Marquis of Newcastle was certainly aware of their coming, though he inflated their numbers to more than 3,000,[12] but they had only gotten the length of Richmond on 6 July when they encountered Rupert in his retreat from Marston Moor. Unabashed Montrose supposedly begged another 1,000 cavalry from him for a renewed expedition to Scotland, but was rebuffed and as Clavering had no intention of going there either he instead soon found himself kicking his heels again in Carlisle.

Tibbermore

Then, at last, his luck changed, for Antrim's men had finally arrived. On 27 June 1644, their commander, a Colonsay MacDonald named Alasdair MacColla, sailed from Passage near Waterford in the south of Ireland with something just over 2,000 men.[13] According to John Spalding, who was to encounter them frequently enough over the next couple of years, they were 'brocht wp in Wast Flanderis, expert soldiouris, with ane yeires pay'.[14] That may very well have been true of the officers, for just as the Scots employed veterans of the Swedish service, the Irish had men enough who had served with the Spanish army in Flanders. The rank and file however were mainly recruited by Antrim in Ulster, but there were also Connaught men among them and Anglo-Irish Catholics from the Pale – enough to make a mockery of the Victorian belief that they were all of them exiled MacDonalds. Far from being a wild Gaelic warband they were indeed expert soldiers, but at first they were in trouble.

Landing in Ardnamurchan in the west Highlands, on 8 July, MacColla immediately applied himself to the capture of Mingarry Castle. The siege lasted a week and then leaving behind a garrison he marched eastwards in the hope of joining with the Marquis of Huntly or any other Royalist leader. Unfortunately as he had feared it was already too late. Huntly, having disbanded his forces at the end of April, was in hiding in the far north of Scotland, and neither Sir James MacDonald of Sleat nor the Earl of Seaforth would call out their men to join the invaders. All he could secure was free passage towards Badenoch, where on 22 August he halted at Ballachroan and was joined by the MacDonnells of Keppoch and some MacPhersons under Cluny's son. Nevertheless there was no disguising the fact that he was in trouble. He was in fact in the classic predicament of a mercenary commander stranded in hostile territory without an employer for his hungry men. With the Laird of Grant and Lord Gordon blocking his path into Strathavan and Strathbogie MacColla had no alternative but to turn south into Atholl and there his fortunes changed dramatically. Having learned of MacColla's arrival in Scotland, Montrose had secretly ridden north from Carlisle with just two companions, arriving in the area just as the Shire Committee was issuing its mustering instructions on 26 August. Thus quite fortuitously the local Royalist sympathisers were able to raise their own followers under colour of this official levy and instead of mustering at Perth brought them to a rendezvous at Blair Atholl. Afterwards both MacColla and Montrose were given to recounting that both parties were on the point of setting about each other there when the latter turned up in the nick of time, but an Irish Officer later let the cat out of the bag by laconically stating that he and his men marched to Blair Castle 'where the Lord Marquess of Montrose came unto and joined them with some other small forces.'[15] Be that as it may the royal standard was formally raised at Blair on 29 August. Next day a detour to Buchanty brought another rendezvous with a second local contingent led by Montrose's kinsman, Lord Kilpont, and Sir John Drummond, a younger son of the Earl of Perth.

As a result the king's army in Scotland may have numbered upwards of 3,000 men when it came in sight of the government's forces arrayed at Tibbermore,[16] a wide expanse of open moorland just to the west of the fair city of Perth on the morning of 1 September 1644. Far from being heroically outnumbered, it might even have been larger than its opponents. Most sources seem to agree that notwithstanding the inevitable straggling and his leaving garrisons behind in Kinlochaline and Mingarry, MacColla's three Irish regiments standing in the centre still mustered about 1,500 men. The right wing was commanded by Montrose, 'on foot with his target and pike', but its exact composition is uncertain. Ruthven cites 700 Athollmen and 500 from Badenoch on the right, although Wishart refers only to the Athollmen under Patrick Graham of

Inchbrackie.[17] On the left wing Kilpont, according to Wishart, had also brought in 500 men, but intriguingly the Irish Officer referred to 'the Lord Kilpunt commanding the bowmen',[18] which might suggest that all of the archers among the various Highland contingents were concentrated under his control. More likely it is simply a reflection of how poorly equipped they all were.

Ruthven says nothing about this, but is emphatic that the two wings, rather than the whole army, were drawn up only three deep. At first sight this might point to the Royalists trying to match the frontage of a significantly larger opposing army, but on closer examination Montrose's real concern appears to have been to avoid being outflanked by the enemy cavalry, for he had none of his own.

As to that enemy, their dispositions were straightforward enough. Command of the whole was supposedly exercised by Lord Elcho despite the fact that according to Wishart he 'had no great character as a soldier'. In the event he confined himself to leading the cavalry on the right, while the Earl of Tullibardine commanded the infantry in the centre, and Sir James Scott of Rossie had the cavalry on the left, facing Montrose. Royalist chroniclers afterwards claimed to have beaten upwards of 6,000 foot and 700–800 horse, but in the circumstances this estimate seems absurdly high. Tullibardine had certainly raised some 800 men in Perthshire at the time of Huntly's rising, but this time round a fair few of those April levies were now standing in the Royalist ranks under Kilpont and Inchbrackie. He will probably have been lucky to have mustered half as many at Tibbermore. Similarly 800 men had been levied in Fife at the same time and formed into a regiment under Lord Elcho, but it was still serving as the garrison of Aberdeen. A further 800 men were now called out from Fife under Elcho and Balfour of Burleigh on 25 August, but there is no evidence that the latter ever arrived, so the number of Fife men must be conjectural. If 400 are allowed for them and another 200 for the Perth burgh militia, that would only amount to 1,000 foot in total. However 800 foot had also been ordered out of Dundee and Forfarshire, and given their close proximity it should have been possible to muster at least 600 of them at Perth by 1 September. While this analysis is clearly unsatisfactory, all the indications are that there probably were no more than 2,000 foot at the most, rather than the 6,000 cited by the various Royalist sources.[19]

All in all therefore the Royalists brought about 3,000 or even 3,200 infantry on to the field against perhaps 2,000 infantry and 400 cavalry. In numbers therefore they were at best about equal, and if Elcho had an advantage in that some of his men were mounted and were supported by a number of small cannon (nine according to the Irish Officer) all or most of them were raw levies, while a substantial proportion of the Royalists were hardened veterans from Ireland.

Describing the fight almost takes rather less time than analysing the two armies. Holding the king's commission and mindful of the defections to him over the past few days, Montrose began the proceedings by sending forward the young Master of Madderty with a flag of truce and a hopeful invitation to submit to his royal authority. Instead, Madderty was promptly arrested and packed off to Perth with a cheerful assurance that he would have his head cut off just as soon as the Irish were dealt with. Then, as those 'Irishes' came within cannon shot, Tullibardine sent out a forlorn hope of musketeers under Lord Drummond.[20] MacColla responded by sending out some skirmishers of his own, and Drummond's men were 'at the first encounter with the Irishes played vpon with hot alarums and continuall fyre'.[21] This tumbled them back in some confusion, and so quickly that Drummond was afterwards accused of treason. Suitably encouraged by this, Montrose thereupon ordered a general attack all along his line. The Royalists we are told quite specifically by Wishart at this point had few long pikes (*hastis longioribus*) or even swords,[22] but the Irish fell on Tullibardine 'with such active and desparat resolution, as there first and second ranks ware fallin to the ground erre the third rank resolued what to do'. Stirring stuff indeed and explained by a difference in tactics.

According to popular legend the Irish rather improbably had only a single round of ammunition apiece, but while they may have been short of it they are unlikely to have been that short. The simplest explanation is that, while the Perth and Forfar levies were laboriously firing rank by rank in extraduction, the Irish simply closed forward, fired a single salvee[23] and charged, sending Tullibardine's 'ontryed men and fresh water souldiours' running in a panic-stricken flight.

On the Royalist right wing the battle was equally brief. As Tullibardine's musketeers advanced, Rossie moved his cavalry obliquely towards some higher ground, but Montrose forestalled him by getting there first and ordered his men to fire a volley. This failed to stop the troopers, for the Athollmen were not so well equipped as the Irish[24] and rather than waste time reloading they immediately came down the hill and 'with shoure of stones for want of more offensive armes, and lastly, with there swordes assailed both horse and foote men so desperatly as they fell first in confusion and disordour'.[25]

By then it was pretty well all over anyway. On the Royalist left neither Kilpont nor Elcho seems to have made any serious attempt to engage each other, although Ruthven suggests that the cavalry after falling back some distance 'strowe to rely and put themselves in better posture to renew the fight' only to be swept away by the broken infantry. Neither side may have been too keen to encounter the other. In contrast to Rossie, a veteran of the Venetian service, Elcho seems to have been regarded as hesitant, while Kilpont's men having defected only the previous day may still have been uncertain as to where their real loyalties lay.

At any event the pursuit was followed all the way into Perth and was supposedly attended both by a considerable slaughter of the fugitives and a thorough plundering of the city. The Irish Officer certainly boasted that:

> ... men might have walked upon the dead corps to the town, being two long miles from the place where the battle was pitched. The chase continued from 8 a clock in the morning till 9 at night: all their cannon, arms, munition, colours, drums, tents, baggage, in a word none of themselves nor baggage escaped our hands, but their horse, and such of the foot as were taken prisoners within the city.

However while the Royalists were obviously keen to emphasise the scale of their victory, and the Covenanters equally keen to trumpet the scale of the atrocity, the actual number of casualties may have been quite low. Depending on the authority consulted, there were anything between 1,300 and 2,000 slain, which if true would rather improbably have accounted for nearly all of Tullibardine's infantry. Sir John Braco on the other hand deposed that coming across the field on the Tuesday after he saw just thirty or forty bodies lying there, and Ruthven and Spalding are more or less agreed on a figure of 800 to 1,000 prisoners. If so, while discounting Wishart's claim of 2,000 dead, we accept his entirely reasonable statement that 'a larger number were captured', that might point to a much more realistic death toll of around a hundred – and most of them were killed not in the battle but running away from it.[26]

In the immediate term the Royalists were able to reclothe and re-equip themselves, but with another army concentrating against them at Stirling under Argyle and the Earl of Lothian they soon headed eastwards to Dundee. The city was summoned to surrender on 6 September, but answered defiantly, and Montrose then chose to head north to Aberdeen in the hope of raising Huntly's people.

Aberdeen: The Craibstane Rout

Instead Montrose found another army thrown across his path just outside the burgh. On 6 September, hearing of the disaster at Perth, all the available fencibles from the Mearns, Aberdeenshire and Banffshire had been ordered to assemble at Aberdeen by 9 or 10 September and the Morayshire fencibles by 12 or 13 September. Unfortunately, with the Royalists already moving north through their territory, the Mearns fencibles refused to turn out, while farther north a mighty row had broken out among their leaders. A number of local lairds obeyed the summons readily enough, including the Earl of Erroll's people from Buchan under James Hay of Muriefauld, the Earl Marischal's Aberdeenshire tenants under James Keith of Clackriach, and a Formartine contingent led by John Udny of Udny, who ironically had fought for the anti-Covenanters in 1639. Others were also brought in by the Forbes lairds and Lords Fraser and Crichton, but all of them were untrained and poorly armed. Just three regular troops of horse turned up, two commanded by Captain Alexander Keith and Sir William Forbes of Craigievar respectively, and a third led by none other than Lord Lewis Gordon! The latter belonged to a regiment being raised by Huntly's eldest son and heir, Lord Gordon; however Lord Gordon and the rest of his men remained up north because the Forbes lairds, who were traditionally at odds if not actual feud with the Gordons, were trying to squeeze him out of the picture. First they had conspired to have a regiment of foot to be raised in Gordon's name reassigned to Lord Forbes,[27] which understandably upset him, and then a number of them made it clear that they would not serve under him. Unsurprisingly he stayed in the north, or rather moved at a pace carefully calculated to give the appearance of obedience while ensuring he would not arrive in time.

Nevertheless the local commanders, Provost Patrick Leslie of Aberdeen and Lord Burleigh, were able to assemble an army around the regiment of regulars from Fife commanded by Lieutenant-Colonel Charles Arnot, which had been serving as the garrison, and the Aberdeen Militia, itself commanded by a professional soldier, Major Arthur Forbes. Between them they accounted for about 1,000 well-armed foot. Adding the men brought in by the northern lairds and the fencibles under Udny, Muriefauld and Clackriach, Leslie and Burleigh may therefore have had as many as 1,500–2,000 foot, and about 300 horse, but as at Perth they were all of them very largely untried and as would soon become apparent there was also a fatal absence of effective leadership.[28]

This time around, as he approached the city, Montrose swung inland from Stonehaven by the infamous Slug Road (A957), thus avoiding the fortified bridge, which had given him so much trouble in '39, and instead crossed the Dee farther upstream at the Mills of Drum on 11 September. At first the Covenanters responded by pulling back from the bridge and occupying the high ground above it at Two Mile Cross, but this was soon felt to be too exposed and the following night they retired into Aberdeen. Montrose, having himself advanced to the Two Mile Cross once again sent in a summons demanding the surrender of the city and its garrison in the name of the king. At Perth, his messenger was summarily tossed in jail, but this time around the provost hastily convened a council meeting to debate the response, while both commissioner and his drummer were liberally plied with drink. As the burgh was quite indefensible there were really only two options, to submit or to fight a battle. As the first was out of the question the army began moving out and into its fighting positions even as their reply was being written out – albeit with much scratching and amendment.[29]

If there had to be a battle in the open field, the place they chose was the best possible one for many kilometres – a long flat-topped ridge about a kilometre south of the burgh, falling steeply towards the valley of the How Burn. It is steepest at its northwestern end, where it overlooked a complex of buildings and ponds forming the Justice Mills, which thereby provided one of the alternative names by which the battle is known. About a hundred metres downstream from the mills the How Burn was crossed by the Hardgate, the main road into the town from the south. The road tackles the face of the ridge head on and although steep the going along was and is easier than on the adjoining slope on either side. At the top, it then splits close by an ancient boundary marker known as the Craibstane, and it is here that the musketeers of the Aberdeen Militia were posted and ever afterwards ruefully referred to what followed as the Craibstane Rout.[30]

Southwards and eastwards from the Craibstane the ridge curves in a steep-fronted crescent for another 150 metres or so but then becomes progressively lower in the direction of the river Dee. Unsurprisingly most of the cavalry were placed on this left flank, while the three troops of regulars were posted on the right. The placing of the infantry is a touch more obscure, although the Fife regiment was evidently on the left, the Aberdeen Militia in the centre and the northern fencibles under Udny, Muriefauld and Clackriach on the right. Ruthven at one point does refer to the 'barrones of the name of Forbese, with those of Buchan' standing on the left, but it is clear he is speaking of cavalry rather than infantry, for he later comments that the horsemen were 'almost composed of lordes, barrones, and gentlemen of qualitie'.

At any rate they were still deploying as Montrose's commissioner passed through the lines, bearing the council's reply at about eleven o'clock, on Friday 13 September 1644. It was then as they passed close by the Fife regiment that one of the soldiers 'aganes the law of nationis' pistolled the drummer. At this, in Spalding's words, Montrose 'grew mad, and becam furious and impatient . . . quicklie merchand fra the tua myll cross to meit ws, chargeing his men to kill and pardon none'.[31]

First he had to win the battle and began by deploying his men on what is now Willowbank on the other side of the How Burn valley. This time around they were certainly outnumbered. After Tibbermore nearly all the Highlanders had variously returned to Badenoch, Atholl and Lochaber in order to secure their plunder, while Kilpont's men disbanded themselves after a quarrel that saw him murdered by his own second-in-command, Stewart of Ardvorlich. This left Montrose with no more than 1,500 infantry by the time he came in sight of Aberdeen, almost all of them Irish, and perhaps 60–80 cavalry – little more than Moss-troopers – who came in under Nathaniel Gordon and Sir Thomas Ogilvie.

The rebel left, which was probably to the west of the Hardgate, was nominally commanded by Colonel James Hay, a professional soldier who had been with Huntly in the spring and comprised some thirty troopers under Nathaniel Gordon and a hundred Irish musketeers commanded by Captain John Mortimer, a Lowland Scot serving in Colonel Manus O'Cahan's Irish Regiment. The right wing, commanded by Sir William Rollo, comprised Sir Thomas Ogilvie's troopers and another hundred infantry, who seemingly included some bowmen, and must therefore have been Highlanders – perhaps Keppock's men. MacColla himself was with Montrose in the centre at the head of the three Irish regiments, while some small cannon, taken at Tippermuir, were planted on the relatively high ground by the Hardgate, at a range of about 300 metres away from the Craibstane.

Infuriated or not by the shooting of the drummer, the Royalists faced a daunting prospect. They were outnumbered, and with little or no prospect of turning the Covenanters' flanks it was going to have to be a frontal assault, straight up the road. Before even that could be attempted however the Upper and Lower Justice Mills in the valley bottom, just to the west of the road, were going to have to be cleared. Thus the battle began with an attempt by Hay and Gordon to drive a detachment of musketeers out of the Justice Mills. In this they were successful but immediately counter-attacked by a troop of lancers. Gordon's Moss-troopers were outnumbered but 'the Irishes at a neere distance, gave such a continuall fyre as they fand that service too hote for them, and therefore makes a retreat. This gave courage to the Royalistes, for they leift there lances behind them.' It was a similar story on the right where the Lords Fraser and Crichton twice essayed half-hearted attacks against the Royalists, but

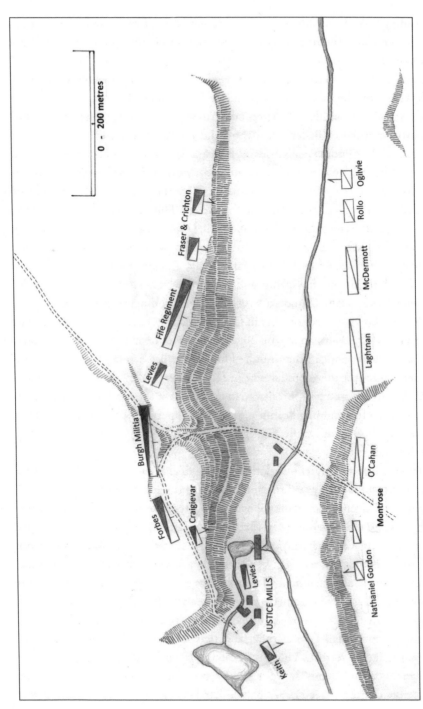

MAP 3: *Aberdeen 1644: The Craibstane Rout.*

were unsupported, not according to Ruthven 'for want of good will to fight, but for want of experience, not knowing that it was there time to charge; and this errour came chiefly for want of a generall commander, whose ordours they should obey'.[32]

Consequently the Covenanters continued to fritter away their advantage in numbers in a series of piecemeal attacks. A body of 400 foot came next. These were presumably such of the northern fencibles who were not already fighting down among the buildings and gardens at the mills. By Ruthven's reckoning the attack was the crisis of the battle:

> Those making a compasse about befor they ware perceived, wines the syd of a hill that lay to the north of this small winge of the Royalistes; and yet want of experience stayes them there, where they ware so fare advanced that, if they had charged roundly forward, they had gone neere to have carried that dayes victorie to overthrow Montrose whole armie; for they had not only takin his canon, but the body of his maine battell was so farre advanced to joyne with there enemies, as they had fallin in there reire upon their backes directly.[33]

Instead as soon as Captain Mortimer's little band of musketeers 'playes upon them lustelie', they halted and a firefight developed at long range. Then when Nathaniel Gordon fetched another detachment of musketeers to reinforce Mortimer, they were in turn attacked by Lord Lewis Gordon and his eighteen troopers who trotted up, fired their pistols and caracoled away again – fairly ineffectively though it is hard to see what else such a small group might have done in the circumstances. Next, aiming to go one better, the main body of the Irish were then directly charged by Sir William Forbes of Craigievar's own troop. Notwithstanding the Irish mercenaries 'being so well trained men as the world could afford no better, oppins thee rankes receiving him, and closes againe immediately by command of there worthie McDonald, and then on all quarters gives fyre vpon'.[34] Of itself this may not have been decisive, but before Craigievar's men could pull themselves together they were hit by all of the Royalist cavalry, for Sir William Rollo, profiting by the inactivity of the Covenanters opposing him, brought Ogilvie's little troop across from the right and pitched in behind Nathaniel Gordon's Mossers. The fight was probably a brief one, but dramatic enough, for Sir Thomas Ogilvie had his horse shot from under him and Ogilvy of Inverquharity suffered a lance thrust in the thigh, before the Covenanters broke, leaving behind both Craigievar and his second-in-command, John Forbes of Lairgie as prisoners.[35] Suitably encouraged, Mortimer's detachment then rushed the northern infantry still standing uncertainly on the hillside above the Justice Mills, 'routes them, and cutes all there foote in pieces'.

By now the battle had been going on for more than an hour, and the Royalist advance was otherwise effectively stalled at the bottom of the steep slope. Neither side at this stage may have been suffering very many casualties, but there was an understandable reluctance on the part of the Irish infantry to tackle the climb in the teeth of a heavy artillery and musket fire. However something was going to have to be done, and Wishart has Montrose floridly exhorting:

> We shall gain nothing, my men, by fighting at a distance. Who can distinguish the strong from the weak, the coward from the brave? Get to close quarters with yon feeble striplings; they will never withstand your valour. Fall on them with sword and musket butts. Crush them; drive them off the field and take vengeance on the traitor rebels![36]

With an air of declaring that with one bound Jack was free, he then concludes that on hearing those words they instantly hurled themselves on the Covenanters and routed them utterly.

It was not of course quite that simple. Rather more convincingly an anonymous contemporary sheet has Montrose briefly ordering his troops to 'lay aside their Muskets and Pikes, and fall on with Sword and Durk', while both Spalding and Ruthven emphatically declare that the fighting was prolonged – 'disputed hard' according to the latter. Instead of a wild charge up the steep face of the brae, it must have been a much slower but unquestionably determined surge up the line of the Hardgate to the crest of the ridge by the Craibstane. It was therefore the unfortunate Aberdeen Militia who bore the brunt of the assault – and suffered worst as the Covenanters' battle line was split asunder. Only the Fife regiment held together: 'being miserablie rent and torne, they, lyk bold and weell trained souldioures, make there retreat in order, and too boldly resolves to march south, by crossing Die; but the major generall, perceiving there designe, takes furth foure hundredth Irishes, and following them so rudely, falls in amongst them, as few or none esceaped'.[37]

As with most military units caught up in similar disasters, reports of the Fife regiment's demise are a little exaggerated and it turned up again soon afterwards, serving under General Baillie. The cavalry and most of the northern levies also seem to have gotten away, but the Aberdeen Militia were not so lucky. When the line broke they fled back along the Hardgate towards the town, which, as Spalding bitterly related: 'wes our toune's menis distraction; whairas if they had fled and not cum neire the toune thay micht have been in better securitie: bot being commandit be Patrik Leslie provest to tak the toune thay war undone, yit himself and the pryme covenanteris being on horsbak wan saiflie themselffis away'. Naturally enough the Irish went howling after them. At Tibbermore they had few pikes or swords, but that was before that they had re-equipped themselves with the spoils, and now they went 'hewing and cutting doun all maner of man thay could overtak within the toune, upone the streites, or in thair houssis, and round about the toune, as oure men wes fleing with brode swordis but mercy or remeid'.[38] Ruthven went so far as to reckon that: 'In the bodie of the maine battell all the citizens . . . ware killed', but John Spalding, meticulously recalling each one of them by name, sorrowfully accounted for 118, most of whom 'wes no covenanteris; but harlitt out sore against thair willis to fight against the Kingis lieutenant'.[39]

Aberdeen had been plundered on a number of occasions before, by both sides, but it had almost been a quasi-judicial process, not unlike a visit by the bailiff's men calmly fining individuals for the crime of supporting the wrong party. This time it was different. Montrose left the battlefield and returned to his camp that night:

> . . . leaving the Irishis killing, robbing, and plundering of this toune at thair pleasour. And nothing hard but pitifull houlling, crying, weiping, murning, throw all the streets . . . Sum wemen they presssit to defloir, and uther sum thay took perforce to serve thame in the camp. It is lamentabill to heir how thir Irishis who had gotten the spyll of the toune did abuse the samen. The men that they killit thay wold not suffer to be bureit, but tirrit [stripped] thame of thair clothis, syne left thair naikit bodies lying above the ground.

Despite half-hearted orders to prepare to march, the killing and plundering were still going on next day when Montrose re-entered the town: 'cled in cot and trewis as the Irishes wes cled'. In a grotesque ceremony Montrose had his commission from the king formally proclaimed at the market cross, together with another demanding that the king's lieges should come in and swear allegiance under pain of the fire and sword that was being ruthlessly meted out even as the herald spoke.

Two days later, laden down with plunder, which in the Irish Officer's words 'hath made all our soldiers cavaliers', they eventually straggled out to Kintore and then westwards into the wild fastness of Rothiemurchus. The Marquess of Argyle was just three days behind them, and Scotland had become Germany.

Chapter 5

Bitter Winter

The Fall of Newcastle
and the Ravaging of Argyll

Even as Argyle was doggedly marching in pursuit of the Royalists the ripples of
the twin débâcles at Tibbermore and Aberdeen were reaching far into England.
The great and glorious victory at Marston Moor was followed by the surrender of
York on 16 July, but it was not until 7 August that the Scots army was sufficiently
rested and recovered to march north again. David Leslie, with most of the
horse, was sent into Cumberland and Westmorland to deal with the remaining
Royalists there and ultimately to secure Carlisle. The main objective of course
was Newcastle upon Tyne, and in the meantime much of the preparatory work
for a siege had been carried out by a second army under the Earl of Callendar,
who crossed the border on 25 June with 6,000 foot and 800 horse.

Taking in Morpeth while passing, Callendar at first swung south of the city to
mop up minor Royalist garrisons earlier left behind – in Hartlepool and Stockton
– and reinforce the ill-defended depot at Sunderland. That done he established
a new camp on the south side of the Tyne and on 27 July seized Gateshead.
Callendar had hoped to do so the night before, sending Sir James Ramsay's
Regiment of Horse and 800 commanded musketeers, but they misjudged their
time and daylight discovered the Royalists waiting for them on the Windmill
Hill above the town. Still determined, Callendar then brought up the whole of
his force, dislodged them and chased them back down through the streets to
the fortified bridge over the Tyne, linking the town with Newcastle.[1] There he
was stopped, and for the next three months the bridge would be barricaded at
both ends, with the Scots holding the southern side and the Royalists holding
the northern one. Beyond that Callendar contented himself with erecting five
batteries on the newly won high ground, from where he could harass the exposed

city on the other side of the gorge. There he remained until Leven arrived and delivered a formal summons on 16 August.[2]

The mayor, John Marley, refused, though he can have had precious little hope of relief and presumably saw it was his simple duty to deny the Scots possession of the place for as long as possible. To defend the town he had, according to William Lithgow, 800 men of the City Trained Band and a further 900 'volunteers' scraped up from the unemployed and anyone else he could lay his hands on, together with a number of Scots Royalists ranging from the Earl of Crawford to Montrose's future biographer Dr William Wishart.

Leven and Callendar considerably outnumbered the defenders of course, and it is a measure of Marley's isolation that the Scots were able to readily assemble some 3,000 local colliers and keelmen as a labour force for the siege works.[3] As Newcastle was fundamentally a friendly city, it was hoped to be liberated in as intact a state as possible rather than shattered by a bombardment from the Gateshead batteries. As it was, any sense of urgency evaporated when a breathless messenger arrived from Edinburgh on 3 September, bearing news of the disaster at Tibbermore, and orders recalling three of Leven's regiments immediately. Whether he captured the city or not, Leven could not afford to march south again until the crisis at home was resolved, so he might as well do the job properly rather than in haste.

The chief problem was evidently a shortage of ammunition, for a considerable quantity had already been expended in the siege of York and replenishment from Scotland was hindered by 'the late troubles faln out at home by the landing of the Irish Rebels which hath diverted much of our supply from thence'.[4] Leven's English colleagues duly obliged by sending some up by ship, and in the meantime reliance was placed on mining rather than artillery. There was no shortage of skilled labour for this on either side, and the garrison of course responded by countermining. After 'drowning' four mines in quick succession at the beginning of October the Royalists celebrated by ringing bells all night long, but by 14 October matters were drawing to a head. Leven's ammunition had been replenished, and he was confident enough to issue another invitation to surrender.

Next day Marley returned a suitably ambiguous response, simultaneously expressing his determination to hold out and his willingness to talk, and then demonstrating both by a series of delays until on 18 October, with winter drawing ever closer, Leven finally lost patience. Callendar's guns were openly brought across from Gateshead and the Scots infantry equally ostentatiously

moved into their assault positions around the city. That night the final
ultimatum was delivered: the Royalists had until 8 a.m. the next morning to
surrender. Accordingly at daybreak, Leven's guns opened up, before briefly
falling silent at the appointed hour to allow a reply. Astonishingly Marley still
tried to prevaricate, and as soon as his envoys had returned within the walls the
bombardment resumed in earnest.

The city was still defended only by an outdated mediaeval stone curtain wall
with a ditch but no protecting embankment in front of it.[5] Until now it had only
been a shortage of ammunition that hindered Leven from levelling it, and by 10
a.m. his infantry were stood to arms waiting for the mines to explode and for the
guns to shoot them in as they assaulted the breaches.

There were four assault columns. The first was on the west side of the city
covering the area between the Westgate and White Friars Tower. It comprised
three brigades: the Lord Chancellor's and Buccleugh's regiments, which were
tasked with getting in by the Closegate, down by the riverside; the Edinburgh
Regiment and General of the Artillery's Regiment, which were to storm a breach
opened by a mine at the White Friars Tower; and the third brigade – Stewart's
and Tullibardine's regiments – was to tackle the Westgate.

The second column was assigned to the northern side of the city and the
formidable Newgate – a miniature castle in itself. This comprised five regiments,
including William Baillie's, Lord Coupar's, the Earl of Dunfermline's and
Hepburn of Waughton's.[6]

The third column, again posted on the northern side of the city, was tasked
with taking the Pilgrim Street gate and the Carliol Tower to the east of it. It
comprised Cassillis' and Kilhead's regiments, the Earl Marischal's, Yester's and
Home of Wedderburn's Merse Regiment.

Finally, the fourth column, that of the Earl of Callendar, was to get in by
the Sandgate at the eastern end of the quayside. To accomplish this, Callendar
was given Sinclair's, Livingston's, Aytoun's, Niddrie's and the Master of
Cranstoun's regiments.[7]

There was a minor setback during the afternoon when Leven was advised
about 3 p.m. that two of his mines, those being prepared at the White Friars and
Sandgate, were in imminent danger of being countermined, so he ordered them
blown prematurely. The walls were successfully breached at both points, but as
the assault was not timed to go in until 5 p.m., when the light began to fail, it
was necessary to concentrate his fire on the breaches to prevent the defenders
retrenching behind them.

Fortunately for all concerned when the assault did begin it turned out to be a brutally short business. The only serious resistance was encountered at the Newgate, and the whole affair was over within two hours and the loss of only about a hundred men, including, inevitably, a number of officers, such as Major Robert Hepburn of Wedderburn's Regiment. A hard struggle had been anticipated at the Sandgate, but Callendar got his men in at once, and sending Livingston's Regiment north to scour the walls he led the rest 'with flyeing culloures and roaring Drummes' through the streets to seize the marketplace and at that point resistance collapsed throughout the city. The militia almost literally evaporated, dispersing to their homes, and as one Scot put it: 'sate down by their fathers fire side, as though they had carried no armes'. A number of the more committed Royalists and Scots refugees flung themselves into the castle, not with any thought of prolonging resistance there but rather to secure themselves in the mediaeval equivalent of a panic room until the fury of the assault subsided and they could find someone to accept their surrender. It was all in fact something of an anticlimax, for the swift end of the fighting, allied to the knowledge that they were entering a friendly city, meant that the attackers were never allowed to get out of hand. There were no horrors such as had lately been visited on Aberdeen, and when Marley finally came out of the castle two days later he had to be placed in protective custody to secure him from the fury of his own townspeople.[8]

The undoubted triumph was published widely abroad and gratefully acknowledged by *Mercurius Britannicus* for one,[9] which cheerfully declared: 'Did I not tell you that the Scots meant to send us coales this winter? And now the fulfilling of this Prophesie cannot but be very comfortable this cold weather . . . though our London Wood Merchants (perhaps) grow chill upon the business.' But it was late enough, given the earlier hopes that the Tyne might have been opened back in February, and too late for the Scots to play the important part in the war that their intervention had once portended. Instead it was the Earl of Manchester's army (and of course Oliver Cromwell), which had stepped into the breach after the summer's Parliamentarian disasters in the south and from now onwards the Scots were to be increasingly sidelined politically, especially as their troubles multiplied at home. And there was also another, more insidious, problem. Tynemouth Castle surrendered without a fight on 27 October, in large part because further resistance after the fall of Newcastle would have been futile, but also because a virulent plague – typhus – had broken out among the garrison. Once the sick and dying men came out it spread to Leven's men and all too many of them in turn carried it into Scotland. There matters were going from bad to worse.

Fyvie

Argyle had successfully hustled the Royalists out of Aberdeen just days after their bloody victory. This was not surprising since he had no fewer than three regiments of his own clan levies from Argyllshire (supposedly amounting to 3,000 men, although realistically no more than half that number), and more importantly he also had two good infantry regiments recalled from Ireland – the Earl of Lothian's and Sir Mungo Campbell of Lawers mustering just a little less than 800 men between them. Shortly afterwards Argyle was also joined by a third regiment of regular infantry, 500 strong, under the Laird of Buchannan. In addition he had three troops apiece of the Earl of Dalhousie's and Sir Frederick Hamilton's regular cavalry regiments, recently sent up from England, and four other troops besides, including Keith's and Craigievar's.

In the face of this formidable threat the Royalists quite literally commenced marching in circles. Moving west to keep ahead of Argyle they found their way into Moray blocked on Speyside by the local fencibles under Grant of Freuchie and another regular cavalry regiment commanded by Lord Gordon. This forced them to turn southwards into Atholl. Doggedly following in their tracks was Argyle, who was at Ruthven in Badenoch when he heard that the Royalists had split up – MacColla having insisted on taking 500 of his men off to the west Highlands, to relieve his garrisons there.[10] Argyle thereupon took the opportunity to split his own forces, throwing a strong garrison (comprising Lawers' and Buchannan's regiments) into Inverness, before setting off in pursuit once more. Montrose thereupon headed south past Perth and then abruptly swung north again back towards Aberdeen. It had a new garrison by now, under Sir James Ramsay, including his own regiment, the rest of Hamilton's and another commanded by Sir James Halkett of Pitfirrane. Rather than fight another battle for the place with just 800 Irish mercenaries and 200 of Inchbrackie's Athollmen, Montrose once again took the westerly Slug Road to the Mills of Drum on 17 October and thence over the hills to Strathbogie.

There, finding that he had a little breathing space, he tried to raise the Gordons, but he was hampered both by Huntly's continued absence and by Lord Gordon's adherence to the government, which naturally inspired a reluctance by many of the Gordon lairds to commit themselves. Nevertheless according to Ruthven in the end he still managed to pick up 200 good infantry from Strathbogie together with 200 Highlanders under Farquharson of Monaltrie, and perhaps another hundred from Strathavan.[11] This was just as well, for Argyle, still following

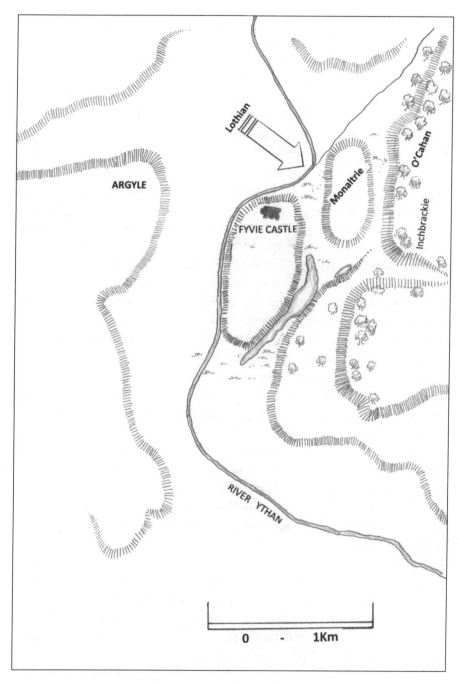

MAP 4: *Fyvie 1644.*

after him, reached Aberdeen on 24 October and pausing only to pick up most of Ramsay's cavalry set off again next day.

At this point one of those intelligence failures which were to dog Montrose's career with distressing regularity nearly resulted in disaster for the Royalists. On the night of 25 October, Montrose abruptly moved eastwards to Auchterless, and from there the next day to Fyvie, near Turriff. Wishart blandly states that Montrose left Strathbogie simply because he had given up on the Gordons, while Ruthven says he did so to avoid eating the place bare. Neither version explains why the move was urgent enough to justify a night march, or why he moved east rather than west. Consequently Spalding's story that he was responding to news of Argyle's approach makes much more sense.[12] Presumably some sort of cunning plan was afoot, but if so it unravelled at once for this part of Aberdeenshire was Covenanting country. Consequently Argyle learned of the move almost as soon as it happened, swung north and, with most of the Royalist cavalry away foraging, caught Montrose unawares at Fyvie on 28 October.

Ruthven helpfully states that the Royalists had the river Ythan on their right and a wood on their left, with what he describes as a 'hollow bruick' to their front, which implies that initially they were facing southwards. However, that was before Huntly's people, having weighed up the odds and perhaps never very enthusiastic to start with, unilaterally decided to break out and head back to Strathbogie while they still had the chance. Anticipating that the rest might follow their lead, Argyle swiftly responded by shifting his own army around to the west, which in turned compelled Montrose to adopt a new position, facing west and adjacent to Fyvie Castle. The castle itself was garrisoned, and ransacked of anything that could be melted down into shot. Most of the Royalists were concealed in the trees, which covered the hillside behind it, and Montrose was still able to make use of the 'hollow bruick', which was evidently the stream that emerges from a prominent re-entrant in the hillside about 300 metres south of the castle. Immediately to the north of this stream, lying between the castle and the hillside, is a low rise then divided by turf walls, which gave an 'appearance like a camp'. Indeed their remains are sometimes said to be represent trenches dug by the Royalists, although they were actually agricultural enclosures. More importantly perhaps the turf walls also hid an area of dead ground at the foot of the hill, where troops could form up unseen from Argyle's position to the west.

As a result the fighting never developed into a general engagement since the Covenanters were unable to determine exactly where the Royalists were located and therefore restricted themselves to a series of rather cautious probing attacks.

Lothian's regulars began promisingly enough with a successful attack on the enclosures, only to be bounced back out again in a prompt counter-attack by Royalist troops lying in the dead ground beyond, variously reported to have been led by Colonel O'Cahan or Donald Farquharson of Monaltrie.[13] Argyle riposted in turn by sending forward five troops of cavalry. This time the Royalists abandoned the position without a fight, but only in order to draw the horsemen into an ambush in the dead ground. Unfortunately the trap was sprung early when Inchbrackie's Athollmen fired too soon from the cover of the woods. The cavalry immediately halted and started to pull back, whereupon the rebel infantry emerged from the trees and rushed forward with a loud shout, reoccupied the enclosures and killed Captain Alexander Keith as his troop tried to cover the retreat. Another probing attack by both infantry and cavalry was made sometime during the afternoon, but it never seems to have gotten properly underway for Argyle was reluctant to send his raw Highland levies blindly into the woods and considered his regular infantry too weak to carry the enclosures.

Desultory skirmishing therefore continued for another two days before a shortage of fodder for his cavalry forced Argyle to break contact,[14] whereupon a greatly relieved Montrose hurriedly decamped in the opposite direction, first to Turriff (which he plundered) and then westwards into Badenoch. Argyle pursued him as far as Strathbogie, but by then the rebel army was melting away. Despite boasting of a great victory at Fyvie the Royalists had effectively been run into the ground, and many were now at the end of their tether. Recognising this, Argyle offered safe conduct to any who would lay down their arms, though even he could hardly have expected that the first to accept would be Nathaniel Gordon, who not only changed sides again on 3 November but also brought in Forbes of Craigievar by way of insurance.[15] Within days Montrose admitted defeat and on 6 November fled south to Blair Atholl again. Despite his victories at Tibbermore and Aberdeen the uprising had failed to take off. The insurgents had slaughtered, plundered and burned their way round in circles, but were still effectively confined within the Highland line and so closely harried as to prevent any real accession of strength. When Argyle settled his men into winter quarters and left for Edinburgh and a conference with Leven on 21 November, there was every reason for confidence that the onset of winter would be sufficient to finish the rebellion.

Inverlochy

Instead Alasdair MacColla came roaring out of the west and reignited it as never before. Not only had he successfully relieved his beleaguered garrisons at Mingarry and Kinlochaline, but he had also recruited 800 MacDonalds of Clanranald and Glen Coe, 'well armed with habershones [mail coats] muriones and targates; for offensive armes they had gunes, bowes, swords, and aixes, called of some Lochaber aixes' and brought them back with him to the rendezvous at Blair Atholl.[16] He also brought his own agenda, insisting in the face of Montrose's strong objections that their combined forces should launch a midwinter raid deep into Argyllshire. Unusually mild weather left the mountain passes open and as MacColla himself afterwards reported:

> From *Castle-Blaire* we marched to *Glanurghyes*, called *McCallin McConaghy*, which lands
> we all burned, and preyed from thence to *Lares*, alias *Lausers*; and burned and preyed all his
> country from thence to *Aghenbrack's*, whose lands and country were burned and preyed;
> and so throughout all *Argyle*, we left neither house nor hold unburned, nor corn nor cattle
> that belonged to the whole name of Campbell.[17]

And all this devastation was inflicted at the beginning of winter too, forcing hundreds, if not thousands, of starving, homeless refugees out into the bitter snows. By 13 December Argyle's own burgh of Inveraray was captured. Argyle himself had been there, but news of the rebels' approach forced his undignified flight to Dumbarton in search of an army, and as it happens there was one ready and waiting. On Leven's advice Lieutenant-General William Baillie had been appointed as commander-in-chief in Argyle's place, and on 20 December he was ordered by the Estates to march his regulars westwards and, meeting Argyle at Rosneath, promptly fell out with him. Having suffered the indignity of being chased out of his own home, Argyle announced that he intended to lead the expedition. When Baillie pointedly declined to take any orders from him, Argyle changed his tack, arguing rightly enough that the devastated countryside could not support the whole army anyway. Argyle therefore settled for borrowing a contingent of regulars to stiffen his own levies, while Baillie took the rest off to Perth and sent orders to the Earl of Seaforth to concentrate the northern Fencibles at Inverness.

The rebels meanwhile had roamed off into Lorne and Lochaber. When Montrose and MacColla, learning that the Inverness garrison had been reinforced, halted at Kilchummin (modern Fort Augustus) on 31 January they

MAP 5: *Inverlochy 1645: 'Over the hills the nearest way'.*

soon discovered that Argyle was coming up behind them at Inverlochy. Both ends of the Great Glen were therefore blocked, but they were by no means trapped since there was nothing to prevent them from marching up Glen Tarff and across the Corrieyairack Pass into Speyside. Instead Montrose was once again persuaded by the MacDonalds to double back on his tracks and attack Argyle.

Eschewing a straightforward advance, which would be detected almost immediately, the rebels first marched due south up Glen Tarff as though making for Badenoch. They then turned aside and moved parallel to the Great Glen as far as Glen Buck, before climbing another 300 metres followed by a steep descent into Glen Turret. After that although there were still many weary kilometres in front of them the worst was over. At Keppoch the Royalist advance guard evicted one of Argyle's outposts and rested for three hours in a still extant barn while the rest of the army caught up.[18] Setting off again they then forded the river Spean and pushed on by moonlight before finally throwing themselves down, exhausted, above Inverlochy. It was the early hours of 2 February 1645, Candlemass Day and in just thirty-six hours they had marched as many kilometres through the hills in midwinter and were about to fight an army which may have been twice their size.

The few remaining hours of darkness were spent in skirmishing, which Spalding thought was initiated by the Royalists lest Argyle's army should steal away rather than fight, but it was more likely the other way round and that it was the Campbells who were trying to feel out the army, which was massing in the woods. As it was, by now the Royalists had only about 1,500 men divided into four 'divisions'. Alasdair MacColla took command of the right at the head of Laghtnan's Irish regiment, which was probably still about 400 strong. In the centre were some 500 Highlanders largely drawn from the western clans – MacDonalds of Clanranald, Glengarry and Glencoe; and MacLeans and Appin Stewarts – and also including the Athollmen under Inchbrackie. The left wing was formed by a second Irish regiment under Lieutenant-Colonel Donoghue O'Cahan, and in reserve, behind the centre, was the third Irish regiment, McDermott's,[19] and perhaps some more Highlanders, including a few Gordons under Captain John Gordon of Littlemill. Nearby was a small troop of about fifty cavalry under Sir Thomas Ogilvy, and that was it.[20]

Below them Argyle was aboard his galley, safely moored offshore. Understandably enough he had opted for its relative comfort rather than shiver in a tent and had in the meantime turned command of the army over to an experienced soldier, Sir Duncan Campbell of Auchinbrec. Less creditably he was to remain out there throughout the battle. While the Royalists cheerfully seized on his behaviour to cast unkind aspersions on his character, their appearance was so unexpected that it is likely Argyle did not realise what was happening until it was too late. Be that as it may, Auchinbrec did his best with what was estimated at some 3,000 men.

According to Gordon of Ruthven there was a strong body of Highlanders posted a little way in front of the main body, armed with guns, bows and axes.[21] This was presumably Argyle's own regiment, recalled from Ireland, for although Ruthven refers to the rest as being 'prime men', such a particular description clearly implies that the clansmen standing behind them were actually much less well-armed levies – not improbably made up of refugees from the Royalist harrying. The wings of the army comprised sixteen companies of regulars borrowed from Baillie's army and formed into two provisional battalions under Lieutenant-Colonel John Roughe of the Earl of Moray's Regiment and a Lieutenant-Colonel John Cockburn. If 400 men are credited to each then the main body could have amounted to some 2,000. Set back a little from the main body, two light cannon were set on a slight eminence, and the left wing of the army was anchored on the ruined Inverlochy Castle, which was itself garrisoned by fifty musketeers.

The battle, as related by MacColla, began at dawn:

> Which on both sides being pitched and their cannon planted, the fight began; the enemy giving fire upon us on both sides, both with cannon and muskets, to their little avail. For only two regiments of our army, playing with musket shot, advanced till they recovered *Argyle's* standard, and took the standard bearer: at which their whole army broke; which were so hotly pursued both with horse and foot, that little or none of the whole army escaped us, the officers being the first that were cut off.

The other Royalist sources likewise confirm that far from beginning with a wild Highland charge, the battle was opened by a firefight between the Irish veterans and the Lowland musketeers on both flanks. O'Cahan seemingly went in first and as instructed by MacColla held his fire until the very last moment before firing a single crashing volley into the regulars, which 'fyred there beards' and followed it up with a physical assault with swords. 'Our men . . . came immediately to push of pike and dint of sword, after their first firing,' wrote Montrose to the king. '[They] could not stand it, but, after some resistance at first began to run, whom we pursued for nine miles together, making a great slaughter.'[22] The reference to fighting at push of pike may at first appear surprising, but fifty years later pikes rather than broadswords would still be the weapon most frequently mentioned in Almerieclose's description of the clans gathered at Dalcomera. Significantly too it was only after the regular troops on both flanks had been beaten by the Irish that Montrose sent his Highlanders forward against Argyle's clansmen.

That strong battalion standing in the van gave way almost at once, but at first seems to have held together and as the Royalists 'followed there charge in a close bodie, with such strength and furie' was physically pushed back into the second line, where the whole lot burst apart and began running. All sources agree that the pursuit was a bloody massacre. A considerable number of the Lowland troops rallied at the castle, despite a spirited intervention by the Royalist cavalry, which saw Sir Thomas Ogilvie fatally shot through the thigh, and successfully negotiated their surrender. According to Ruthven, 200 Highlanders who were with them were slaughtered out of hand. In all as many as 1,500 were said to have died, including Auchinbrec and a number of other prominent Campbell lairds, which amounts to an unlikely half of the total number engaged. Whatever the true figure there is no doubting that the power of Clan Campbell was all but shattered for a generation. For their part the Royalists boasted of just three or four dead, but the 200 wounded confessed in Montrose's despatch suggest that it was not quite a walk-over.[23]

Nevertheless there was no denying it was a famous victory, and for the first time it brought in substantial numbers of recruits. Inverness was still too strong to attempt, but turning aside into Strathspey the Royalists were joined at Ballachestall (Grantown on Spey) by John Grant of Freuchie with 300 men. As usual this was just a matter of making their peace with what was for the moment the winning side, but much more significantly on 19 February Lord Gordon defected to the rebels at the head of his regular cavalry regiment, delivered up the city of Elgin which he had been charged with defending, and thereafter devoted himself to raising his father's people for the king's service.

By the beginning of March Montrose was able to move southwards from Aberdeen with about 3,000 infantry. Rather less than a third of them were Irish by this time, and the only Highlanders were the small regiments commanded by Graham of Inchbrackie and Farquharson of Monaltrie. Full half of the infantry were Lowland Scots, including the Strathbogie Regiment, which was to earn itself something of a reputation as a fighting regiment in the coming months. For the first time too Montrose was able to field an effective force of cavalry. What was more, while some of the 300 troopers were survivors of Ogilvie's faithful little troop, the majority were not the rude multitude of 'bonnet lairds on cart-horses' imagined by John Buchan and other popular historians, but Lord Gordon's regulars – and it would show. In the meantime they allowed themselves to become careless.

On 26 February the Earl of Balcarres rode into Aberdeen at the head of his veteran cavalry regiment with orders to rendezvous with the local forces and secure the place ahead of General Baillie, who was now marching northwards with six regiments of foot. However Balcarres found the garrison in a pretty shocking state and hearing soon afterwards that the Royalists were on the move again pulled them all out, leaving the burgh wide open. Nathaniel Gordon, who had evidently been instrumental in managing Lord Gordon's defection, immediately rode in, released all the prisoners from the tollbooth and with the aid of 100 Irish dragooners under Captain Mortimer, won a useful little skirmish at the Bridge o' Dee. So far so good, and having secured a large quantity of arms, estimated at 1,800 muskets and pikes in the tollbooth, they all went back to rejoin Montrose who had demanded a muster of the Aberdeenshire fencibles at Inverurie on 15 March. Surprisingly enough the wapinschaw went ahead as advertised and was by all accounts well attended, albeit somewhat overshadowed by an ominous upset two days before.

Emboldened by their earlier success Nathaniel Gordon and John Mortimer had ridden back into Aberdeen with about eighty-odd troopers, all intent on a little 'mirryment'. Donald Farquharson of Monaltrie went with them too. As they carelessly scattered themselves around the burgh without giving a thought to security, someone sent off a messenger to alert Sir John Hurry, the commander of Baillie's cavalry.

Hurry was a decidedly colourful character who had been general drill master of the Aberdeen Militia as long ago as 1627, and by the time he ended his life on the end of a rope in 1650 had probably changed sides more frequently than anyone else. In 1640, if not earlier, he came home from Germany to serve in the Scots army, was instrumental in betraying Cochrane's attempted coup in the following year and in 1642 obtained command of one of the troops of horse being raised in England to go to Ireland. Instead, like Nathaniel Gordon he fought in the Parliamentarian army at Edgehill before defecting to the Royalists the following summer with news of a pay convoy carrying £21,000 in silver. The attempt on it miscarried, but Prince Rupert took a liking to him and he was still with the Royalists at Marston Moor, before coming home via another brief spell in the Parliamentarian army towards the end of the year. While his character might be deplorable there was no doubting his ability, as Hurry now demonstrated.

At the time he was lying at North Water bridge on the North Esk and eagerly accepting the invitation at once hastened northwards with eight score horse and foot, mainly drawn from Balcarres' Regiment, which had been largely raised in the area. Hurry proceeded to deliver a textbook operation which could have been lifted straight out of the pages of John Cruso's *Militarie Instructions for the Cavallrie*.[24]

Arriving outside Aberdeen at about eight o'clock on the evening of Friday 15 March, Hurry first secured the gates before galloping into the streets as noisily as possible. The Royalists, dispersed throughout the burgh, were taken completely by surprise and offered little or no resistance. Nathaniel Gordon and a few others, grown old in such wickedness, made off at once, probably by the back yards. Others, inevitably, made the fatal mistake of running out into the street and among them was Farquharson of Monaltrie. As soon as he appeared he and his companions were surrounded by horsemen demanding their names, and in an ill-timed moment of bravado Monaltrie answered proudly and began tugging out his sword. Not surprisingly he was promptly pistolled. His cousin, slower off the mark, was wounded and taken prisoner, but otherwise few other Royalists were killed or captured. Instead Hurry, well aware that time was of the essence in such affairs, contented himself with securing their horses before retiring southwards again as quickly as he had come. Afterwards a furious Montrose levied a swingeing fine on the burgh, while Alasdair MacColla gave Monaltrie a soldier's funeral in St Machar's cathedral with 'the trailing of pickes and thundering vollie of muskets'.[25]

It was little enough consolation that Hurry in turn appeared to get the worst of a skirmish at Halkerton Wood near Fettercairn a week later, for he was able to alert Baillie to the fact that, as soon as the Royalist army crossed the river Dee, its new Aberdeenshire levies began drifting away in appreciable numbers. Bolstered by this happy news Baillie took up a strong position at Ruthven on the river Isla. Montrose duly came up, decided against forcing a crossing and then after some shuffling retreated into the hills and occupied Dunkeld. There even more of his men took the opportunity to slip off home, and Montrose realised he had to do something positive before the army disintegrated completely.

Dundee
Misled by a false report that Baillie had crossed the river Tay at Perth, Montrose decided to regain the initiative. Sending the baggage train and artillery back to Blair Atholl with most of the Irish, he marched eastwards towards Brechin on 3

April. Stopping at Blairgowrie after darkness had fallen, Montrose then picked out 600 'light armed musketeers' – half of them Irish and half Strathbogie men under Lord Lewis Gordon – together with 150–200 troopers of Lord Gordon's Horse. While the rest of the army continued on its way, he and MacColla turned south for Dundee, arriving shortly before dawn.

The burgh was protected by a wall and there was no chance of just sweeping straight in, so once it was properly light Montrose roused Lieutenant John Gordon and sent in his usual summons. Just as at Aberdeen the magistrates and the military governor, Lieutenant-Colonel Cockburn,[26] at first treated the envoy courteously enough and promised a written answer, but before they could do so the Royalist assault began prematurely and Gordon was flung into the tollbooth. At first the attack went well and the Irish quickly broke in by the West Port or gate, while Lord Gordon forced the North Port. Traditionally the Royalists are then said to have dispersed in an orgy of drunken plundering, but it is clear from what happened next that fighting was still going on late into the afternoon. Ruthven for his part allows they had gotten the length of the marketplace, but Wishart unequivocally states that Montrose was still standing on a hillock watching the progress of the fighting in the streets when word came that General Baillie was not on the other side of Perth at all but just three kilometres away and coming on fast!

Needless to say this news produced absolute consternation and drunk or sober Montrose sent off 400 foot at once 'with orders to march as rapidly as possible without breaking ranks' while the remaining 200 under Lord Lewis Gordon followed as a rearguard and then Montrose after them, with the cavalry riding 'in open order, with intervals to admit the light musketeers should occasion arise'.[27] According to legend the last of them tumbled out through the East Port just as Baillie stormed in by the west, leaving the unfortunate Lieutenant Gordon still locked up in the tollbooth![28]

Happily, Baillie and his men were themselves exhausted by their forced march from Perth. In order to save the burgh he had left his infantry behind on the road and now took the understandable decision to wait for them before embarking on a pursuit of the Royalists. By the time the infantry had come up and horses and men were fed and watered, darkness had fallen. However Sir John Hurry, commanding the cavalry, soon caught up with the Royalist rearguard, which was then still only a few kilometres east of the town.

There was a brief fight, but in the dark Hurry was unwilling to press forward without infantry support and allowed the Royalists to break contact once again.

By midnight, according to Wishart, they were not far from Arbroath, a tolerably vague estimate which most likely means they had reached Elliot Water, just by the coast some twenty-two kilometres out of Dundee. From there, after a brief rest they faced about and again according to Wishart marched southwest and then north. Presumably, if they had been following the main road (now the A92), this means they must have doubled back along the coast to Panbride, just short of Carnoustie, before turning due north and crossing the main road at Muirdrum *behind* Hurry, who all unknowing was still pressing on towards Arbroath.

The Royalists now had a clear road open to a rendezvous with the rest of their forces at Brechin, but Baillie and Hurry must already have learned of it from stragglers. When Hurry arrived in Arbroath to find no trace of the Royalists he immediately turned north, and for a time there was a real prospect that they might be caught between Hurry's cavalry and Baillie's infantry marching up the road to Forfar. Instead Montrose sheered off again at Guthrie and struck off across country to get over the South Esk at Careston, just a little to the west of Brechin. Hurry for his part appears to have turned cautious and remained at Guthrie until daylight, ignoring repeated orders from Baillie to drive the rebels westwards.[29] Thus dawn found Baillie at Forfar, and the Royalists safely out of the trap. Hurry it is true did eventually get on their track again, but after another rearguard action at Edzell they disappeared up Glen Esk and beyond any practicable pursuit.

In later years Montrose's conduct of the retreat, aided as it was by a healthy dose of local knowledge, would justifiably be lauded as one of his most celebrated achievements, but at the time the Royalists were too well aware that in reality it was merely the difference between defeat and utter disaster. No sooner were they safely back in the hills than it all fell apart. Lord Gordon took his men back to Strathbogie, while Alasdair MacColla went to Braemar, perhaps to rally Monaltrie's people. Within days Montrose's own forces were reduced to less than 500 men, and on 17 April Baillie attacked him at Crieff and chased his troops all up Strathearn. The only bright spot was news that Huntly's second son, Lord Aboyne, had broken out of the beleaguered garrison at Carlisle and was on his way home. Knowing him to be a far more committed Royalist than his elder brother, Lord Gordon, Montrose risked a swift foray southwards three days later as far as Doune Castle, near Stirling, before picking him up at Cardross House and hurrying north to a rendezvous with MacColla on Deeside and a growing crisis in the northeast.

The timing of Aboyne's return was far more critical than anyone had realised, for after the failure to trap Montrose at Dundee Hurry and Baillie parted in no very good humour. A deputation from Aberdeenshire had turned up at Brechin on 5 April and pressed Baillie for the urgent assistance of some regulars. He reluctantly agreed to send Hurry north with two veteran infantry regiments – the Lord Chancellor's and the Earl of Lothian's – together with some 160 cavalry drawn from Sir James Halkett's Regiment. Not even a mutiny among Lothian's men at Aberdeen on 15 April could slow what rapidly turned into a triumphant progress. Calming the mutineers by producing their back pay and a fresh issue of clothing, Hurry sent orders for the Earls of Seaforth and Sutherland to muster their men at Inverness and set off to meet them, gathering the Aberdeenshire and Banffshire fencibles under Forbes of Millbuie and Crichton of Frendraught into a regiment of foot under Lord Findlater, and a regiment of dragoons for himself.

In the face of this growing cavalcade Lord Gordon prudently suspended his own recruiting and retired into the hills by way of Auchindoun and then rode to meet with Montrose. As soon as the Royalist leaders were reunited they agreed their first priority had to be the destruction of Hurry's army – an entirely predictable response, which suited Hurry just fine. He crossed over the river Spey on 3 May, and at a meeting in Elgin, with Seaforth (representing the northerners) and the Laird of Innes (representing the government's local supporters), it was resolved to turn and fight as soon as all three contingents could be combined.

Confident of victory the last thing Hurry wanted to do was to scare off the rebels before this promising concentration was complete and so he lingered at Elgin until the rebels too crossed the Spey late on 7 May – or more likely 8 May – and then retired very slowly through Forres. Hurry may not have been a military genius, but he was a very competent professional soldier and like the earlier raid on Aberdeen his fighting retreat was very much a textbook operation. Covered by his cavalry, his infantry steadily fell back in three- or five-kilometre bounds, halting each time to then cover the retiral of the cavalry before moving back another three or five kilometres. For the Royalists it was a slow and frustrating business. Hurry held the initiative throughout the day and while losing fifteen or sixteen troopers seemingly had no casualties amongst his infantry. Montrose's losses are largely unknown but they were obviously sufficient to keep him at a respectful distance. One casualty who can be identified however was young James Gordon of Rhynie, wounded during the crossing of the Spey and then subsequently murdered in his bed by some of the Laird of Innes' men – a pointless killing that only led to reprisals by Lord Gordon's men in the coming battle.

Montrose's own account has in the past been interpreted to mean that he actually pursued Hurry all the way to Inverness on 7 May, retired back to the village of Auldearn, just outside Nairn on 8 May and was attacked there by Hurry on the morning of 9 May. This seems rather unlikely. Montrose himself actually claimed that his running fight with Hurry's rearguard covered twenty-two kilometres, while Ruthven (who was evidently present) afterwards wrote that the first clash occurred at Forres. Assuming both are correct, and there is no reason to doubt it, this would suggest that Montrose followed Hurry no farther west than Cawdor, while Ruthven clearly states that the rebels actually halted at Auldearn. The obvious inference of course is that after that first action at Forres Montrose and the cavalry pushed on as far as Cawdor, before falling back again to rendezvous with the slower-moving infantry in Auldearn at or shortly after nightfall.[30]

Unfortunately Montrose had unwittingly broken contact with Hurry just as the latter was about to be significantly reinforced.

Chapter 6
We Gat Fechtin' Oor Fill
Auldearn and Alford

Auldearn

The night of 8 May found the Royalists quartered in and around the small village of Auldearn. From the evidence of subsequent events it would seem that the village itself was occupied by one of Lord Gordon's units – William Gordon of Monymore's newly raised regiment from Strathavan – and by Colonel Laghtnan's Irish regiment. The rest of the army however was widely scattered somewhat to the east of it. John Spalding's account blandly but rather tellingly states that they camped 'commodiously', which rather suggests that with the weather coming on to heavy rain Montrose and most of his men spread themselves far and wide around the countryside, seeking shelter in houses, cottages and barns over a very broad area. At any rate after the battle began next morning it certainly appears to have taken some hours for them all, Montrose included, to come together again.

When the Royalists last saw Hurry's army at dusk it had still been marching away from them, down the road to Inverness, and there was a natural but dangerous assumption that he would not stop until he got there. Accordingly the Royalists merely contented themselves with setting a strong 'watch' or picquet, but even then the sentries were poorly supervised in what turned out to be a dark night of pouring rain. By morning all of them seem to have crammed themselves into the shelter of Auldearn village with Monymore's Strathavan men. Consequently shortly before dawn an angry Alasdair MacColla rousted out half a dozen of them 'as God would have it' and ordered them to scout down the road at first light. What they thought of their assignment may easily be guessed, but as Ruthven remarked they saved the rebels from having their throats cut, for borne on the wind they heard a 'thundering report' of musketry.[1]

Somewhere to the west of Cawdor, Hurry had rendezvoused in the dark with the Inverness garrison and Seaforth's northern levies, then immediately turned around and marched back again, across country this time, hoping to surprise the rebels in their beds. In this he might well have succeeded had he not halted about six kilometres short of his objective in order to let his men clear and reload their muskets, before launching the assault. This was the 'thundring report' heard by MacColla's scouts, who, warned by the noise of the volley, raced back to rouse their sleeping comrades.

The modern village of Auldearn largely lies on an east–west axis, but in 1645 it was a longish straggle of cottages and yards running *south* from a point between the twin mounds marking a long-vanished motte-and-bailey castle on one side[2] and a steep hill crowned by the kirk on the other. While some modern accounts speak of its lying along a low ridge-line the original village street is actually situated on a westward-facing slope, which descends surprisingly sharply from the backs of the houses into a marshy 'bottom' formed by the Auldearn burn and its feeders. These small streams together with a fairly wide swathe of wet and boggy ground on each side formed a horseshoe, or rather almost a circle, enclosing a surprisingly prominent piece of relatively high ground called Garlic Hill, lying immediately to the west of the village.

This low hill, rising only about fifteen metres above its immediate surroundings, was partly covered in gorse bushes and turf-walled enclosures. At first sight of no great military significance in itself, it severely hampered the visibility of anyone not actually sitting on the top of it, and the shallow, boggy ground around it discouraged anyone from straying off it. Ultimately these constrictions would be compounded by the fact that the ground also rose a little on the outer sides of the horseshoe – again not by much, but sufficient to mask from view what might be happening beyond, where the Royalist army was frantically reassembling. All that Hurry could see as he deployed his forces in the grey light of dawn at the farm of Kinnudie, was a body of infantry formed up on Garlic Hill, with the village at their backs.[3]

According to Wishart:

> in front of the village he [Montrose] stationed a few picked foot soldiers, men of experience and prompt to act, along with his cannon, mounted by some small dykes, which had been cast up there. The right wing he entrusted to Alastair MacDonald with 400 foot stationed on ground which happened to be defended by dykes and ditches, brushwood and rocks

... he had [no centre] but a small body stationed under cover of the dykes before the
village made a show of one.[4]

In fact this description although outwardly plausible compresses rather too much
of the action and requires such a degree of correction that, allied with MacColla's
prominence in the ensuing events, it raises a real doubt that Montrose himself was
anywhere near the battlefield when the fighting began. The fact of the matter is
that referring to MacColla's command as the right wing is more than a touch
disingenuous. Throughout the morning he and his men were the only Royalist
troops actually on the field, and they only became the right at some time during
the afternoon – and possibly quite late in the afternoon at that.

The ever-meticulous Spalding claimed that in total the Royalists were 3,000
strong, while Hurry reckoned, or at least assured his own men, that they had only
about 2,000 infantry, besides 300 cavalry. On the other hand Montrose himself
claimed to have had the staggeringly low total of only 1,400 men, both horse
and foot. Astonishing as this figure sounds, it may not have been so very far from
the truth, particularly since it seems likely that a good many of those who had
been mustered with the army on the previous day never actually came into the
fight.[5] James Fraser, who seems on the whole to be a reliable witness, credits Lord
Gordon with having brought in 1,000 foot in addition to his 200 cavalry, and
Spalding agrees, adding 400 dragooners or mounted infantry. In addition there
were probably no more than about 700 Irish and Highlanders, although once
again most of them were quartered well to the east of the village, and MacColla
seemingly 'for all his diligence, could hardly get two regiments drawen wpe,
on of the Irishes, and on of Huntlie, when the enemie wer com in sight'. The
latter were the 200 raw recruits of Gordon of Monymore's Regiment, and it is
unlikely that the Irish (probably of Laghtnan's Regiment since it included his
own lifeguard company) mustered much more in order to give him the 400-odd
claimed by Wishart.

Hurry obviously had considerably more men right from the outset. For a
start he had no fewer than five regiments of regular infantry under his command:
Lothian's; the Lord Chancellor's; the Earl of Findlater's; and by now two more
from the Inverness garrison – Sir Mungo Campbell of Lawers' and the Laird of
Buchanan's. The victorious Royalists afterwards crowed that all five were well
trained and indeed the best troops in the kingdom, but this was true only up to
a point. Lawers', Lothian's and the Lord Chancellor's regiments were certainly
veterans, but Buchannan's although raised in 1644 had never seen action, and

nor had Findlater's, which had only been commissioned at the beginning of March 1645.[6]

If each of these regiments had mustered an average of 500 men, Hurry would have had 2,500 regulars at his disposal, but this is almost certainly far too high and no more than 400 apiece for the three 'old' regiments might be nearer the mark. Buchannan's moreover provided only a detachment, probably no more than 200 strong, since the greater part of the regiment was left guarding Inverness.[7] How successful Findlater's recruiting had been, in what was a disputed area, is impossible to say, but in the circumstances he will probably have been lucky to bring about 300 men to Auldearn.

Besides these 1,700–2,000 regulars, Hurry also had two newly raised regiments brought in by the Earls of Seaforth and Sutherland. Seaforth at least still had some 300 men in July, but that was after they had been savaged at Auldearn, so there could well have been as many as 400–500 there, and Sutherland may have brought the same from Strathnavar.[8] In addition there were also several hundred hastily assembled local levies, including the Laird of Grant's men and the Frasers from Beuly. All in all therefore Hurry could have had something in the region of 3,000 infantry of very variable quality.

His cavalry are less easy to reconstruct; some chroniclers estimate he may have had as many as 600 or 700, but once again this is probably too high. The best of them were the 160 troopers of Sir James Halkett's Regiment, but there were also three troops of Morayshire cavalrymen under a Major Drummond, which probably represented that part of Lord Gordon's Regiment that did not go over to the Royalists in February,[9] and Campbell of Lawers may also have had a little troop of his own. In addition there were those 400 dragooners Hurry had picked up in Aberdeenshire, but they figure in none of the accounts of the battle and so presumably stayed safely in the rear. Discounting the dragoons, it seems most unlikely that Hurry could muster more than 300 cavalry. Even then some of them were probably a touch seedy at that, for Ruthven rather sniffily claimed that while the Royalist cavalry were gentlemen their opponents 'wer bot troopers tain upe of the common multitude'.

Notwithstanding, Hurry ought to have had more than enough men to brush aside the 400-odd Royalists immediately to his front, but his problem was the decision to try to funnel his army over the dry ground of Garlic Hill. This meant fighting on a narrow frontage, which nullified much of his advantage in numbers. Nevertheless MacColla was still horribly outnumbered, and was immediately attacked by one of Hurry's regiments – almost certainly Sir Mungo Campbell

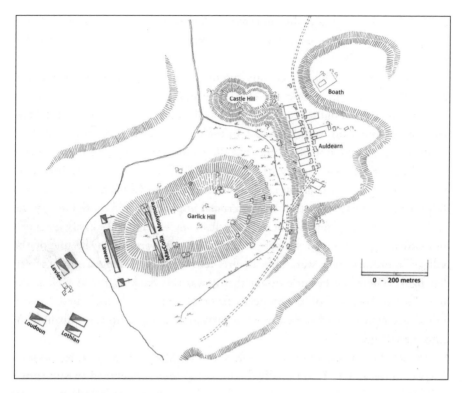

Map 6: *Auldearn 1645: Early morning.*

of Lawers' veterans from Ireland – supported by two troops of horse. The rebels opened fire first according to Fraser, but soon got the worst of the firefight. Macolla's own ensign was slain by the first volley, and although his distinctive yellow banner was immediately raised up again three more men were shot down in quick succession while holding it aloft. 'So efter a brave and long maintained resistance, he is forced a reteir to som yards of the toun.'[10]

As the Royalists tumbled back Hurry prudently kept his men in hand. Aside from any damage wrought in the initial encounter, they will have needed to reform their ranks and files after getting through the enclosures, and they might also have required a replenishment of ammunition. Ideally fresh troops should have been fed forward, but the constricted nature of the ground evidently prevented this. How long the pause lasted is unknown, but it at least gave MacColla time to barricade the village itself, which was in fact a far stronger position than a casual reading of contemporary accounts would suggest. With the momentum of Lawers' attack slowed by the marshy ground and then stopped entirely by the steep slope beyond, MacColla was able to make a stand, and a firefight – described by one eyewitness as 'continuall shot' – once again rippled up and down the line.

At least one Highland account suggests that the two regiments under MacColla's command were completely intermingled at this point and that his own Irishmen and Highlanders were spread all along the line to prevent the raw Gordon recruits from running away. In the circumstances a certain amount of confusion was no doubt inevitable, but the consensus actually seems to be that the village proper was largely held by MacColla's own men, while Nathaniel Gordon occupied the adjacent castle hill with William Gordon of Monymore's Regiment. The latter position was of crucial importance and quite literally the cornerstone of the defence. Not only was it strong enough to be easily defended in its own right, but also, because it projected westwards from the line of the village, Gordon's men were able to fire very effectively indeed into Lawers' left flank. There can be little doubt that it was this flanking fire as well as the unexpected steepness of the slope in front of him which frustrated Lawers' initial attempts to get his men moving forward again and up the embankment into the village.

In fact this combination was so effective that MacColla decided to mount a hasty counter-attack. Traditionally this move has been condemned by Montrose's biographers, who contend that MacColla's role was simply to hold Hurry's men in check while the marquis carefully positioned the remainder of his army for what would be the decisive counter-attack. According to this interpretation MacColla foolishly jeopardised the cunning plan by going forward too soon and so risking destruction before Montrose was ready.

In reality there was no carefully thought-out ambush in preparation and no evidence at all that MacColla was ordered by Montrose or anyone else to remain quietly on the defensive inside the village. The Royalists had been badly surprised, and Montrose had more than enough on his hands pulling his scattered army together. Until such time as he could assemble and bring up the rest of the army MacColla was on his own, and it was up to him to fight his battle as best he could.

Furthermore it is very difficult to be precise about how long this phase of the battle (or indeed any other episode of the battle) had lasted. With two notable exceptions, contemporary accounts almost invariably compress the battle into a few sentences and perhaps inadvertently create the impression that it was a fast-moving affair and all over very quickly. However those two accounts which do provide any sort of frame of reference are quite explicit in stating that the battle lasted all day. One report that reached Edinburgh stated that the fighting had raged for twelve hours, while James Fraser, who left the only known account by one of Hurry's men, confirms this by recording that the defeated army eventually withdrew across the river Nairn at How Ford, just three kilometres away from the battlefield *under cover of darkness*.[11] It has to be accepted therefore that the dramatic episodes recorded in the various accounts sometimes represent quite extended periods of time interspersed by equally lengthy pauses in the intensity of the fighting as each side regrouped for a renewed effort.

Therefore, assuming that first light in the overcast conditions would have been around 7 a.m. it is unlikely that the battle got underway until some time between 8 a.m. and 9 a.m. This may mean that in very general terms MacColla did not repulse the first attack on the village until 10 a.m. and then, given the time necessary to organise it, may not have counter-attacked much before 11 a.m.

At any rate when his attack did go in it began promisingly enough but then quite literally got bogged down in the same marshy bottom which had slowed Lawers' attack in the first place. Patrick Gordon of Ruthven, who was evidently an eyewitness, explicitly stated that: 'the ground wpon his left hand being all quagmyre and bushes, was in this second charge extreamly to his dissadvantage, wher his men could nether advance in order, not fynd sure footing to stand, nor marche forward to helpe ther fellows'.[12]

Clearly therefore this was no wild and impetuous Highland charge, or else Ruthven would not have stressed the difficulty in advancing 'in order' or more critically of bringing the left wing up to support the centre and right, which appear to have fought their way up into the enclosures on the forward slopes of Garlic Hill. Lawers for his part retired back up to the top of the hill, reorganised and then counter-attacked in turn – this time with two regiments. Once again however this must have taken some time to organise. Indeed both common sense and an overwhelming weight of precedent from countless similar episodes in military history would indicate that it probably took about an hour to get everyone in place, particularly since this time – which in all likelihood was at or shortly before midday – the attack was much better co-ordinated than the initial one.

Once again Lawers' own veterans led the assault in what was rapidly turning into a grudge-match. Many if not most of Seaforth's Highland levies were armed with bows, and so Lawers seems to have positioned them behind his own regiment so that they could shoot over their heads. This would bring an indirect fire down on the objective, and at the same time attempt to suppress that deadly flanking fire from the castle hill.

Perhaps for that reason this second attack was eventually more successful:

> The enemie, coming wp two regiments in a full body, flanked with horsemen, did charge the major (MacColla) in that deficult place; and the rest of ther maine battell following, on(e) regiment still secunding ane other; yet efter a strong and absteinat resistance, he mainteines his station with invinceible curage a long tym, till, opprest with multitude, and charge wpon charge, he was forced to give ground, and with great deficulty, befor he could reteir his people in good order, or kepe them from confused fleight.

The salient points which emerge from Ruthven's narrative are once again that the fighting on the hill was prolonged and that, albeit with some difficulty, MacColla eventually succeeded in retiring in good order back into the village. This time Lawers' men finally scrambled up the steep slope, broke into the yards and drove MacColla's people back into the houses and outbuildings from where they maintained a furious and often hand-to-hand resistance.

Hemmed in, MacColla had a number of pikes thrust into his round targe, but hacked off their heads, only for his sword to break in his hand. Ruthven rather picturesquely claims that he actually 'brak two swords', after which he was handed a third by his brother-in-law, Davidson of Applecross – who in the best heroic tradition was then himself cut down. As Applecross died, MacColla regained the temporary safety of a doorway, covered by another of his men, named Ranald Mackinnon, who pistolled an over-eager pikemen but then had an arrow shot through both his cheeks. Dropping the empty pistol Mackinnon tried to draw his sword, only to find it had stuck in the scabbard and then received a number of superficial wounds before staggering into the house. According to the bards a pikeman tried to follow him, but as he stuck his head through the door MacColla promptly cut it off. All the while, we are told, he was cursing the Gordons who he thought had let him down, although in reality it was their flanking fire from the castle hill which was still preventing Lawers from completely overrunning the village.

Nevertheless, although Lawers could not get his cavalry over the dykes and into the village, his infantry alone should have been sufficient to do the business. The pressure was simply becoming too great, and in what must have been a brief pause, as Lawers marshalled his men for the final assault, MacColla recognised that a total collapse was perhaps only a matter of minutes away:

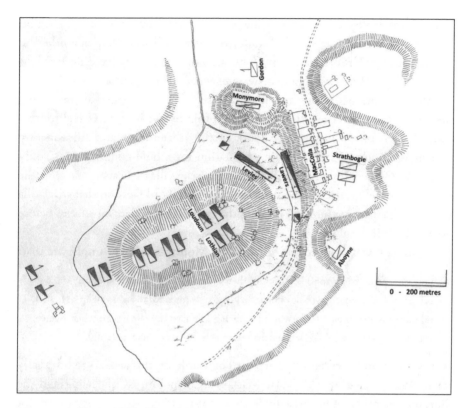

MAP 7: *Auldearn 1645: The crisis.*

. . . then for griefe was he ready to burst, seeing non to second him, and saw no hope of
victorie, but all the simptoms of a disasterous and dreadful overthrow. Wherefor he called
to those that wer about him, 'Ach, messoures,' said he, 'sall our enemies by this on dayes
work be able to wreast out of our handes all the glorie that we have formerly gained. Let it
never be said that a basse flight shall bear witness of it, or that our actiones should seem to
confesse so much; but let us die bravely; let it never be thought that they have triumphed
over our courage, nor the loyaltie we ow to our soveraigne lord, and let us hope the best.
God is stronge enough.'

And whill he whispered these words for he would not speak aloud, least the enemies
might imagine of yielding, behold how gratious Heavin and the Devyne Power did
assist him.[13]

The crisis of the battle had now been reached. MacColla still, however tenuously,
held the village, and Nathaniel Gordon the castle hill. Hurry's army meanwhile

had still not deployed into a battle line but was pretty largely stacked up behind Lawers' Brigade on Garlic Hill – 'on[e] regiment still secunding ane other' as Ruthven put it. Unfortunately, with his attention obviously fixed on the fight for the village, Hurry was quite unaware of what was happening beyond it.

All this time Montrose and his officers had been engaged in mustering the rest of the rebel army. Traditionally, as told by Wishart, he is said to have concealed his men a little to the south of the village in an area subsequently known as 'Montrose's Hollow' in preparation for a bold counter-attack, only to see MacColla defeated and driven back into the village. Fearing the worst he then handsomely retrieved the situation by telling Lord Gordon that MacColla was driving all before him and inviting the cavalry to emulate his success before he snatched all the glory.

In his own very brief report on the battle Montrose himself simply said that:

> they the enemy being confident both of their men and their number fell hotly on, but being beat back, seimed to coole of their fury, and only intended to blocke us up (as it wer) till more number should come which perceiving I divided myselfe in two wings (which was all the ground would suffer) and marched upon them most unexpectedly.[14]

At first sight, and as certainly interpreted by Gardiner, this appears to be exactly what Wishart later wrote – that MacColla's men formed one wing and the Gordons the other. What actually happened was rather less straightforward, for the two 'wings' actually came up on either side of the village.

The first, led not by Lord Gordon but by his younger brother Aboyne, attacked from the south, against Hurry's right flank. The result was devastating. It was supposedly covered by a troop of horse under Major Drummond, but he promptly panicked and, ordering his men to wheel to the left rather than to the right, avoided combat by riding over his own infantry.[15] According to Ruthven, Aboyne followed him into the shattered ranks and took four or five colours, so presumably the regiment ridden down was not Lawers' own but one of the supporting ones, most likely the Lord Chancellor's, for it was particularly badly cut up in the battle. Although presented as Montrose' cunning ambush this particular cavalry charge was not the decisive moment in the battle, for it was followed by another as Lord Gordon appeared from behind the castle hill, on the northern side of the battlefield, leading his own regular cavalry regiment:

> 'My Lord Gordon by this time charges the left winge', said Ruthven, 'and that with a new form of fight, for he discharges all shooting of pistoles and carrabines, only with

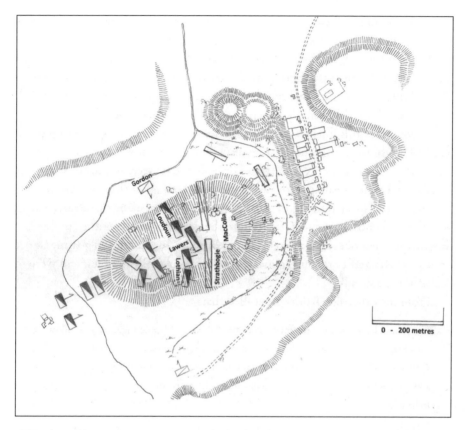

MAP 8: *Auldearn 1645: Counter-attack.*

ther swords to charge quhyt throwgh ther enemies, who wer so many in number, and so stronge and weell horsed as if by a desperat charge they had got them not broken, it was too apparent that they might recover the day. But Aboyn having overthrowen the right winge, and the main battell left bair on that syd, and seing Montrose and McDonnell joyned to give a new charge, the great body began to stagger, all their hopes being in ther left winge; and that my lord Gordon charges so soundly with swords only, as if they scorned to be resisted; they had all sworn to go throw or dye.[16]

Having summarily disposed of the single troop of horse on the left wing Gordon then charged straight into the flank of the unfortunate infantry, presumably Lawers' retreating brigade, and evidently drove the fugitives due southwards. According to Fraser, many of them were killed around the farms of Kinsteary and Brightmony, more than a kilometre to the southeast of the village and in quite the opposite direction they would have followed if broken by Aboyne's men charging out of 'Montrose's Hollow'.[17]

In the meantime Hurry could only brace himself to meet a renewed assault by fresh Royalist infantry. Fraser vividly recalls the horror of those standing on Garlic Hill as Montrose now brought his infantry up on MacColla's left and they saw the Strathbogie Regiment sweep around the southern end of the village.[18]

Accounts of this final stage of the battle, as the Royalists stormed up on to Garlic Hill for the third time, are tantalisingly brief, but it was evidently a savage fight. Montrose, laconic as ever, relates only that there were 'some hot salvyes of musket and a litell dealing with sword and pike'; but all of the other chroniclers emphasise the sheer ferocity of the fighting. Spalding states that Hurry's men were 'for the most part cut af, fighting to the death most valiauntlie'; and Fraser sorrowfully describes how the rebels 'run throw them, killing and goaring under foot . . . Lairs and Lothians regiment stood in their ranks and files, and were so killed as they stood'.

From the other side Ruthven recalled that:

> you should have sein how the infantrie of the Royalists, keiping together and following the charge of the horsemen, did tear and cut them in pieces, even in rankes and fyles, as they stood, so great was the execution which they made efter the horse had shanken and quyt astonished them, by persueing rudly throw them, as it was very lamentable to behold.[19]

Campbell of Lawers' Regiment lost its colonel, together with Lieutenant-Colonel William Campbell, and at least four of the company commanders – Captain Campbell, Captain William Bruce, Captain Cashore and Captain Shaw.[20] The Earl of Lothian's Regiment lost four company commanders – Captain William Douglas (one of the nine nephews of Douglas of Cavers said to have been killed there), Captain Alexander Drummond, Captain Gideon Murray and Captain Sir John Murray[21] – thus obliquely confirming Ruthven's account of their being overrun. Even worse hit may have been the Lord Chancellor's Regiment for a bare 100 men survived to fight at Kilsyth in August, which strongly suggests that it was they who were ridden down by Lord Gordon's cavalry and pursued southwards.

Both Lord Findlater and his second-in-command, Walter Ogilvie of Boyne, escaped from the battlefield, but nothing further is heard of his regiment, which presumably disintegrated. The raw northern levies also appear to have suffered quite badly, although the evidence for this is largely anecdotal. Robert Grant, the eldest son of Grant of Shewglie in Glen Urquhart, was killed, as was a Captain Bernard McKenzie together with most of his company from the Chanonry of Ross in the Black Isle, while Fraser records that his own chief, Lovat, was left with eighty-seven widows to support.

Just as the fighting has tended to be somewhat compressed, so too was its ending. While chroniclers were prone to emphasising the carnage wrought in the pursuit, the southward drift of the fugitives towards Brightmony and Kinsteary evidently drew far too many of the Royalists in the same direction, as Hurry fell back due westwards in a fighting retreat over the river Nairn at Howford. By that time the last of his rearguards were over the river, darkness had fallen and the Royalists were probably pretty glad to see him go, for their own losses had been heavy. Ruthven rather airily quotes sixteen dead, fourteen of them MacColla's men, while Spalding gives '24 gentlemen hurt to Montross, and sum few Irishes killit, which is miraculous'. The significant word however is *gentlemen*, which to all intents and purposes may be translated as officers.

Gordon of Sallagh on the other hand while recording twenty-two gentlemen killed, which is broadly consistent with both Ruthven's and Spalding's accounts, rather more realistically includes another 200 common soldiers, to which must be added an unknown but certainly greater number of wounded.[22] Just how many of them there were can be guessed from the fact that shortly afterwards it took a whole day to get the baggage train and wounded across the Spey and into the relative security of Bog of Gight Castle. If two to three times as many men had been wounded as were killed, then well over a third and perhaps as many as half of the Royalists were rendered *hors de combat* in winning their famous victory.

There is certainly no doubting that they had been crippled. While Hurry eventually retired unmolested to Inverness, still with a fair number of men including the remnants of Campbell of Lawers' Regiment,[23] the Royalists paused only long enough to recover their wounded and scavenge the battlefield before retreating in the opposite direction first to Elgin and then recrossing the Spey on 14 May to lick their wounds at Birkenbog, near Cullen.

Alford

General Baillie meanwhile had been engaged in what he later described as 'ane innecessary voyage into Athole by order of the Committee', which commenced on 3 May. His objective seemingly was the Royalist depot at Blair Castle, which not only served as a base hospital but was also enticingly stuffed full of accumulated plunder and prisoners. The attractions of the place were obvious, but without artillery he could do nothing, and as soon as decently possible he set off for the north with 2,000 foot and 100 horse, intended to join with Hurry. Unfortunately the Committee of political advisers, which he had been saddled with ever since his falling out with Argyle, insisted that the Lowlands could not be left undefended. Accordingly the Earl of Lindsay remained behind with his own and two other regiments, while Baillie went on to cross the Dee with just Glencairn's and Callendar's regiments, only to receive unconfirmed reports of a battle on 11 May. Prudently he halted to wait for further news and reinforcements. The latter turned up a week later in the shape of the Earl of Balcarres at the head of his own veteran regiment of cavalry and two provisional battalions of 'redcoats' drawn from the regiments of the Scots army in Ulster, under the command of Colonel Robert Home. Even with this very solid reinforcement he was still inclined to be wary, since he lacked reliable intelligence of the rebels' whereabouts until Sir John Hurry broke out of Inverness with his remaining cavalry on 20 May.

At that point the balance of affairs abruptly shifted. Not only did Baillie now know exactly where the Royalists were, but for the first time he also learned that their curious and quite uncharacteristic inactivity proceeded from their shattered condition after the battle. Moreover, widely dispersed as they were, they were clearly vulnerable to a sudden offensive – and so it proved. On 21 May Montrose received 'haistie advertesment' that Baillie was marching north. His initial reaction was to move forward with whatever troops were immediately at hand, and he began digging in at Strathbogie (Huntly) Castle that evening, but later that night he decided discretion was after all the better part of valour and hastily decamped westwards to Speyside.[24]

Baillie was soon on the rebels' track and caught up with them at Glenlivet, which shows he must have been marching hard, but they shook him off again at nightfall. Next morning Baillie's scouts deduced by the trampled grass and heather that the rebel army was making for Abernethy. Setting off again he seems to have come up with them somewhere near Aviemore 'in the entrie of Badzenoch, a very strait country, where, both for unaccessible rocks, woods, and the interposition of the river, it wes impossible for us to come at them'. Reluctantly, at this point Baillie had to admit defeat. His men had done all that was asked of them and more, but now they were exhausted and starving, the cavalry complaining that they had had no food for forty-eight hours. With the rebels posted in an unassailable position Baillie had no alternative but to pull back to Inverness and refit.

As soon as Baillie had marched out of sight Montrose sought to capitalise on his isolation by lunging southwards, hoping to break out of the hills into the seemingly undefended Lowlands. Instead he found himself confronted by another force under the Earl of Lindsay, dug in along the river Isla at Newtyle in Angus. Whatever hopes he might have entertained of forcing this position were then abruptly dashed by the news that Baillie had moved out of Inverness again and commenced devastating the Gordon recruiting grounds in the northeast. Lord Gordon thereupon insisted on heading north with all his men, leaving Montrose with just 200-odd Irish mercenaries and no alternative but to retreat back into the hills and take refuge for a time at Corgarff in upper Strathdon.

Baillie meanwhile had returned safely to Aberdeen and there parted company with Hurry, who retired from the army pleading a diplomatic indisposition – being unable to stomach serving under him. Unfortunately any pleasure at their parting was quickly ruined by a summons to rendezvous with Lindsay near Aberdeen. The earl brought bad news. The Committee of Estates was dissatisfied with Baillie's handling of operations and rather astonishingly considered him to be insufficiently determined in his pursuit of the rebels! Instead a new army was to be assembled under the Marquess of Argyle, and Baillie, now relegated to a purely defensive supporting role, was ordered to give up his own 'Irish' Brigade – the 1,200 veterans drawn from the Scots army in Ulster – and 100 of Balcarres' Horse, in exchange for a mere 400 men of the Earl of Cassillis' Regiment of Foot.

This nonsensical plan was soon abandoned. First Argyle once again declined command of the new army, and then Lindsay took off on another 'unnecessary voyage' into Atholl, while Baillie – far from remaining on the defensive – was ordered to take his badly depleted little army north again and link up with the Earl of Seaforth. Predictably, despite receiving a substantial shipment of muskets and pikes with which to re-equip his levies, Seaforth failed to appear, and the general was falling back on Aberdeen when he ran into the Royalists at the village of Keith on 24 June. Fortunately, having had some warning of their approach, he took up a good position by the kirk and the discomfited rebels were once again reduced to challenging him to come down and fight them in the open. Naturally enough he refused their playground invitation, and to his surprise they immediately began retreating southwards. Intrigued he got his scouts out again and discovered that the challenge had been a bluff; Alasdair MacColla had gone off to the west with most of the remaining Irish and the Royalists were just as weak as he was. Determinedly setting off in pursuit, at about noon on 1 July Baillie caught up with them at the foot of the Correen Hills, where Montrose turned at bay on some rising ground either at the Suie Foot or Knockespock. Instead of attacking however Baillie 'turned aside about three miles to the left' to rendezvous with a contingent of Aberdeenshire reinforcements at Leslie Castle, whereupon a greatly relieved Montrose continued his retreat down the Suie Road to Alford, spending the night at nearby Asloun Castle.

Thus the morning of 2 July 1645 found the Royalist army posted on top of a large, rather rounded eminence known as Gallows Hill, overlooking the road just to the south of the swift-flowing river Don. That much is certain, but otherwise there is some considerable dispute as to where the battle was actually fought. There was a natural assumption that Baillie and his men would follow the Royalists down the Suie Road. The influential historian John Buchan not only postulated that they did so but then also presented an extraordinary picture of their duly crossing at Boat of Forbes and trying to outflank the Gallows Hill position (in the mistaken belief that it was held only by a rearguard) only to have the Royalists descend on them like the proverbial wolf on the fold.

Instead, while Montrose himself was reconnoitring the ford, word came to him that Baillie was indeed outflanking him – but by crossing a quite different ford 'a mile distant from Alford'.[25] This is explicitly confirmed by a contemporary Aberdeenshire ballad – very evidently composed by one of the unfortunate Forbes levies – for Baillie, having spent the night at Leslie, marched due south from there, parallel to but at some distance to the east of the Suie Road. Furthermore, far from rushing blindly in pursuit of the rebels, the ballad specifically relates that Baillie formed his men in order of battle at Mill Hill – a farm still lying on the road that crosses Correens between Knock Soul and Satter Hill, very near to where it comes down to cross the Don by the ford at Mountgarrie a kilometre or so due east and downstream from Boat of Forbes.[26] The fact that Baillie had halted to form his men in order of battle before crossing at Mountgarrie also confirms that he was deliberately advancing to contact, and the Royalists for their part hastily shifted around to their right to face him.

A frontal attack on the hill was obviously out of the question, so once he was across Baillie halted on the low-lying How of Alford. This is a fairly flat area adjacent to the tiny village of the same name, which prior to the coming of the railway amounted to little more than a small inn and a few houses.

Baillie's army can be partially reconstructed by reference to both his own detailed report and some other official papers. He had at least six regiments of regulars – Cassillis', Elcho's, Lanark's, Moray's, Glencairn's and Callendar's – of which the first at least mustered about 400 men. The probability is that in total

Baillie had about 2,400 infantry, although it is likely that there may also have been a seventh regiment, made up of Aberdeenshire levies under one or other of the Forbes lairds. At any rate Baillie himself reckoned that he was outnumbered by about 2:1 and therefore drew them up in only three ranks deep in order to avoid their being outflanked.[27]

As to the cavalry protecting his flanks, Baillie makes reference in his report only to Balcarres' Regiment on the left and Halkett's Regiment on the right, totalling a mere 260 men. However the Royalist accounts, perhaps predictably credit him with twice that number. It is probably significant that Baillie also refers to his cavalry regiments being drawn up in three squadrons rather than the two, which was the normal practice in the Scots army. Presumably therefore the two additional squadrons were some of the Aberdeenshire levies picked up at Leslie the day before (they certainly included Forbes of Craigievar's men), and Baillie may therefore have had something approaching 400 cavalry after all.

On the other hand the composition of the Royalist army is not at all clear, but there is fairly broad agreement that Montrose disposed of some 200–300 cavalry commanded by Lord Gordon and his brother Aboyne, and something over 2,000 infantry.

The main battle or centre, according to Ruthven, comprised the Strathbogie Regiment and 'Huntly's Highlanders' – a rather elastic term which certainly encompassed James Farquharson of Inverey's 'standing regiment' from Deeside as well as William Gordon of Monymore's 200 Strathavan men. In total the Gordon contingent could have been about 1,000 strong and to all intents and purposes was made up of regulars, or at least veterans who could be relied on to do what they were told by Inverey, who seemingly had the command of the whole. Oddly enough however Montrose's chaplain, George Wishart, claims that the centre was commanded by MacDonald of Glengarry, assisted by Lieutenant-Colonel George Drummond of Balloch and the quartermaster-general, George Graham. While this statement was explicitly refuted by Ruthven it does at least point to the slightly surprising presence of a MacDonald contingent, which may have added another 200 or so to the front line.

Since Baillie, despite his protestations to the contrary, clearly had more cavalry than the Royalists, the remaining Irish mercenaries were parcelled out on the wings to support the rebel cavalry: Laghtnan's Regiment with Lord Gordon on the right; and O'Cahan's with Aboyne on the left. In addition there was also a reserve placed behind the centre under the command of Lord Napier, although its composition is entirely uncertain.

Baillie, understandably enough, was far from keen on the idea of attacking and afterwards complained that he was 'necessitate to buckle with the enemie' despite his assessment that he was outnumbered. Just why he was 'necessitate' was not explained, but there seems to have been a pretty widespread rumour that he was

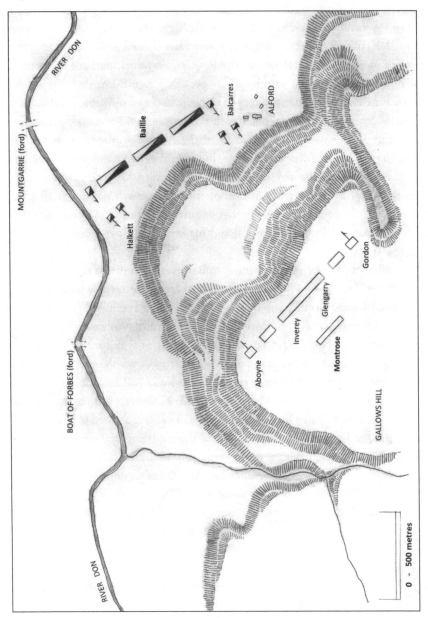

Map 9: *Alford 1645.*

hustled into it by Balcarres' forwardness.[28] At any rate all the sources agree that the battle began with a clash between the latter's regiment and Lord Gordon's.

With the slope in their favour Lord Gordon's men initially threw the Covenanters back, but then were in turn brought to a stand after Balcarres committed his second squadron. Baillie himself then tried to intervene by ordering Forbes of Craigievar's squadron to charge the rebels in flank, but instead Craigievar simply moved up behind Balcarres to add his weight to the press. In the end it was the intervention of Gordon's supporting infantry that proved decisive. As the Irish infantry got in among the near stationary mass of horses with dirk and sword, Balcarres' formation fell apart and his troopers scattered in panic.

The fighting on the other wing is rather more obscure, but the indications are that Halkett's troopers never came into contact with Aboyne's men at all. Instead both sides contented themselves with an ineffectual exchange of pistol and carbine fire, until Lord Gordon, swinging right around the rear of Baillie's infantry, broke in on Halkett's men from behind. Unfortunately in the understandable confusion that followed Lord Gordon was killed – according to local tradition shot in the back by either one of his own men, or more likely by one of Aboyne's troopers.

It was the end too for Baillie's infantry. Commanded by Lieutenant-Colonel John Kennedy of Cassillis' Regiment, they had thus far held their own in a firefight with the Royalists, and now, as Wishart admits, they still 'fought on doggedly, refusing quarter, and they were almost all of them cut down'.[29] But it was Baillie himself who pronounced their epitaph: 'Our foot stood with myselfe and behaved themselves as became them, untill the enemies horse charged in our reare, and in front we were overcharged with their foot.'[30]

Baillie's army was substantially destroyed. The contemporary Aberdeenshire ballad relates how the Royalists 'hunted us and dunted us and drove us here and there, until three hunder o' oor men lay gasping in their lair'. The author must however have been talking only of the Aberdeenshire forces for there are indications that Baillie's losses were much higher. Only a hundred apiece of Cassillis' and Glencairn's regiments survived to fight at Kilsyth six weeks later, and while the survivors of Callendar's Regiment missed that particular disaster this may have been because their losses at Alford were even greater. At any rate while 800 reinforcements were allocated to each of the former in August, Callendar's was granted 850. Elcho's, Lanark's and Moray's regiments were also substantially destroyed, and in total Baillie may therefore have lost upwards of 1,000 rather than 300 men.

Once again Royalist losses may also have been comparatively high in what was evidently a hard-fought fight. Wishart ludicrously claims that Montrose had not a single common soldier killed, but Fraser refers to 'a considerable losse upon Montrosse his side'. Ruthven speaks of seven officers being killed, besides Lord Gordon, which if we apply the same 1:10 ratio implied in Sallagh's account of Auldearn might suggest a total of 80–100 dead.[31] Whatever the true number the most serious loss was undoubtedly that of Lord Gordon, for while his younger brother Aboyne was a more committed Royalist, his relationship with Montrose was far less cordial and would soon become acrimonious.

In the meantime, at long last Montrose had a victory that he could exploit. There was still an army under the Earl of Lindsay to the south of him, but he knew that Seaforth and the northern levies would not stir beyond Inverness, and now, with Baillie's army also destroyed, he was able to move south with his rear secure. There was all the more necessity for this for the king had been very badly beaten at Naseby in Northamptonshire a few weeks earlier, and it was imperative that Montrose do something to relieve the pressure on him.

Nevertheless it was a slow business. Once his elder brother was buried in Aberdeen with all due ceremony, Aboyne agreed to march south but first insisted on raising more men. In the meantime he extracted a promise from Montrose that he would not fight until he was reinforced – which rather suggests the marquis's colleagues were by now rather wary of his predilection for rushing into fights without sufficient men or adequate reconnaissance.

Unfortunately he then proceeded to do just that. At Fordoun in the Mearns, MacColla rejoined him with 1,400 men of the western clans and 200 of Inchbrackie's Athollmen. Encouraged by this substantial accession of strength Montrose immediately essayed a raid on Perth. There was in fact some justification for this for with plague (the same typhus that originated in the Tynemouth garrison) raging in Edinburgh a parliament due on 24 July was to meet at Perth instead. Establishing himself in the nearby Methven Wood, Montrose then mounted a series of fairly ineffectual demonstrations over a period of about a week before an unlikely pairing of Baillie and Hurry chased them out. As at Dundee the pursuit was botched, once again because Hurry's cavalry failed to move as fast or as determinedly as expected, and the only loss to the Royalists was the slaughter of many of their camp-followers abandoned in the woods.

There was however another and more important result. Baillie finally decided he had had enough and resigned on 4 August.

Chapter 7

High Noon

Kilsyth and Philiphaugh

William Baillie of Letham[1] had been a professional soldier for all of his life, first in the Netherlands and then in the Swedish service before coming home to Scotland, serving under Leven at Marston Moor and Newcastle, and then taking over as commander-in-chief in Scotland on Argyle's resignation. In fairness to Baillie he exercised some considerable skill in carrying out this office, but whether, given a free hand, he could have encompassed the ruin of the Royalist cause is an open question. To employ a well-worn cliché, in his own mind at least those in front of him might be his opponents, but his enemies were behind him. And what was more some of those Baillie regarded as his enemies were very powerful men indeed, as he afterwards complained:

> Because I would not consent to receive orders from the Marquis of Argyle (if casuallie we
> should have mett together) after I received commission to command in chief over all the
> forces within the Kingdome, my Lord seemed to be displeased, and expressed himselfe
> so unto some, that if he lived, he should remember it; wherein his lordship indeed hath
> super-abundantly been alse good as his word.[2]

Kilsyth

It was not just Argyle of course, and the picture that emerges from his lengthy and extremely detailed report into the causes of the defeat at Kilsyth is of a man constantly at odds with his political masters. It is difficult to determine whether Baillie's undoubted intransigence in the latter days of his command was a consequence of the breakdown between them, or more likely the cause of it. Suffice it to say that wherever justice lay, by the summer of 1645 Baillie was becoming increasingly irascible and now, exasperated by his failure to trap Montrose in Methven and by what he regarded as constant political interference in military operations, he resigned as commander-in-chief. His 'dimission' was duly accepted, but as neither Hurry nor Lindsay would touch the job he was instructed to serve out his notice until 8 September, while Robert Monro was fetched back from Ireland to take his place.

At the same time and for the avoidance of all doubt it was clearly laid down that for the future: 'the directing of the Warre shall be by Parliament, or Committee of Parliament; and the actual managing and executing of the directions to be by the Commander-in-Chiefe, as he will be answerable to the Parliament or ther Committee'.[3] It sounded straightforward enough, but while a parliament or Committee sitting in Edinburgh might direct Leven in England or Monro in Ireland to pursue a particular objective by whatever means necessary, Baillie now found that Committee quite literally riding at his elbow and interfering in the day-to-day management of those directions. It was obviously an uncomfortable position, but once again it may be enquired whether the Committee wished themselves on him entirely of their own volition or whether they were constrained to do so by his stubborn and increasingly unco-operative attitude. At all events while their influence and frequent interference were certainly unhelpful it would be unwise to regard Baillie as an entirely innocent victim in what followed.

In the meantime Aboyne at last came south to rendezvous with Montrose at Dunkeld, bringing with him 400 cavalry and 800 good infantry to take part in the culminating act of the campaign. As Montrose pushed southwards once more, Baillie dug in at Bridge of Earn only for the Royalists to bypass his fortified camp and head for the Mills of Forth, above Stirling, on 11 August. Exactly what their objective was is now unclear for they were still avoiding a fight. As even Montrose can hardly have been contemplating pushing south into England at this stage, the likelihood is that they were simply intent on doing as much damage as possible in the Covenanting heartland, spreading the revolt and thus relieving pressure on the king by forcing the withdrawal of the Scots army from England.

Delayed by an errant infantry brigade, which incontinently marched home to Fife, and by another falling out with his political masters, Baillie was slow in getting after them, but crossed Stirling Bridge on 14 August. By now it was clear that the Royalists were heading towards Glasgow rather than Edinburgh, and Baillie's scouts soon reported them to be encamped near Kilsyth on a high meadow overlooking what is now the A803 road. Following cautiously Baillie marched by way of Denny and encamped that night at a farm called Hollandbush. What happened next bears careful consideration, for as at Auldearn the generally accepted version of events told in secondary sources fails to stand up to scrutiny.

Next morning, Argyle came to Baillie's quarters and not unreasonably enquired of him where the rebels were. Baillie replied that they were still sitting at Kilsyth and that the army was quite close enough if they were not going to fight. Although Baillie makes no mention of the fact in his evidence there may have been an underlying assumption at this point that action should be deferred until further reinforcements came up under the Earl of Lanark. However, no doubt mindful of the Royalists' tendency to cut and run (and exasperated by an increasingly petulant Baillie), Argyle and the rest of the Committee insisted on an immediate advance. In the circumstances it was a reasonable enough decision, for Lanark was still at Glasgow. Therefore, still anticipating that the Royalists intended to ambush him, Baillie left the road and 'marched with the regiments through the corns and over the braes, untill the unpassible ground did hold us up'.[4]

At this point he was evidently deployed along the line of the present road between the modern village of Banton to the A803 at Kelvinhead, for it is clear from Baillie's narrative that the army was halted on a reverse slope since he had to gallop over the brae to look at the ground. The industrial revolution came early to this area, and much of it is pockmarked with eighteenth-century coal and iron workings and a reservoir serving the Forth and Clyde canal. Notwithstanding these superficial scars it is easy to see how unattractive the uneven lie of the land must have seemed to Baillie for that reservoir conceals a deep glen, which would have made a formidable obstacle in itself.

This was unfortunate for Baillie was actually sitting on the rebels' left flank and otherwise poised to inflict a memorable defeat. The Committee thought so too and as he related:

> It was asked of me by the Lords, but by whom in particular I have forgot, if we could not draw up on the hill on our right hand? I shew them I did not conceive that ground to be good, and that the rebels (if they would) might possess themselves of it before us. Their Lordships then desired that some might be sent to visit the ground; which was done. In the meantime I went with my Lord Elcho and Burghlie to the right hand of the regiments. Not long after I was sent for by the other noblemen, and I desired the Lord Elcho and Burghlie to go with me, conjecturing they would press our removing; which at our coming they did, alleadging the advantage might be had of the enemies from that field, they being, as

I supposed, already upon their march westward. I liked not the motion: I told them if the rebels should seek to engadge us there I conceaved they should have great advantage of us; farder if we should beat them to the hill, it would be unto us no great advantage: But, as I had said upon like disputes near unto Methven and the Bridge of Earn to us the loss of the day would be the loss of the Kingdome. This wes not satisfactory: and therefore I gathered the voices of such of the Committee as wer there, namely the Marquess Argyle, the Earles of Crawford[5] and Tullibardine, the Lords Elcho, Burghlie and Balcarras; who the rest wer I remember not; but all agreed to draw unto the hill except Balcarras.

How much hindsight was being employed here is difficult to say but it is clear that there was a real problem. In order to avoid an ambush Baillie had taken the army off the road only to effectively march into a dead end: 'where I doubt if on any quarter twenty men on a front could either have gone from us or attack us'. This presented some unpalatable choices: they could move to the left, back on to the road and fight on a battlefield of Montrose's choosing; or they could sit tight, wrangling among themselves while the Royalists slipped out of their grasp yet again; or finally they could avoid the 'impassible ground' by striking northwards to seize the high ground at Auchinrivoch behind the enemy's left flank.

It is little wonder that Baillie, having inadvertently gotten the army into a hole, should have been so defensive and difficult at the council of war, but there was no real alternative to this bold move and initially it went well enough. Many secondary sources deride it as having been foolishly carried out in full view of the Royalists, but, as Baillie's own very detailed account makes clear, during the early part of the march his army was still concealed on a reverse slope. Moreover, for their part the Royalists, as Ruthven admits, were taken by surprise, learning that Baillie's men were 'within three myles befor he [Montrose] knew of there approach'. Far from being poised to attack as Baillie's men began their turning movement, they themselves were still hastily forming themselves up in order of battle and busily pulling white shirts over their clothing by way of a recognition sign.[6] If they moved swiftly enough Baillie's men were well placed to win the race for the high ground, but instead it all went wrong.

All too conscious of the importance of moving fast, Baillie instructed a Major John Haldane to march directly to the hill with a composite battalion of musketeers and there establish himself in a stone-walled enclosure, probably at Wester Auchinrivoch. Then once everyone else was following in their wake he again rode up to the crest 'to see the posture of the enemie, who were embattled in the meadow and sundries of them disbanded were falling up the glen through

PLATE I: *King Charles I, as depicted by Wenceslas Hollar in 1644, striking a suitably martial pose with a splendid depiction of an seventeenth-century army behind him.*

Argyle a muckle Scotch Knaue in gude faith Sir.

PLATE 2 ABOVE: *Archibald Campbell, Marquess of Argyle, as depicted on a contemporary playing card.*

PLATE 3 LEFT: *James Graham, Marquis of Montrose, in an engraving of his portrait by Honthurst.*

PLATE 4 BELOW: *This gentleman reviewing his somewhat motley levies could belong to any of the armies.*

PLATE 5 ABOVE: *Alexander Leslie, first Earl of Leven, and arguably the finest soldier of the period.*

PLATE 6 RIGHT: *Contemporary illustration of a typical cavalry trooper, wearing no armour beyond his helmet and buff leather coat, but well provided with firearms.*

PLATE 7 LEFT: *In contrast to the formal portrait with armour, Montrose was described at the Craibstane Rout as wearing 'a coit and trewis as the Irishis were clad'.*

PLATE 8 BELOW: *Huntly Castle, in the district of Strathbogie, was the abode of George Gordon, Marquis of Huntly – Montrose's great rival.*

FOR GOD THE KING AND AGANIST ALL TRAITTOURIS

C R

GOD SAVE THE KING

PLATE 9 TOP LEFT: *Strathbogie Regiment colours 1644 — yellow with red lion rampant.*

PLATE 10 CENTRE LEFT: *Irish brigade colour — white with a red cross, and in the canton a red saltire on yellow.*

PLATE 11 BOTTOM LEFT: *Irish brigade colour — yellow with the risen Christ and a red saltire in the canton.*

PLATE 12 BELOW: *George Keith's Regiment 1648 — red with a white saltire.*

PLATE 13 BOTTOM RIGHT: *Fraser's Firelocks colours 1648 — blue with a white saltire and the arms of Old Aberdeen.*

VIVAT CAROLUS REX

CR

AEQVVM EST PRO CHRISTO MORI

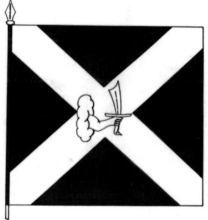

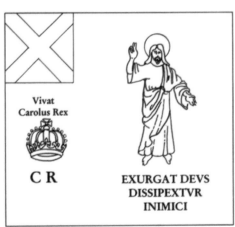

Vivat Carolus Rex

C R

EXURGAT DEVS DISSIPEXTVR INIMICI

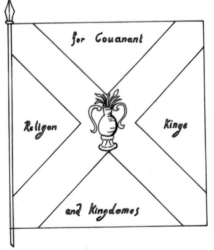

for Couanant

Religon

Kinge

and Kingdomes

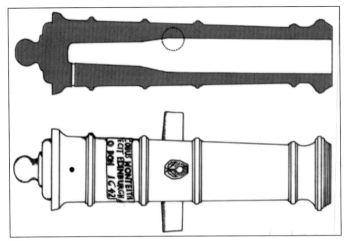

PLATE 14 LEFT:
Bronze cannon 1642.

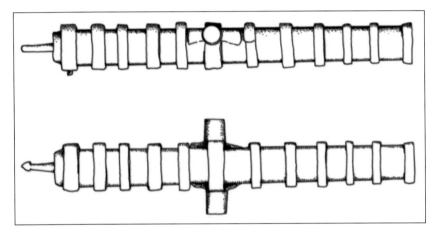

PLATE 15 ABOVE: *Tin and iron core of leather gun.*

PLATE 16 BELOW: *Double-barrelled leather gun.*

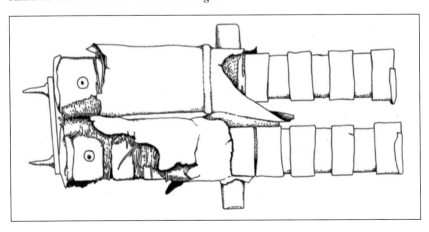

PLATE 17 RIGHT: *Soldier with Lochaber axe, a timeless figure actually sketched in 1745 but quite indistinguishable from his forebears of a century before.*

PLATE 18 BELOW RIGHT: *Highland bowman.*

PLATE 19 BELOW: *Scottish musketeer as depicted by Georg Koler of Nuremberg in 1631.*

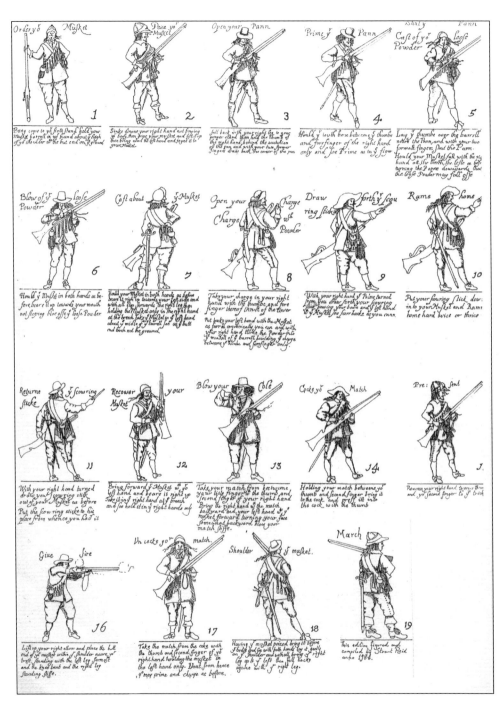

PLATE 20: *While this broadsheet depicting the musket drill of the period looks intimidating it was intended as a step-by-step guide, and in battle the process was a good deal quicker than suggested here.*

PLATE 21 ABOVE: *Auldearn – Boath Doo-Cot on Castle Hill.*

PLATE 22 BELOW: *Alford – the ford at Mountgarrie where Baillie crossed in 1645.*

PLATE 23 LEFT: *A somewhat unflattering depiction of Oliver Cromwell.*

PLATE 24 RIGHT: *Highland piper.*

PLATE 25: *A splendidly romantic but far from accurate depiction of a struggle between a Highland soldier and some of Cromwell's men, perhaps at Inverkeithing in 1651.*

PLATE 29 ABOVE: *Another of Forbes' colours, this time a yellow saltire on green.*

PLATE 26 ABOVE LEFT: *Forbes' Regiment colours 1650 or 1651 – a silver bear's head on white.*

PLATE 27 CENTRE RIGHT: *Balfour of Burleigh's Regiment colours 1650 – black with the maiden of Burleigh in the centre and a white saltire in the canton.*

PLATE 28 BELOW: *Colonel John Innes' Regiment colours 1650 – white with a cockerel in its proper colours.*

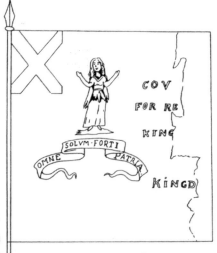

PLATE 30 BELOW: *Montrose's foot colours 1650 – black with the severed head of King Charles I.*

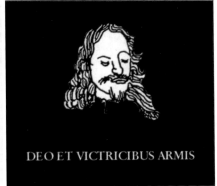

PLATE 31 RIGHT: *The Laird of Warreston [sic], a contemporary caricature of the Scottish politican Archibald Johnston of Wariston.*

Laird of Warreston an arrant
Knaue Au my Saul man.

PLATE 32 BELOW: *The Scots holding their young king's head to the grindstone — a telling political cartoon, which also provides a splendid illustration of a Scottish foot soldier.*

THE SCOTS HOLDING THEIR YOVNG KINGES NOSE TO Y GRINSTONE

Come to the Grinstone Charles tis now to late:
To Recolect, tis presbiterian fate:.

Iou Couinant pretenders must Ibee
The subiect of Iouer Tradgie Comedie

Jockie

Stoope Charles

PLATE 33 LEFT:
Major–General John Lambert.

PLATE 34 BELOW:
Colonel George Monck.

PLATE 35 BELOW: *Panoramic view of the battlefield of Dunbar, from the top of Doon Hill.*

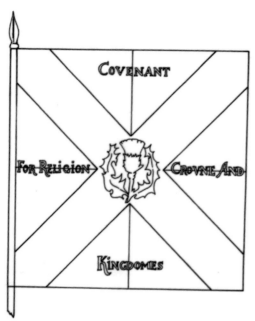

PLATE 36 ABOVE: *Colonel William Stewart's Regiment colours – white saltire on a field quartered red and blue.*

PLATE 37 ABOVE: *Preston of Valleyfield's Regiment colours 1650 – a black unicorn crest on a white field.*

PLATE 38 BELOW: *The Dunbar medal, struck for the officers of the victorious English army.*

PLATE 39: *King Charles II, as portrayed after his Restoration in 1660. He pointedly refused ever to set foot in Scotland again after his eventful year as the guest of the Covenant.*

the bushes'. This ought to have been encouraging enough, for it confirms Ruthven's version that the Royalists were still in some confusion at this point. Unfortunately, as soon as Haldane saw the skirmishers filtering up through the bushes, he promptly swung his men around to attack them head on, and to his horror Baillie 'saw Major Halden leading up ane partie of musqueteers over the field, and towards a house [Auchinvalley] near the glen, without any order from me; neither did they come off when I sent Colonel Arnot and thereafter Routmaster Blair, to Major Halden for that purpose'.

In fairness to Haldane he was responding to a clear and immediate threat and one moreover which rapidly escalated as the original Royalist party – some Highlanders under Ewen Maclean of Treshnish – were reinforced first by Glengarry's Macdonalds and then by MacColla himself with the rest of the western clans.

Recognising that for good or ill the battle was well and truly begun, Baillie quickly rode to the front. In his evidence Baillie provides a unique insight into the sequence and nature of the orders given to his 3,500 infantry and 300 cavalry, and also more than a flavour of the confusion and excitement as his army moved resolutely into the attack:

> He [Balcarres] asked me what he should do? I desired him to draw up his regiment on the right hand of the Earl of Lauderdale's. I gave order to Lauderdale's both by myselfe and my adjutant, to face to the right hand, and to march to the foot of the hill, then to face as they were; to Hume to follow their steps, halt when they halted, and keep distance and front with them. The Marquess [of Argyle] his Major, as I went toward him asked what he should doe? I told him, he should draw up on Hume's left hand, as he had done before. I had not ridden farr from him, when looking back, I find Hume had left the way I put him in, and wes gone at a trott, right west, in among the dykes and toward the enemy. I followed [Home] alse fast as I could ride, and meeting the Adjutant on the way, desired him he should bring up the Earl of Crafurd's regiment to Lauderdale's left hand, and cause the Generall-Major [John] Leslie draw up the regiments of Fyfe in reserve as of before; but before I could come to Hume, he and the other two regiments, to wit, the Marquess of Argyles and the three that were joyned in one,[7] had taken in an enclosure, from whilk (the enemy being so neer) it wes impossible to bring them off.

From the other side of the battlefield Ruthven confirms this sequence of events, relating how a 'strong partie from the estates armie was send before to ingadge the Royalists; and this partie consisted of thrie regiments, that of the reide cottes and other tuo, in the middle whereof were placed tuo troupes of horse, and one of lanciers to flanke them'.[8] Thus instead of straggling along in a column, Baillie's army was now drawn up in three distinct bodies facing the enemy. Under his personal command up among the stone- or turf-walled enclosures by Auchinvalley were some 1,600 regulars, belonging to Home's and Argyle's regiments and that little band of survivors under Lieutenant-Colonel John

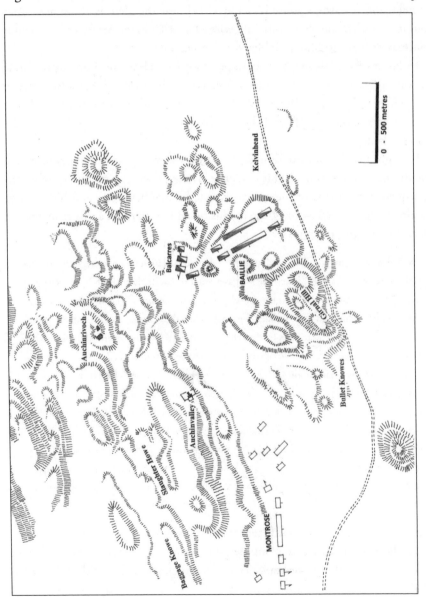

MAP 10: *Kilsyth 1645.*

Kennedy. Behind Baillie and to his right were a further 800 infantry of Lindsay's and Lauderdale's regiments under Major-General Holburne, and Balcarres' 300 cavalry, while somewhere to his left rear were the three rather shaky Fifeshire regiments, commanded by the lairds of Fordell, Ferny and Cambo, all under Major-General John Leslie.

Immediately facing them were 1,600 or so Highlanders under MacColla – but instead of roaring down on Baillie's hapless infantry, the clansmen found themselves pinned down under a furious storm of musketry:

> The rebels foot, by this time, were approached the next dyke, on whom our musqueteers made more fire than I could have wished; and therefore I did what I could, with the assistance of such of the officers as were known unto me, to make them spare their shott till the enemy should be at a nearer distance, and to keep up the musqueteers with their pickes and collors, but to no great purpose.

Nevertheless, with the Highlanders halted on the far side of the Auchinvalley enclosures, all was going to depend on what happened farther to the north on what had now become Baillie's right wing. Alexander Lindsay, Earl of Balcarres, was a competent and determined cavalry officer and he did his best to hook around into the Royalist rear. At first all that stood in his path was a small troop of cavalry commanded by a 'Captain Adjutant' Gordon. Undaunted by the odds, the Royalists immediately charged and briefly checked Balcarres' advance. However the imbalance in numbers soon told against them, but just as they were on the point of being surrounded Viscount Aboyne came to their aid with his personal lifeguard.

It was obviously an adventurous ride, for sheering away from Harie Barclay's as yet unengaged lancers the Royalists collided momentarily with the pikemen of Home's 'reide' regiment, and were shot up by its flanking musketeers before finally reaching Gordon's beleaguered troop. Unsurprisingly, by then they were in pretty poor shape and Balcarres drove them well back and up on to the high ground behind Montrose's original battle line. There at last the Covenanters were halted when Nathaniel Gordon and the Earl of Airlie counter-attacked with the main body of the Royalist cavalry. Ominously the area is still marked on modern maps as 'Slaughter Howe'. No longer closed up, their horses blown and their pistols empty – and badly outnumbered – Balcarres and his men were tumbled back down the hill again and out of the fight. Worse still, the victorious Royalist troopers then turned on the now-exposed right flank of Baillie's infantry and so provided the opportunity for MacColla and his Highlanders to get into action.

Once again, it was Baillie himself provided the most vivid account of what followed:

> In the end the rebells leapt over the dyke, and with downe heads fell on and broke these
> regiments . . . The present officers whom I remember were Home, his Lieutenant Colonel
> and Major of the Marquess's regiment, Lieutenant Colonel Campbell, and Major Menzies,
> Glencairne's sergeant Major, and Cassillis's Lieutenant Colonel with sundry others who
> behaved themselves well, and whom I saw none carefull to save themselves before the
> routing of the regiments. Thereafter I rode to the brae, where I found Generall Major
> Hollburne alone, who shew me a squadron of the rebells horsemen, who had gone by and
> charged the horsemen with Lieutenant-Colonell Murray and, as I supposed, did afterward
> rowt the Earle of Crawfurd, and these with him.

With his front line overwhelmed by the rebel infantry, and Lindsay's and Lauderdale's regiments seemingly dispersed by the rebel cavalry, Baillie and Holburne 'galloped through the inclosures' to find the reserves only to discover that they too were gone. So swift was the collapse that one of the charges afterwards levelled against Baillie was that his men were so unprepared they had not yet lit the slow-match for their muskets, to which he responded that: 'The fire given by the first five regiments will sufficiently answer what concerns them: and for the other three (the Fife levies), I humbly intreat your Honours to inform yourselves of Generall-Major Leslie, the adjutant, and the chief officers of these severall regiments: if they doe not satisfie yow therein, then I shall answer for myself.'

Fire they might well have done, but it can have been no more than a token volley, and with the Royalist cavalry all engaged on the northern side of the battlefield and MacColla's Highlanders fully occupied in dealing with Baillie's regulars it must have been the Gordon foot under Farquharson of Inverey and Laghtnan and O'Cahan's Irish mercenaries which routed Leslie's Fife Brigade. At any rate it was all over very quickly, and the whole army completely disintegrated. Baillie and some of his officers tried to rally the fugitives at 'the brook', presumably where the road crosses a stream at Auchincloch a kilometre or more east of the battlefield, 'bot all in vaine', so they made their way up to Stirling where they were eventually joined by the cavalry, who were badly shaken but otherwise largely unscathed.

In fact Baillie's regular infantry units may also have held together fairly well in the retreat and were consequently left well alone, for even the 'three that were joyned in one' survived to have their ranks filled out again with new recruits and sent into England. It was a very different story with the three Fife regiments. Dissolving into a panic-stricken rabble they were pursued for kilometres by the exultant clansmen, and hundreds were ruthlessly cut down. Ruthven provides a curiously precise figure of 5,469 buried afterwards, but as this exceeds the number of soldiers brought into the field by a very large margin there must have been a considerable element of double counting somewhere, and no doubt a fair number of non-combatants and innocent countrymen included in the dead as well. Materially, the Royalists also got 'there whole stuffe, the baggage, and thrie piece of ordinance, one whereof they called Prince Robert, because it was taken from him at the battell of Yorke, and they ware in wse to shoote this at there solemnities'.[9]

Royalist casualties are unknown. Ruthven states that: 'the [Royalist] foot armie had gotten little to doe, being last in coming vp, and therefore they did most of the execution [in the pursuit]', which would certainly suggest they had few casualties. Whether he was including the western clans in this is uncertain. Although pinned down for a time they were also well sheltered by the dyke until that last gallant rush, and so it is quite possible that most of the Royalist casualties were among their cavalry, albeit there were probably far more knocks than fatalities except among the horses.

Be that as it may, notwithstanding the beating they had just dealt out, the Royalists showed no inclination whatever to follow what remained of Baillie's army to Stirling. Instead, after resting on the battlefield for two days, Montrose chose to move off in a diametrically opposite direction. On learning of the battle the Earl of Lanark had abandoned Glasgow and like Argyle fled to Berwick. Albeit one of his regiments, led by a tough professional named Sir John Browne, remained in the field and harassed the rebels sufficiently for Sir John to be awarded £100 sterling: 'In thankful remembrance of good service with his dragoons against the rebels since 15th August last.'[10] The temptation proved too much for Montrose, and while despatching some cavalry under Lord Napier and Nathaniel Gordon to Edinburgh he moved with his infantry on Glasgow.

The triumph was short-lived. A number of prominent Royalists including the Earl of Crawford and Dr Wishart were released from the Edinburgh Tolbooth, but the castle gates remained firmly shut. Then, with the city still gripped by typhus, Napier and Gordon pulled out again as quickly as they had arrived. Glasgow too was occupied but briefly. With the government scattered as comprehensively as its soldiers, Montrose saw an opportunity to fill the resulting power vacuum by summoning a new parliament in the name of the king – one that could instruct Leven's army to withdraw from the English war or even change sides. It was a beguiling prospect, which promised much, and as this parliament was to meet in Glasgow rather than plague-ridden Edinburgh on 20 October there could be no question of sacking the city in the meantime. The magistrates were duly persuaded to promise a substantial sum of 'storm money' to compensate the disappointed soldiery, while Montrose drew them off to a camp at Bothwell, and there it all fell apart.

The money never appeared of course. The soldiers fell to marauding, and by the end of the month most of the clans had gone home. Of itself this was not too serious, for although Montrose is popularly believed to have led a Highland army, until Kilsyth most of the fighting had been done by MacColla's Irish mercenaries and by the 'standing regiments' raised in Atholl and Huntly's country. What followed was far more significant. First, MacColla, who had been deservedly knighted after the battle led a large-scale raid on Kilmarnock and the Ayrshire coast and then announced that he too was going into the west to accomplish the recovery of Kintyre. From the very beginning Antrim and MacColla had their ambition firmly fixed on re-establishing the power of Clan Donald in Kintyre and the Isles and had pledged their support for the king's war to achieve it. Now was the opportunity and it was not to be wasted idling at Bothwell. Reluctantly Montrose had no alternative but to let him go, taking 120 of the Irish with him as a lifeguard. Belatedly realising that inaction was doing more damage than Baillie's muskets, Montrose decided to march on Edinburgh after all. Next day at Calder Castle the Gordons also turned for home.

Philiphaugh

This time Montrose had no one to blame but himself. Huntly was returned from his hiding place in the far north and had sent to recall Aboyne to defend the Gordon country against a resurgent threat from the local Covenanters. At first Aboyne was persuaded that his duty to his king took precedence but already he was upset by the publication of an account of the campaign, supposedly written by Montrose's confidant Sir William Rollo, which accorded scant acknowledgement of the Gordons' role, and then the marquis himself made the fatal mistake of appointing the Earl of Crawford to command the Royalist cavalry. As one of the great earls of Scotland Crawford was always going to lend the Royalist cause a far greater degree of respectability than a younger son of an ancient but marginalised house. He was also an experienced, if not always lucky cavalry officer who had led one of Prince Rupert's brigades, and still had the commission granted him when he rode north with Montrose early in 1644, but he had played no part in subsequent events and with the exception of the Earl of Airlie's little troop and Mortimer's Irish dragooners all the cavalry he was to command were Gordons.

Little wonder then that Aboyne should heed his father and lead his men home, while Montrose carried on only as far as Dalkeith. Edinburgh was still gripped by plague, and this was sufficient excuse to halt his advance and avoid the embarrassment of knocking on the gates with just a single regiment of foot at his back. Instead he turned south, hoping to raise large numbers of cavalry in the borders for at Bothwell many of the local magnates had submitted to the king's general and promised to raise their men. At first the signs were good. The Marquis of Douglas joined him at Galashiels on 7 September with around 1,000 Moss-troopers, but neither the Earl of Home nor the Earl of Roxburgh appeared. By 10 September Montrose was at Jedburgh, and perhaps contemplating a raid into England, when disturbing news reached him. Lieutenant-General David Leslie had passed through Berwick four days earlier with at least four regiments of infantry and six regiments of cavalry hurriedly recalled from England.

Having already parted with Baillie and as many regiments as he could spare to secure Scotland against the Royalist insurgency Leven and his army had then spent much of the year in the north. The English Parliament wanted the army to join in an offensive against the strategically important Royalist stronghold of Chester, but with the situation in Scotland growing ever more critical, especially after Auldearn, Leven was reluctant to move far from the border. Nevertheless it was politically imperative that the English alliance be maintained and so he compromised by crossing the Pennines into Westmorland, a move that simultaneously allowed him to cover David Leslie's wearisome blockade of Carlisle and interpose between a possible attempt by the king to cut his way through to Scotland, but which at the same time left him conveniently positioned to march on Chester if circumstances allowed. In the event a Royalist thrust into Yorkshire appeared for a time to be a more realistic possibility and so Leven recrossed the Pennines to a rendezvous with Lord Fairfax at Doncaster. There he learned the end of the war was in sight.

The destruction of the king's army in the north at Marston Moor had freed that of the Eastern Association to turn south and quite literally ride to the rescue of London, shorn of its defenders in twin disasters at Cropredy bridge and Lostwithiel during the summer. Another battle at Newbury was indecisive, but what followed was not. Dismayed by the failure of no fewer than three combined armies to gain a victory there, Parliament reorganised or 'new modelled' them into just one army and gave the command to the most successful of its generals – Sir Thomas Fairfax – with Oliver Cromwell as his second-in-command. At Naseby, in Northamptonshire, on 14 June 1645 this new army utterly destroyed the king's principal army. Eager to follow up this triumph Fairfax next moved against the king's army in the west and to cover his rear Leven was ordered down into the Severn Valley.

As ever Leven remained reluctant to be drawn even farther south, but on 2 July he marched from Nottingham, crossed the Severn at Bewdley and pushed south to besiege Hereford by the end of the month. With his last armies disintegrating around him the king skirted Leven's outposts and lunged northwards for Yorkshire after all, hoping to raise again the army lost on Marston Moor the year before. He got as far as Doncaster, but by then David Leslie was in pursuit with eight regiments of horse, one of dragoons and 500 mounted infantry, so the king turned south again, stormed Huntingdon out of sheer frustration and then returned to Oxford. By now Hereford was on the point of falling.

On the night of 28 August two sergeants, Thomas Innes and William Brown, were paid thirty shillings apiece for plumbing the ditch around Hereford. Based on what they discovered it was drained and two mines blown under the walls. All was ready to storm the place, but as the king cautiously approached with his last remaining soldiers on 3 September he found the Scots were gone. Leven had learned of the disaster at Kilsyth and was heading for home. Exactly what he intended to do when he got there, especially if he were to find a Royalist parliament sitting in Glasgow, might be an interesting question, but David Leslie's cavalry brigade was ahead of him and in Berwick by 6 September.

There Leslie conferred with Argyle before marching rather cautiously along the coast road towards Edinburgh, with scouts out across the border hills sniffing for news of the Royalists. By the night of 11 September he had gotten the length of Gladsmuir, halfway between Haddington and Tranent where he was joined by at least two other cavalry regiments, Kirkcudbright's and Barclay's,[11] and next day turned due south to Soutra and so over the hills to Galashiels.

In the meantime Montrose had pulled out of Jedburgh and was heading westwards to avoid him, presumably with a view to passing into Upper Clydesdale from where he could either cover Glasgow or get back above the Forth. By the afternoon of 12 September he and his men were at Selkirk. Unaware that Leslie was closing in, many of the officers found comfortable quarters in the burgh, while the rest of the army scattered itself along the north bank of Ettrick

Water for nearly three kilometres along a narrow bottom called Philiphaugh. Security was seemingly limited to a single troop of cavalry left as a rearguard three kilometres away at Sunderland Hall, and at some point during the night this was snapped up by Leslie's advance guard as it forded the Tweed. Only the commander, Alexander Charteris of Amisfield, and two or three others got away. When they reached Selkirk, Amisfield's report that they had been attacked by Leslie's men was dismissed as a drunken brawl, and no attempt was made to rouse the army.

Undisturbed, Leslie and his men appear to have spent the rest of night 'invironed with woodes in a deep walley',[12] presumably the valley of the Tweed between Linglie Hill and Meigle Hill, just a little upstream from Sunderland. Some of his men must have been left behind in England to rejoin Leven for he had marched from Berwick with just six cavalry regiments: his own, the Earl of Leven's, John Middleton's, Lord Kirkcudbright's, Lord Montgomery's, and Hugh Fraser's Dragoons. Muster reports from the following January and the records of a bounty paid to the Philiphaugh regiments suggest that the first two may have had something in the region of 550 officers and men apiece, while Middleton's had about 400, Lord Kirkcudbright's 600 and Lord Montgomery's 470. By this time Fraser's 400 dragooners were also riding as cavalry in all but name, so in total Leslie ought to have had just under 3,000 cavalry of his own. In addition however he had been joined at Gladsmuir by at least two other units – the Earl of Dalhousie's and Colonel Harie Barclay's Horse – and perhaps also some of Balcarres' men. These may have added another 350 or so, but they were evidently in pretty poor shape and may have been left in reserve. On the other hand Leslie also had 500 mounted infantry of Lord Coupar's Regiment under a Captain Grierson.[13]

Ironically the following morning dawned grey and misty, and had any notice been taken of Amisfield's warning the Royalists might have still been able to escape under cover of the fog. Montrose, according to Ruthven, did intend to pull his men together at first light, but having sat up all night preparing despatches for the king he overslept. Instead just a single patrol was sent out at daybreak under Thomas Ogilvy of Powrie. When he returned with the happy news there was not an enemy within sixteen kilometres, they all remained where they were, displaying no urgency to go anywhere.

All the time Leslie was closing in. With a very comfortable superiority in numbers he divided his army in two at the Linglie Burn, about a kilometre north of Selkirk. One wing led by Lieutenant-Colonel James Agnew of Lord

Kirkcudbright's Regiment crossed the river Ettrick and made for Selkirk itself, while the rest, according to a reliable local ballad tradition, swung around the base of Linglie Hill and went straight for the rebel camp.

The fight, according to his official report, began at 10 a.m. and just minutes before that Montrose's scoutmaster, Captain Blackadder, had burst in on his lordship at breakfast 'in a great fright, assureing him that a great armie of his enemies ware aduancing, and allreadie within a myll of the toune'.[14]

Montrose thereupon flung himself on to the first horse he could catch and galloped across to Philiphaugh, where as so often before he found 'all in uproar and confusion'. The large body of cavalry encamped on the haugh was not only untrained and inexperienced, but also most of their officers, like Montrose, had taken themselves off to find beds in Selkirk the night before. Presumably they were then trapped there by Agnew's men, for Wishart says that many were absent and never reached the field. Consequently the troopers were now scattered all over the haugh in loose bodies of fifty, sixty, a hundred or even 200 men and making no attempt to form a battle line. Even the veteran Irish, recognising perhaps that the battle was already lost, were in some disorder with a great many of them intent only on securing their own baggage.

The result was that Laghtnan and O'Cahan could bring up only about 200 infantry, less than half their number. Of the 1,200 horse: 'He fand only his old souldioures, Airly his troupe, and Collonell Gordoune, both which amounted not to a hundredth and fyftie; with those of Crawford, Ogilvie and some other noble cavelyres, being nyne or ten in number, did raige themselves vpon the generalles right hand, the foot on the left, and a ditch before them.'[15]

This was largely confirmed by the anonymous W. H. of the so-called Haddington despatch, who wrote that: '. . . according to their usuall manner thay had made choice of a most advantageous ground wherein they had intrenched themselves, having upon the one hand an unpasible Ditch, and on the other Dikes and Hedges, and where these were not strong enough, they further fortified them by casting up Ditches, and lined their hedges with Musketeers'.[16] Just how much fortifying was actually done in the circumstances is open to question. The remains of 'trenches' can still be seen, but as at Fyvie these were most likely agricultural ditches and banks. The 'unpasible' ditch may possibly have been the Linglie Burn, joining the Ettrick just north of Selkirk itself, but was more likely to be the prominent re-entrant of the Philhope Burn, for it appears the Royalists also had two cannon planted where it joins the Ettrick.

At any rate W. H. states that the main fight began when three cavalrymen from each side came forward to skirmish and after banging away at each other for a quarter of an hour the Royalists fell back and instead 200 musketeers came out 'but were forced by ours to retreat in great disorder'. This rather suggests that with Leslie's opening attack having been made on the Selkirk side of the river the Irish came hurrying up to counter-attack only to run into the 500 musketeers of Lord Coupar's Regiment, who sent them tumbling back to the ditch.

After these preliminaries there then seems to have been a pause before the battle began in earnest, perhaps because Leslie was still trying to develop the rebel position in the fog. The front between the enclosures occupied by the Royalist infantry and the river Ettrick was relatively narrow, and so when Leslie moved forward again he could deploy only one cavalry regiment at a time. For an hour or so 'it was hotly disputed'. His first attack was repulsed, as was the second, but in the process many of the Royalist cavalry, led by Gordon and Ogilvy, found themselves trapped on the wrong side of the ditch and at around noon, with nowhere else to go, they broke out to the north.

This left Montrose with just forty or fifty horse besides the border levies still hanging about uncertainly in the rear. With Agnew now having finished mopping up in Selkirk and moving upstream, Leslie was confident enough to ignore him and instead he wheeled to his right and 'charging very desperately upon the head of his own regiment, broke the body of the enemy's Foot, after which they all went in confusion and disorder'.[17]

With more and more cavalry coming up all the time, Montrose and his immediate party decided it was all over and so retired at a 'soft gallop', splitting up into three groups to confuse their pursuers. The border levies may have been a little slower off the mark, for the Haddington despatch tells how the Royalist horse rallied again, 'which occasioned their total overthrow'. Amidst the confusion, Montrose's adjutant, Stewart, also managed to rally about a hundred of the Irish at Philiphaugh farm, but then surrendered on promise of quarter. With that, the battle ended, but not the killing. Coldly equivocating that quarter had been promised only to the three senior officers – Stewart, O'Cahan and Laghtnan – Leslie proceeded to have all his Irish prisoners shot. There were about a hundred in all, and that seemingly did not include a large numbers of camp-followers, who were also murdered, either on the spot or over the next few days.

The senior officers among the prisoners, who eventually included Nathaniel Gordon, were also executed in the end, except for Stewart who somehow escaped. As for the rest, a surprising number got away. In fact Wishart contends that: 'Almost none of the horse, and very few of the foot, excepting those who had surrendered on terms, fell in fight. As they were not more than 500 in all, and of those 250 rejoined Montrose before the next day, all armed with their swords, we may conjecture that those who were missing did not exceed that number.'[18] This boast might be as optimistic in its own way as the Haddington despatch, which claims there were 'between two and three thousand killed', but the fact remains that, while crippled, Montrose refused to accept defeat and still had enough men to prolong the agony. By 19 September he was safely back in Atholl.

At Dunkeld Montrose was rejoined by Inchbrackie, but appeals to MacColla went unanswered, and so Montrose marched northwards with some 800 infantry and 200 cavalry to try and link up with the Gordons again. Instead he found himself in the middle of a local civil war, which had little to do with national politics and everything to do with deep-seated family rivalries.

The End

Returning home after Kilsyth, Aboyne had quite fortuitously surprised and captured the entire Committee of War for the northeastern sheriffdoms near Fettereso on 14 September, and then followed up this unexpected coup by installing William Gordon of Arradoul as governor of Aberdeen.[19] The burgh militia were also ordered to be called out as a garrison, but the arrival of Major-General John Middleton with 800 men of his own and Lord Montgomery's regiments at the end of the month was greeted with relief rather than musket balls. At first Middleton was understandably wary of venturing farther with his little brigade, but his presence provided sufficient impetus for a revival of pro-government activity in Aberdeenshire led by the Master of Forbes.[20]

It was against this unpromising background that Montrose reappeared and persuaded Aboyne to meet him at Drumminor Castle with some 1,500 infantry, and as many as 500 cavalry under his younger brother, Lord Lewis Gordon. So far so good, but the marquis 'fynding himselfe now stronge eneugh to giue his enemies a day' announced that he intended to march south again, rather than confront Middleton, who by then was lying at Turriff. Aboyne reluctantly agreed, but then Montrose repeated his earlier mistake by insisting that the Earl of Crawford be acknowledged as commander of the cavalry, whereupon Lord Lewis Gordon proceeded to assert his independence by undertaking an unauthorised raid on one of Middleton's outposts at Kintore.

The raid was spectacularly successful. Middleton's men, considerably outnumbered, fell back to Turriff in such a panic that he in turn fled northwards to Banff. There he was uncomfortably close to Strathbogie, and this was sufficient excuse for Lord Lewis Gordon to return there. This in turn left Montrose with insufficient cavalry support for his proposed march southwards, so he reluctantly turned back to Alford from where Aboyne also returned to Strathbogie. Left with just Inchbrackie's men and the last remaining Irish mercenaries Montrose then moved over the mountains to Dunkeld. Then with the aid of a few recruits levied by Robertson of Inver Montrose tried to threaten Glasgow – a move aimed at least in part in a vain attempt to save the lives of the Royalist officers captured at Philiphaugh. David Leslie however had done his work only too well. Glasgow was heavily garrisoned and fortified, and a strong line of outposts established along the Forth crossings. Dalhousie's Regiment was based on Stirling, while Lord Montgomery's and Colonel Hugh Fraser's regiments lay in Clackmannan and Lord Kirkcudbright's was pushed forward to reoccupy Baillie's old fortified camp at Bridge of Earn. From there contact could also be maintained with both the Dundee garrison and with the Earl of Moray's Foot, who were watching the Highland passes out of Atholl.

Gradually the noose was tightening, and at the beginning of January 1646 Colonel Harie Barclay arrived in Aberdeen with his own regiments of horse and dragoons, Colonel Robert Montgomery's Horse and also two regular infantry regiments which had come north with Leslie – Colonel William Stewart's and Viscount Kenmure's. There they halted until the spring, while the battered but indefatigable Aberdeenshire levies were reorganised into a regiment of horse under the Master of Forbes and a regiment of foot under Colonel George Forbes of Millbuie.[21]

On the far side of the river Spey Montrose was vainly trying to raise a new army, while the Gordons engaged in a petty round of raid and counter-raid against their neighbours. The war was clearly lost, but they were still fighting on because they were afraid to stop. Only the Earl of Crawford, based at Banff, presented any threat to the growing concentration at Aberdeen. At first he made life distinctly uncomfortable for Barclay, with a series of raids pushed down Deeside by Farquharson of Inverey and from Fyvie Castle by Captain Blackadder, but eventually Barclay decided enough was enough and riposted with an even heavier raid on Banff, which sent the rebels tumbling back across the Spey.

By the end of April relations between the Royalist commanders had deteriorated to the extent that Huntly and Montrose were operating independently of each other when the latter embarked on a futile and quite pointless siege of Inverness. It was also reckless for Major-General John Middleton had come north to supersede Barclay and was then lying at Banff with a cavalry brigade and Millbuie's Foot. Huntly on the other hand, having allowed his infantry to winter at home, had not yet concentrated his forces and was unable to cover the siege when Middleton suddenly lunged forward with his cavalry. Crossing the Spey late on 7 May and pausing only long enough at Elgin to feed and water his horses, Middleton pushed straight on through the night to Inverness, taking the Royalists completely by surprise. Alerted only by Middleton's trumpets, Montrose's men abandoned their guns and fled westwards without attempting to fight.[22]

With that, the campaign was all but over. After hanging around for a few days Montrose swung around to the south and took refuge in Speyside, while Huntly suddenly displaying unwonted energy struck south with 1,500 horse and 2,000 foot and stormed Aberdeen on 14 May. Approaching from the north his men seized the barricaded Gallowgate port and charged down the length of the street with two troops of horse. However once out of the narrow Gallowgate and into the rather wider Broadgate they were counter-charged by a Major Forbes and started to get thrown out again until Lord Lewis Gordon slew him in personal combat. Then the governor, Lieutenant-Colonel Hew Montgomery, intervened with his own regulars and by 'maine strength' forced the Royalists out.

Twice more the Royalist cavalry attacked without success, but then a body of musketeers broke in through the back yards and Montgomery's men broke and fled at last. There were according to Spalding some eighty killed in all, and in addition Montgomery left 350 of his men behind as prisoners.[23] 'It was thought', said one chronicler, 'to be one of the hottest pieces of service that happened since this unnatural war began, both in regard to the eagerness of the pursuers and valour of the defenders.'[24] It was also seven years to the day since the civil wars had begun with the Gordons' victory over the Covenanters at Turriff in 1639. Three weeks later it was officially all over, when word arrived from the king, ordering the last of his forces to lay down their arms.

In reality the worst was yet to come.

Chapter 8
An End and a New Beginning

When King Charles sent those instructions for his followers to cease fighting he was the guest of the Scots army! This was not quite so extraordinary as it first appears for all was not well in the alliance against him. From the very beginning there had been shifting coalitions of power and influence among those opposed to the king, but in the months leading up to the new modelling of the Parliamentarian army those differences had sharpened dangerously.

The New Model army is popularly imagined to have been something special – an elite force created to replace the shambolic bands of amateurs that had gone before – but at a basic level all it was intended to do was amalgamate the more or less shattered remains of three old armies into a single, reasonably large, new one, organised, trained and equipped exactly as those that had gone before. The intricacies of the project need not concern us here, beyond the all-important fact that, while there were still not enough ordinary soldiers to go around, there were certainly far too many officers available to fill the greatly reduced number of vacancies. The new modelling therefore turned into a political contest between the two principal factions in the English Parliament – the Presbyterians and the Independents – as to which should nominate the officers to lead the army – a struggle won by the radical Independents.

This had a number of important consequences in both the short and the long term, but the immediate one was the breaking of the Solemn League and Covenant. The Scots had entered the war in order to secure their own political revolution by bridling the king of England and establishing Presbyterianism in England. That was the price of their intervention, but the failure to exploit their victory at Marston Moor properly meant that in the following year it was the Independents' army which not merely defeated the king but also so comprehensively destroyed his remaining forces that a negotiated settlement was no longer necessary. Neither was the Scots army.

Not only were their hopes of establishing Presbyterianism dashed but it also became increasing plain that now the Scots had served their purpose the English wanted to be rid of them. Charles therefore sought to exploit this discord by trying to seek an accommodation of his own with the Scots, just as he had done in 1641. Initially his approaches, directed to Leven, were pointedly ignored, but then a complex series of clandestine negotiations, misunderstandings and a healthy dose of cynical betrayal saw him quite literally turn up on Leven's doorstep outside Newark on Trent. Any hopes that the Scots army would declare for the king were blasted when it was insisted first that he order the Royalist garrison of Newark to surrender and then send instructions for his remaining forces in Scotland to do likewise.

Reluctantly Charles complied, but it is symptomatic of the deepening distrust between the Allies that no sooner was Newark rendered up than Leven swiftly marched north to avoid the all too real possibility that the English army (as the 'New Model' had to all intents and purposes become) would get between him and Scotland. By 13 May both he and the king were safely at Newcastle upon Tyne, and there they would remain until 30 January 1647, when the first instalment of the outstanding subsidy money was paid over by an all but bankrupt Parliament and all Scots troops then returned home. The king was ruthlessly left behind.

In the meantime only Montrose had obeyed Charles' injunction to 'disband all your forces' and after some hesitation had patched up an agreement with Middleton to leave Scotland under safe conduct by 1 September 1646. Huntly for his part initially submitted, but then raised his people again in response to secret orders from the king to have a force ready in anticipation of his return to Scotland. That was never a realistic prospect, and it was only the weakness of Middleton's forces that allowed him to survive until March 1647; even so it was not until November that he was eventually captured. By then it was no more than a matter of tying loose ends, for unsurprisingly it was the problem of MacColla which had been accorded the greater priority as the war ground to its close.

Joined by the Earl of Antrim and fresh troops from Ireland MacColla had indeed taken over the Kintyre peninsula, to the continuing embarrassment of Argyle. Antrim in obedience to the king's orders subsequently went home, but MacColla was at first reluctant and encouraged in that reluctance by the fate of his Lamont allies, who had surrendered in June 1646 only to be executed at Dunoon shortly afterwards. In terms of what had gone before, the brutal killing of upwards of seventy men in cold blood may not have counted for much, but neither did it encourage a negotiated settlement and not until the summer of 1647 were the government forces strong enough to move against the remaining rebels.

As elsewhere the carefully levied and properly equipped but raw regiments which began the war had degenerated into fearsome little bands of veterans owing little real allegiance but to themselves. Astonishingly a muster of the army outside Newark in January 1646 had revealed Leven's forces to comprise 4,136 horsemen but only 2,836 foot exclusive of officers.[1] There were other infantrymen besides of course, occupying garrisons such as Newcastle, and in Scotland itself, but it was an indicator of the way things were going, and in February 1647 as the last of them marched home the army was 'New Modelled' in conscious emulation of the English example.

The cavalry were to be reduced to just fifteen independent troops of horse and three of dragooners, reflecting their anticipated new role as a mounted police force or gendarmerie. There were intended to be just seven infantry regiments, each comprising 800 men in eight companies, of which Sandy Hamilton's, James Holburne's and Ludovick Leslie's regiments were to be largely recruited out of units then serving in Scotland, while Colin Pitscottie's and Walter Scott's were to be formed from the remnants of those returning from England.[2] Reflecting the nature of the campaign ahead, the two remaining regiments were Highland ones, one being Argyle's and the other Colonel James Campbell of Ardkinglas'. Just as the Independents had thrust their own men into the key posts of the English army, so Argyle and what was becoming the Kirk party ensured it was *their* men, headed by David Leslie, who commanded the new one.

Ultimately however the reorganisation failed to live up to expectations, and the foot proved to be a particular disappointment. They were nearly all of them conscripts, and some of the veterans among them had been levied as fencibles as long ago as 1643 under an obligation to serve for forty days. That restriction had long since gone by the board of course, and it was pay, or at least the expectation of it, rather than patriotic duty that sustained them. If the Kirk was puzzled by the absence of 'alacritie and cheerfulness of the souldiers of this new modell', they were soon enlightened as to the cause when the whole lot refused to march out of Dunblane until they received their arrears of pay![3] When they finally did lurch westwards on 17 May, they did so primarily to avoid the plague. It was an inauspicious start, and it was just as well that MacColla, recognising that his position was untenable, decided not to make a fight of it but began shipping his men for Ireland.

On 24 May Leslie's cavalry caught MacColla's rearguard at Rhunahoarine Point and promptly scattered it, claiming to have slain upwards of sixty. They missed MacColla himself, and while Leslie was waiting for his infantry to catch up MacColla got away that night to Islay with most of his MacDonald followers and his Irish. Those left behind took refuge in Dunaverty Castle, and there, having held off one attempt to storm the place, soon surrendered. Just as at Philiphaugh, Leslie, implacable as ever, had them executed out of hand. Next he crossed to Islay, but once again he found MacColla gone, this time back to Ireland, and Leslie settled for MacColla's father, old Col Keitach, whom he found holding on to the castle of Dunveg. By now there was no appetite for a fight on either side and no desire to die with the end of the war so plainly in sight. Col came out to treat, allegedly begging for whisky, and Leslie, keenly aware that he lacked the supplies to sustain his unpaid and near mutinous troops on the island, had him arrested and then offered the now leaderless garrison terms. The last 176 Royalist soldiers filed out on 5 July 1647 to surrender their weapons, and even the Irish were allowed to go home. Col Keitach however was hanged, and his son, Alasdair MacColla, died obscurely in Ireland, stabbed in the back after his capture at the battle of Knocknanus on 13 November.

There it might all have ended but for the king. The fundamental problem was that on both sides of the border men had gone to war to curb the power of the Crown, not to abolish it, yet it was becoming increasingly clear that due to his continuing intransigence there was a very real possibility that this might become necessary.

Parliament had finally lost control of its army when it made the fatal mistake of attempting to have it disbanded without first settling its arrears of pay. Faced with the equally unpalatable choices of being turned off without a penny or volunteering for service in Ireland, they mutinied and marched on London. A scratch force of militia and former officers left unemployed when the new modelling took place two years earlier were hastily raised to oppose them, but at the first whiff of a negotiated settlement they declared themselves betrayed once again and invaded Parliament. In response the Speakers of both Houses fled to the army for protection and the triumph of the Independents was complete.

Throughout this the king remained in negotiation with all parties, constantly playing one off against the other. Ultimately his retention of any real power would require an accommodation with the Presbyterians, and without the army they in turn required a renewed intervention by the Scots. That also in turn required a similar political regrouping north of the border. The Scots Parliament was itself divided into two main factions, led by Argyle and the Duke of Hamilton respectively.[4] Both professed their simultaneous adherence to the Covenant and the rights of the king, but while Argyle's Kirk party, which had the support of the ministers, was prepared to see the king humbled if he would not take the Covenant and establish Presbyterianism in England, Hamilton's party, which included most of the nobility, was more concerned to preserve the existing social order even if that meant accepting compromises on religion. Therefore on 26 December 1647 Hamilton's party entered into a secret Engagement with the king, promising military aid in return for establishing Presbyterianism in England for a trial period of three years and giving up control of the militia for ten.[5]

A new war was inevitable, and on 23 March 1648 two officers named Poyer and Laugherne declared for the king at Pembroke.[6] There was also sporadic rioting in London throughout April and May, and an actual rising at Bury St Edmunds at the beginning of May, when 600 men seized the county magazine, crying 'For God and King Charles'. Five troops of horse sufficed to settle that particular business, but in the north it was a different matter. On 28 April an old (and Catholic) Cavalier named Sir Marmaduke Langdale seized Berwick, and the next day Sir Philip Musgrave took Carlisle. Both gateways to England were now held for the king. Although the local commander, Colonel John Lambert, moved swiftly to suppress a more general Royalist uprising in Northumberland, he was also distracted by the seizure of Pontefract by another disaffected former Parliamentarian officer. Recognising the seriousness of the developing situation Sir Thomas Fairfax prepared to move the army north, only to be diverted by a crisis in the southeast, where Royalist insurgents came dangerously close to seizing London before being penned into Colchester. There Fairfax and the bulk of the army would be tied down until the town's eventual surrender on 28 August, but what of the Scots on whom so much depended?

The problem was that, although Leslie's army had not yet been disbanded, Hamilton was reluctant to use it, dominated as it was by officers who were at the very least sympathetic to Argyle's Kirk party and opposed to intervention. Even with the best will in the world Leslie's army was in any case far too small to be effective. In short a new army was required, and although the Engagement was ratified by the Scots Parliament on 2 March 1648 two months passed before the general levy was ordered on 4 May. By then the English revolts having begun piecemeal were in danger of being extinguished long before the army could be raised, let alone brought across the border.

Levying that army turned out to be a heartbreakingly difficult business. The country was exhausted by both war and pestilence, and there was also obstruction and outright resistance in the Covenanting heartland of the southwest. The colours ordered to be carried by the new army still proclaimed its adherence to the Covenant before the king, but it cannot have escaped anyone's attention that it was not the English Presbyterians who were taking up arms in the king's name, but the Cavaliers and that rather too many of them were noted Catholics. Such men would never accept Presbyterianism as the price of Scottish intervention.

Ministers denounced the Engagement from the pulpit, and in Glasgow the magistrates refused to raise any levies, but when an unscrupulous professional soldier named James Turner was sent to quarter his men on the burgh he found that to be 'ane argument strong enough ... to make the hardest headed Covenanter in the toune to forsake the kirk'.[7] Others however were less easily cowed, and orders had to be issued forbidding men to leave the country since many were slipping across to Ulster in order to escape the levy. Notwithstanding this, some hundreds of men continued to flee from Lanarkshire into neighbouring Ayrshire and there rallied on Mauchline Moor, near Kilmarnock.

Whether at this stage they were actually ready to mount an uprising remains uncertain, although there were no doubt some calling for one. At any rate Major-General John Middleton and the Earl of Glencairn were promptly sent with ten troops of horse to deal with the would-be insurgents on 12 June, only to find an estimated 1,200 horse and 800 foot waiting for them. No one was keen to start fighting however, and when a deputation of ministers came forward Middleton readily offered a written assurance that if the Covenanters dispersed peacefully no further action would be taken. Unfortunately, when the ministers returned to broadcast the terms some bright spark pointed out that Middleton had only offered an amnesty to the 'cuntrie people' and not to the deserters from the Lanark fencibles. Whether he had actually intended to make that distinction is unclear, but at any rate they were still arguing among themselves when Middleton sent a Captain Grieve across to see if they were minded to co-operate. As luck would have it the first group he rode up to were Lanarkshire men, and in response they shouted they would fight.

Middleton's patience had run out by now, so he immediately obliged them by ordering a forlorn hope or advance guard to charge. They did so briskly and the rabble were at first driven back, but the troopers soon lost their cohesion and according to one story some of them even dismounted to plunder those they had cut down. Inevitably the rest of the now angry mob closed in around them, and Middleton had to ride to the rescue with the rest of his little force. Once again they were at first successful but as resistance stiffened both he and Colonel William Hurry[8] were wounded and their men driven back. Meanwhile Middleton's superior, the Earl of Callendar, had become increasing concerned at the reports filtering back. Leaving his infantry at Kilmarnock Callendar hurried forward with 1,000 horse and pausing only long enough to form them into a proper battle line he charged the Covenanters for the third time, this time scattering them completely.

In all there were about ten or twelve killed and as many as fifty or sixty wounded in the pointless skirmish, but while it left the Engagers (as Hamilton's party was now become) in the ascendancy for the time being it was an uncomfortable pointer to the future. The Committee of Estates even recommended planting garrisons in the area, but Hamilton feared to do so lest such a move might provoke the uprising they were intended to prevent. For the same reason offers of assistance from former Royalists in the north were turned down. Conversely the Irish army, which was recalled to provide a veteran nucleus for the new levies, proved equally intractable in its own way. Two regiments refused outright to accept the Engagement and return home, while the others simply refused to move until they received their arrears of pay and even then warned that they would serve under no one but their own commander, George Monro.[9]

The wider question of leading the army brought its own problems. Leven was too old and too sensible to accept the command, while Leslie was too much Argyle's man, and so Hamilton took on the job himself despite a total want of qualification or experience. His second-in-command, the Earl of Callendar, who *was* an experienced soldier, considered himself far better fitted for the appointment and would lose no opportunity to remind Hamilton of the fact. As a sop to the Kirk party both Leslie and Holburn were offered subordinate commands as lieutenant-generals of the horse and foot respectively, but both declined and the appointments went to John Middleton and our old friend William Baillie instead, while George Monro was to be major-general in command of the regiments from Ireland.

Unfortunately while the army was well provided with generals it lacked just about everything else. At one point it had been rather optimistically estimated that by combining Leslie's army, the Irish army and the new levies a total of 40,000 men might be assembled. Instead Hamilton finally crossed the border on 8 July with something in the region of 3,000 horse and 6,000 foot – and no artillery. At first sight the very high proportion of cavalry appears untypical for a Scots army but once again, as at Newark two years earlier, it merely reflected the weakness of Hamilton's army. The old soldiers had all or most of them found themselves horses, the better as one officer acidly commented to go a plundering;[10] there were no veteran infantry, just twenty regiments of reluctant, ill-equipped and untrained conscripts averaging about 300 men apiece.

Musgrave readily opened the gates of Carlisle, but that was nearly as far as English assistance went. Hamilton rested his little army in the city for six days, before pushing south again and running into Lambert outside Penrith on 14 July. Badly outnumbered, Lambert promptly fell straight back to Appleby before the Scots infantry could come up, and there was another skirmish there three days later before Hamilton halted again at Kirby Thore, anxiously waiting for reinforcements from Scotland. He had entered England to assist his supposed allies, but apart from scattered groups of insurgents there was no king's party, and even the men he had were beginning to fall apart – the cavalry marauding in search of food and fodder, and the infantry simply deserting. Worse still when George Monro arrived at Kendal he promptly fell out with everybody else. Hamilton naturally enough wanted him to bring the Irish army forward as quickly as possible, but they themselves had already insisted that they would be commanded only by Monro, and he for his part took this as a mandate to insist that he be placed on an equal footing with the lieutenant-generals. As Monro flatly refused to take orders either from Callendar or from Baillie, Hamilton was at first minded to give way, but understandably enough Callendar baulked at this, and the upshot was that Monro was ordered to wait with his men for the artillery train, still hopefully expected from Scotland.

In the meantime Hamilton decided it was time to get moving again, but he still had no real idea of where he was going or what he hoped to achieve, and so at Hornby on 9 August a council of war was called to debate what to do next. Lambert had been holding the Stainmore Pass, but by now had fallen back to Knaresborough, so crossing the Pennines and linking up with the insurgents based on Pontefract was thought to be a viable option, and both Middleton and Turner argued in favour of it, Turner because:

> I understood Lancashire was a close country, full of ditches and hedges; which was a great
>
> advantage the English would have over our raw and undisciplined musketeers . . . while

> on the other hand Yorkshire was a more open country and full of heaths, where we might
> make better use of our horse, and come sooner to push of pike.

Given that a third or more of the army was mounted it was a plausible argument, but they were most of them mounted on those 'light but weak nags' derided by Lord Saye and Sele. Individually they were probably tough and resourceful veteran fighters, but being organised in small regiments or rather bands comprising only three troops apiece and equipped as light horse lancers they were no match for the large regiments of armoured heavy cavalry deployed by the English army.

Preston

Baillie therefore disagreed and with Callendar professing himself indifferent Hamilton decided in favour of continuing south farther into Lancashire, but meanwhile stayed on in Hornby for nearly a week longer. Then on 14 August Hamilton quite literally lurched forward, and two days later his cavalry were entering Wigan while his infantry were still straggling into Preston, fully twenty-five kilometres behind. This separation may have eased the very real problem of finding covered accommodation for the whole army in the persistent bad weather, which had dogged the campaign from the outset, but it was a fatal mistake. Unbeknownst to Hamilton, Oliver Cromwell – having dealt with the Welsh insurgents – had come north with reinforcements and was closing in fast. Having rendezvoused with Lambert at Wetherby on 12 August Cromwell pushed across the Pennines by way of Skipton and thence down the Ribble Valley to Preston. By his own account he had some 2,500 regular cavalry and 4,000 foot, together with another 500 horse and 1,600 foot belonging to locally raised units, although other sources put his real total at more than 11,000 men. Be that as it may the first news anyone had of Cromwell's approach was when he surprised one of Langdale's patrols at Waddow, near Clitheroe on the morning of 16 August.

Somehow it then took far too long for the news to filter through. Perhaps Langdale at first did not attach any great importance to the report or did not realise the size of the force about to hit him – or the fact he now faced Cromwell rather than Lambert. In any case with the Scots army so badly strung out it may simply have taken some time to get the message through to Hamilton – and by then events were moving so quickly that any such message was out of date. Cromwell on the other hand very quickly learned from his prisoners that he was sitting on the flank of the Scots army and poised to hit them while they were still on the march. By nightfall he had his army closed up in the grounds of Stonyhurst Hall and only then did Langdale, five kilometres away, fully appreciate the danger. There may still have been time for Hamilton to react. If he could concentrate his forces by morning he might match Cromwell's cavalry in numbers if not quality, and with the addition of Langdale's men slightly outnumber him in infantry, even allowing for stragglers and deserters. Unfortunately Langdale failed to convince Hamilton of the seriousness of the situation. Callendar, who had ridden back from Wigan, still believed on the strength of the initial reports that it was only Lambert back again and trying to make a nuisance of himself and so convinced Hamilton that the proper course of action was to hurry the foot forward to join the cavalry at Wigan rather than halt at Preston and bring the cavalry back again. It was a perfectly sensible argument but based on false intelligence, and as a consequence Langdale's insurgents were left on their own to deal not with Lambert but with Cromwell.

In the circumstances Langdale did surprisingly well. At daybreak he started falling back on Preston, but his rearguard was soon engaged and he was forced to halt and make a stand astride a sunken lane three kilometres short of the town. It was a strong position with hedged and ditched enclosures on either side of the lane, and after weeks of heavy rain the going was extremely soft, which inhibited Cromwell from using his considerable superiority in cavalry to outflank him. Accordingly, Langdale packed his pikemen into the lane, deployed his musketeers in the hedgerows, and then galloped off to Preston in search of reinforcements.

By now the Scots infantry were already crossing the bridge over the Ribble, and Callendar forcefully argued that they should keep going, either because he remained unconvinced that Cromwell was really at hand or more likely because his first priority was reunite them with the Scots cavalry. In the circumstances he may well have been right, and Hamilton gave way. Langdale was to be effectively hung out to dry as a sacrificial rearguard, while Callendar got the rest of the army away. As it was, with the aid of a small party of Scots cavalry, Langdale held on among the hedgerows through most of the day, and it was some time around five in the evening before he was finally forced back and out on the open road leading to Preston.

At this point Hamilton evidently lost his head or at least any grip on reality. Getting the army across the narrow bridge had been a time-consuming business and was not yet complete when Langdale's line collapsed. Now, when it was far too late, he decided to fight after all. He deployed the remaining foot on Preston Moor, sent Turner forward with a reinforcement and ammunition for Langdale and sent orders recalling the cavalry from Wigan. An incredulous Callendar thereupon galloped up from the bridge and furiously pointed out that standing on the open moor without cavalry support was asking for trouble at the best of times and with a swollen river at their backs and most of the army on the wrong side of it, nothing short of suicidal. In his altogether more sensible view they needed to get everyone across the river, in order to take up a proper defensive position and wait for Middleton and the cavalry.

As usual Hamilton gave way to his subordinate and has ever since been criticised for abandoning Langdale to his fate, but as events rapidly proved it was already too late. Even as Callendar hurried the last of the infantry over the bridge Cromwell's men were pushing into the streets of the town, and by the time Langdale managed to disengage the Scots rearguard the north end of the bridge was already under attack. Hamilton, with more honour than common sense, had still waited for Langdale on the moor, attended only by his lifeguard and so found himself cut off. Ordering his lifeguard to break out to the north and find Monro, he and Langdale fought their way down to the river and swam.

In his absence Callendar and Baillie were hurriedly patching a proper battle line together along the high ground overlooking the river Darwen close by its confluence with the Ribble at Walton-le-Dale. Once they were all in place Callendar then sent forward 600 musketeers to try and bring off the two brigades under Colonel George Keith, who were still holding the Ribble bridge. Unfortunately as they tried to cross the flat ground between the two bridges they came under heavy fire and fell back. Nothing daunted, Keith, the Earl Marischal's younger brother, gamely held on for another two hours, but eventually his position was carried 'at push of pike', he himself was captured and such was the momentum of the attack that the English pushed on to take the Darwen bridge as well – and with it part of the Scots baggage train, still stuck at the bottom of the hill.

By now darkness was falling, and Cromwell decided to call it a day. He had won a useful tactical victory, but his men were exhausted and many were dropping away to find dry quarters in Preston, while the hardier ones were plundering the Scots baggage train. On the morrow he was going to have to get his men over the Darwen and then assault a strongly posted Scots army holding the high ground. At the same time, prisoners taken from Hamilton's lifeguard had alerted him to the fact that Monro's army was still somewhere behind him and he therefore had to contend with the twin possibilities that either Hamilton might shift eastwards in order to recross the Ribble at Whalley (the next bridge upstream) in order to link up again with Monro, or stand fast and wait for Monro to fall on the English rear. Accordingly after some discussion the Lancashire forces under Colonel Assheton were detached to cover both the bridge at Whalley and the Lancaster road, while Cromwell prepared to attack Hamilton next morning only with his regulars.

Had it happened it might have been a harder-fought battle than the one against Langdale's men the day before, but while Baillie and Turner argued that they should stand and fight Callendar successfully persuaded Hamilton to fall back under cover of darkness in order to link up with the still missing cavalry. Whether or not he was right the operation immediately descended into farce for there were then two roads linking Preston with Wigan, one by way of Standish and the other by way of Chorley. Callendar, or his guide, chose the Standish road and so missed Middleton, who inevitably was hastening up the Chorley road instead. Expecting to meet his own infantry Middleton instead blithely rode straight into Cromwell's men in the early hours at Walton-le-Dale, but recovering quickly swung around and conducted a textbook fighting retreat down the Standish road, killing a Colonel Francis Thornhaugh in the process: 'being run through the body, thigh and head by the Enemys lancers'.

Eventually Middleton caught up with the foot outside Standish in the early hours of the morning. Although there was at first some thought of making a stand there it was claimed that the musketeers' powder was wet, and so as Cromwell continued:

> Our horse still pursued the Enemy; killing and taking divers all the way. At last the enemy drew up within three miles of Wigan; and by that time our army was come up, they drew off again, and recovered Wigan before we could attempt any thing upon them. We lay that night in a field close by the enemy; being very dirty and weary, and having marched twelve miles of such ground as I never rode in all my life, the day being very wet. We had some skirmishing, with the enemy, near the town; where we took General Van Druske and a Colonel, and killed some principal officers, and took about a hundred prisoners.

The Scots army was drawn up on Wigan Moor, but by now it was in no condition to fight. In theory it might still have outnumbered Cromwell given that he had been forced to leave Assheton's Lancashire men behind, but the Scots themselves were badly depleted both by the casualties suffered in the defence of the bridgeheads and by the straggling since. Not only were those who remained exhausted and demoralised but they had seemingly lost all their reserve ammunition with the baggage train. A further retreat, or rather flight, was therefore determined on with no clear objective other than remaining ahead of their pursuers.

That night the Scots army set off again, but the rear of the column was still in Wigan when Middleton's covering force was driven in. Turner hastily drew up his brigade in the marketplace to serve as a rearguard, but as Middleton's troopers fell back through the streets towards them it all fell apart. Turner ordered his men to open their ranks to let the cavalry pass through, but instead:

> By now my pikemen, being demented (as I think we were all), would not hear me; and two of them ran full tilt at me. One of their pikes which was intended for my belly, I gripped with my left hand; the other ran me nearly two inches in the inner side of my right thigh; all of them crying of me and the Horse 'They are Cromwell's men . . .' I rode to the Horse and desired them to charge through these Foot. They, fearing the hazard of the pikes, stood. I then made a cry come up from behind them, that the enemy was upon them. This encouraged them to charge my Foot so fiercely that the pikemen threw down their pikes, and got into the houses. All the Horse galloped away, and as I was afterwards told, rode not through but over, our whole Foot treading them down.[11]

While there was no doubting that both horse and foot were in poor shape and extremely brittle, deliberately setting them on each other was hardly calculated to improve matters and only bears out Turner's admission that he too was 'demented'.

Having spent an equally wet and uncomfortable night in that field Cromwell resumed his pursuit at daybreak, and at about noon on 19 August he caught up with the Scots army again at Winwick, five kilometres north of Warrington. By now Baillie had taken the foot in hand and established a strong position on a steep sandstone rise known as Red Bank, blocking the road with pikemen and stuffing the hedgerows on either side with musketeers. Unfortunately the fight that followed is told only from English sources, but it is clear that Cromwell was growing overconfident, and, as John Hodgson related, the Scots 'snaffled our forlorn and put them to a retreat'.

Nevertheless wrote Cromwell: 'We held them in some dispute till our army came up, they maintaining the passe with great resolution for many hours, ours and theirs coming to push of pike and very close charges and forced us to give ground.'[12] A Major Cholmley of Colonel John Bright's Regiment was killed, and the situation was only stabilised by the arrival of Colonel Pride's Regiment. The English frontal assaults were going nowhere, which only invites speculation as to what might have happened if Baillie had persuaded Callendar to hold on to the high ground overlooking the Darwen bridge on the first night of the retreat. Be that as it may, Cromwell next tried feeling his way around the Scots right flank with his cavalry in combination with a renewed attack up the road by Pride's Regiment and 'after a sharp dispute, put these same brave fellows to the run'. The Scots collapse was hastened by the loss of 'a little spark in a blue bonnet, who performed the part of an excellent commander, and was killed on the spot'. Just who he might have been is impossible to determine for none of the Scots' senior officers is known to have been killed in this fight. It is possible therefore that he may simply have been a particularly brave but junior officer, or that he was Baillie himself and that reports of his death were exaggerated. At all events after they were driven back a final stand was made on Winwick Green, just to the north of the church, where the English 'made a great slaughter of them'.

Just what Callendar and Hamilton had being doing all this while is unclear, but when Baillie and Turner brought what remained of the foot into Warrington they found them both gone and the cavalry with them, leaving behind orders to surrender on the best terms Baillie could obtain. At this Baillie completely lost his temper and shouted for someone to shoot him, but was persuaded to calm down after his remaining senior officers offered to sign a paper exonerating *him* from any blame. By now what remained of the army was almost literally melting away, so after drawing them up behind the barricaded bridge Baillie beat for a parley and surrendered on the promise of quarter and civil usage. That night just 1,712 rank and file laid down their arms and surrendered seventy-five colours, but the eventual total will probably have been a great deal higher once the stragglers were gathered in.[13]

It did not end at Warrington of course. Having abandoned his infantry to its fate Hamilton continued to flee southwards, but after narrowly escaping being murdered by his own men finally surrendered with them at Uttoxeter on 25 August. Much good it did him for he was subsequently tried and executed under his English title as Earl of Cambridge. Callendar on the other hand made his escape all the way to Holland, as did Middleton and Langdale, while Turner having been taken prisoner managed to ransom himself. Baillie and the other officers were eventually released (he died at home in 1653), but the rank and file found themselves sold abroad for service in the Low Countries.

The Whiggamore Raid

In the meantime with Langdale having gone south command of the English Royalist forces in the north fell to Sir Thomas Tyldesley, who was then besieging

Lancaster Castle. When news of the first clashes arrived Tyldesley immediately abandoned the siege, gathered those of Langdale's men who had gotten away from Preston and proposed to Monro that they should combine their forces and march south at once. According to Sir Philip Musgrave, had they done so they 'would have made a body of above 7,000 horse and foot'.[14] However, as Monro reckoned he could only depend on his own 1,200 veterans, he flatly refused and instead marched north, correctly anticipating trouble at home.

Ruthlessly, Monro also refused to allow the fugitive Royalists to cross the border with him, for in late August the Westland Covenanters had risen in rebellion. As we have already seen they came close to it in early June, but, with the Engagers assembling an army, had backed down. Within a few days of hearing the news that the Scots army was destroyed at Preston the Westland Covenanters had gathered their forces in open revolt. In what became celebrated as the Whiggamore Raid,[15] several thousand men from Ayrshire and Lanarkshire moved eastwards led by the Earls of Loudoun and Eglinton – and David Leslie.

In response the Estates hurriedly sent orders to Monro, instructing him to hold on to Carlisle and to concentrate the rest of his forces at Berwick, while Hamilton's brother, the Earl of Lanark, was to assemble others at Jedburgh. Clearly Edinburgh was regarded as untenable and Eglinton's Whigs seized the castle without a fight on 5 September. There was no time for congratulation however for Monro rendezvoused with Lanark and instead of trying to retake Edinburgh at a run, swung around the capital to capture Linlithgow instead. Thus situated they were in a position to block any assistance to the Covenanters from the west, while at the same time were well placed to receive their own reinforcements from the Royalist north. A truce was thereupon patched up with both sides agreeing to halt all military movements – an agreement that lasted right up until the moment the Engagers realised that Argyle's forces were approaching Stirling from the west. Tasked with this apparent breach of the truce the Covenanters responded by solemnly pledging that their troops would not enter the burgh, and instead quartered them outside in the New Park. Needless to say the Engagers greeted this particular assurance with scepticism. As it was vital that they retain control of Stirling Bridge and the road to the north, Monro marched on 12 September. Indeed he did more, for it was the general himself who dismounted and quite literally kicked open a postern gate to let his men get into the New Park and scatter Argyle's levies. Thus the two sides were left glaring at each other from Stirling and Edinburgh respectively, both strongly situated, albeit in strategic terms Stirling was by far the more important prize, but neither side was willing to open a full-scale civil war.

The stalemate was broken by Oliver Cromwell, who came up to Edinburgh at the head of a cavalry brigade. The hint could not be plainer. Either Argyle dealt with the Engagers or Cromwell would do it for him. The result was another series of truces and then a negotiated settlement known as the Treaty of Stirling on 27 September 1648. This saw the Estates concede that no Engager accepting the treaty was to be 'injured in life, estate, title or freedom', although those holding public office were to refrain from exercising their duties until a full Parliament met in January 1649 to settle all outstanding civil matters. In return the Engagers agreed to surrender Stirling, Carlisle (still held by the Earl of Callendar's Regiment under Colonel Livingston) and Berwick by 1 October, while for their part Argyle and Leslie agreed to disband all but 1,500 of their men by the same date, and then ten days after that both sides were to disband all of their remaining forces.

Both sides had very carefully stepped back from the brink, and Cromwell departed satisfied. What no one had reckoned on was the execution of the king in London on 30 January 1649, for with that act the rules of the game changed.

Chapter 9
The King in the North

The immediate reaction to the judicial slaying of the king was relatively restrained. The 1649 Parliament in Edinburgh was dominated by the supporters of the Kirk party, and while putting a king on trial was something of an innovation disposing of awkward ones was not. Indeed the late king's grandmother, Mary, had also been executed in England.

While Mary's son James was duly proclaimed only as king of Scots, Charles, the second of his name, was proclaimed after the style of his own recently executed father as both king of Scotland *and* king of England. The Scots had every right to proclaim their own king, but declaring him at the same time to be king of England might be perceived as a dangerous provocation south of the border, although arguably no more so than simultaneously proclaiming him king of France after the style of Plantagenet and Tudor monarchs. In any case the young prince and future king was in Holland at this juncture, having been sent abroad for his own safety when it became clear that the war in England was lost.

Although the proclamation acknowledged the young prince's right to the thrones it was made clear to him that he would not be allowed to set foot in Scotland – far less have either crown placed on his head – unless he first took the Covenant and accepted those restrictions on his royal prerogative which his late father had fatally resisted. English anger was therefore mollified for a time and in any case distracted by the more pressing need to settle the Irish business once and for all.[1]

This was just as well for the Kirk party's hold on Scotland was by no means unchallenged. The north had always been seen as Royalist country, although it is debateable whether this reflected genuine support for the monarchy or rather opposition to the southern-based Kirk party. At any rate rumours were soon rife that Royalist exiles intended to land there and raise the new king's standard. As a precautionary measure a number of suspected gentlemen were immediately summoned to Edinburgh to sign bands of loyalty to the government, whereupon most of them, led by Sir Thomas Mackenzie of Pluscardine, responded by seizing Inverness. The government promptly panicked, despatching David Leslie northwards with every man he could lay his hands on. It also called for the immediate levying of another 4,440 horse and 13,400 foot for the defence of the country against invasion.[2]

In the event the whole affair turned out to be a damp squib. The orders for a new levy were met with an exhausted apathy and at best produced only a few hundred men. On the other hand far from raising the north for the new king, Pluscardine and his followers turned out to be doing no more than resisting arrest. They had established a Committee of War and levied taxes, which no one paid, but instead of recruiting men for a fight they had demolished the fortifications around Inverness and then fled north into Ross-shire at Leslie's approach. Any thought of pursuing them was scuppered by the news that Atholl had also risen under Middleton (who had escaped from an English jail) and Lord Ogilvie, and that the garrison of Stirling Castle had mutinied.

Whether the three outbreaks had a common purpose is unclear, but the situation was momentarily frightening enough for Leslie to offer an amnesty to Pluscardine's people. Not many accepted, but enough of them to let him turn south for Atholl, where the would-be Royalists scattered at his approach. Holburne had in the meantime quieted the mutineers in Stirling, and just by way of underlining their seeming ascendancy the Estates also had Huntly executed. He, poor man, had been languishing in jail ever since his capture in November 1647 and had no part in either the Engagement or what Leslie rightly dismissed as 'the hubbub about Inverness', but an example was needed and so the Maiden (a Scots forerunner of the guillotine) embraced him on 22 March.

Once again this stern measure did far more harm than good. With Huntly's eldest son Lord Gordon dead at Alford and his second son Aboyne having died in exile, it was the wild young Lord Lewis Gordon who succeeded to the chieftainship of the Gordons, and in mid April he brought his people to a rendezvous with Pluscardine, Ogilvie and Middleton at Balvenie on Speyside. Leslie wearily turned northwards again, but on 8 May Colonel Gibby Kerr unexpectedly settled the business. Leslie had earlier left him behind at Inverness with just three troops of horse, totalling no more than 120 men, who were seemingly regarded as no threat to the 1,000-strong rebels until Kerr surprised them in their camp at Balvenie, supposedly killing upwards of sixty and capturing 800, including a number of Irish mercenaries who were ordered to 'bee put to present execution'.[3]

Suitably chastened, Huntly, Middleton, Pluscardine and the others submitted after receiving the usual assurances as to the security of their life, liberty and estates. Meanwhile in Holland negotiations between the Estates and the king were getting nowhere, and as his friends in Scotland had failed to achieve anything Charles decided to improve his bargaining position by unleashing the long-feared foreign invasion.

Accordingly, in September 1649 a pathetically small force of Scots and English Royalists, backed up with a slightly more impressive collection of Danish and German mercenaries, sailed for Orkney and after a long and uncomfortable voyage seized the town of Kirkwall.[4] This was a dramatic enough move in itself, even allowing for the total lack of any opposition to the invaders when they landed. Unfortunately, while Kirkwall was sufficiently inaccessible to afford a certain security for the Royalists, it soon proved to be far too remote from Edinburgh to influence decision-making there, far less in Holland. In March 1650 with negotiations still stalled Charles raised the stakes once again by sending home the feared James Graham, Marquis of Montrose.

Over the winter the original cadre of exiles and mercenaries at Kirkwall had been augmented by some far from enthusiastic Orcadian levies and a further 200 mercenaries. Sir John Hurry, now in the king's service once more, landed near Duncansby Head with the Royalist advance guard on 9 April, and marching swiftly southwards bypassed Dunbeath Castle to seize the strategically important Ord of Caithness – a narrow pass between the mountains and the sea.[5] It was a neat beginning to the campaign but it was also the last time the Royalists would move fast and decisively.

Montrose himself got the rest of his army across the Pentland Firth by 12 April and established a temporary headquarters at Thurso. A number of the local gentry dutifully rallied to the king's standard, but they brought few of their people with them. Leaving 200 of his men as a garrison, Montrose then marched south to join Hurry a few days later. On the way however he paused for three days to capture Dunbeath Castle – and then dropped off another 100 men to hold it. Conversely he failed to take Dunrobin and instead swung inland to Lairg, crossed the hills and came down to the Kyle of Sutherland at Carbisdale on the evening of 25 April. And there he abruptly halted, digging in for what to all appearances would be a lengthy stay.

Why he did so is not at first sight entirely clear. Thus far he had met with little active resistance, for the local commander, the Earl of Sutherland, prudently retired southwards and had he chosen to do so there was nothing to hinder Montrose marching all the way down to Inverness. Yet by comparison with his earlier campaigns his progress was positively glacial. Moreover in another break with the past Montrose was leaving strong garrisons along a line of communications stretching all the way back to his original base in Kirkwall.

Clearly the halt at Carbisdale was not intended as a temporary pause to gather reinforcements before pushing farther south into his old stamping ground in Atholl, but was rather a matter of consolidating his position. The failure of Pluscardine's rising had demonstrated that the Kirk party was firmly in control of the country and that military action alone would not suffice. Advancing farther at this stage would simply plunge Scotland into another destructive round of bloody civil war. Even if Montrose was to emerge victorious there was no saying how much damage it would do to the young king's cause in the process. Instead, it was the threat that Montrose represented which was intended to strengthen the king's hand and give Charles the leverage he required to secure his return without making the humiliating concessions demanded by the Kirk party.

Carbisdale

Thus, having achieved his initial objective of establishing a Royalist presence on the mainland, Montrose was now playing it safe. His campsite was well chosen – a long flat stretch of ground between the deep Kyle of Sutherland and the heights of Craigcaoinichean. At the southern end of the camp, the ground narrowed into an easily defended defile before opening out again into the broad strath of Carbisdale itself. Had he been attacked there even by overwhelming numbers a small rearguard would have sufficed to hold the defile long enough for the army to get away.

Unfortunately it was not only his talent for destruction that made Montrose a liability to the king's cause but also his pathological inability to grasp the importance of proper scouting and security, and this casts real doubt on his popular status as a great captain. As we have seen, at Fyvie he had been unexpectedly trapped by Argyle's army, albeit eventually making his escape. At Dundee he was still in the middle of storming the burgh when Baillie came up in full cry behind him, and any admiration of his subsequent escape has to be tempered by acknowledgement of the fact that he should never have allowed himself to be so badly surprised in the first place. Once or twice might be accepted as the accident of fate, but then there was Auldearn, where the Royalists came so close to having their throats cut in their beds, and Baillie's appearance from a completely unexpected direction at Alford and Kilsyth. All three of those battles eventually resulted in Royalist victories, but not Philiphaugh. While it might be possible to find an immediate scapegoat for that particular débâcle, such as Amisfield or Blackadder, there is no getting away from the fact that ultimately responsibility lay with Montrose – and with Montrose alone – for never learning the lesson that time spent on reconnaissance is never wasted. At Carbisdale on Sunday 27 April 1650 his luck finally and fatally ran out.

At the time Leslie was known to be far to the south, having appointed a muster on Brechin Muir, near Dundee, two days earlier, and Montrose was under the mistaken impression that there was only a single troop of hostile cavalry in the area. Seeing it suddenly dangled as bait in front of him he swiftly broke camp and went after it, hoping for an easy victory.

In fact his opponent, Lieutenant-Colonel Archibald Strachan, had *four* troops of veteran cavalry – his own one, Gibby Kerr's, Sir James Halkett's and the Irish Troop under Captain Cullace[6] – totalling about 230 men, together with thirty-six musketeers under a quartermaster, Shaw, detached from Campbell of Lawers' Regiment.[7] As he marched north from Inverness to rendezvous with the Earl of Sutherland at Tain Strachan was also joined by 400-odd local levies under David Ross of Balnagowan and John Munro of Lemlair.[8]

At a council of war held in Tain that morning some of Strachan's officers piously argued against fighting on the sabbath, but then hearing a report that the Royalists were approaching they put aside their scruples. While Sutherland and his men were hurriedly shipped across the Dornoch Firth to block the coast road and prevent reinforcements reaching Montrose from the north, Strachan marched directly on the Royalists by way of Wester Fearn and after a few psalms exhorted his men in fine style:

> Gentlemen, yonder are your enemies, and they are not only your enemies, they are the enemies of our Lord Jesus Christ; I have been dealing this night with Almighty God, to know the event of this affair, and I have gotten it: as sure as God is in heaven, they are delivered into our hands and there shall not a man of us fall to the ground.

Meanwhile Montrose, learning of this movement, sent forward his own forty cavalry under Hurry and a Major Lisle, and then, perhaps suspecting all was not quite as it seemed, followed after with the main body of his infantry. In so doing he was playing directly into Strachan's hands. Even taking his Highland levies into account Strachan was still badly outnumbered for in total the Royalists may have had as many as 1,200 infantry, albeit far too many of them were raw Orcadian levies. However Strachan had no intention of trying to force the pass, and so by dangling that single troop of horse as bait he easily drew the Royalists out into the open.

In front of them, hidden in the thick patches of broom lining the Culrain Burn he placed the remainder of his cavalry, screened no doubt by the handful of musketeers borrowed from Campbell of Lawers' Regiment. Apart from eighty picked men under Major William Ross, the Highland levies under Ross of Balnagowan were ordered to swing to the left after leaving Wester Fearn, and by crossing the river Carron they came over the hills towards what would be the Royalist right.

When his troopers sprang their ambush at about 3 p.m., the result was all that Strachan could have hoped for. The little band of Royalist cavalry was ridden down at once. Lisle was killed, Hurry was badly wounded and captured, and the survivors driven straight back on the Orcadian levies who without further ado threw down their arms and ran for their lives. They may well have been hastened on their way by the appearance of Balnagowan's and Lemlair's men on the hillside above their wide open right flank. At any rate Montrose's numerical superiority simply evaporated in the first few moments of the battle, and many of the Orcadians drowned trying to flee across the Kyle. Only the German and Danish mercenaries put up any sort of a fight, retiring into a convenient birch wood until, finding themselves menaced by Balnagowan's Highland levies, they promptly surrendered to Strachan's regulars! All in all eleven Royalist officers were killed and a further thirty captured, along with twenty-eight NCOs, drums and trumpets, and 386 common soldiers.[9] Strachan himself was bruised by a musket ball, which struck him on his sword belt, but claimed to have only lost one man in the fight.[10]

Montrose managed to flee from the battlefield, but was driven westwards by his pursuers, rather than north to those garrisons he had carefully left behind. Alone, he lost his way in unfamiliar country and was soon captured, hauled off to Edinburgh and summarily executed there on 21 May. Having been sentenced to death back in 1644 there was no need for a trial. With his bargaining position thus fatally undermined Charles sailed from Holland, duly signed the Covenant on 23 June and next day came ashore at Speymouth on the Scots government's terms.

Having thus decisively defeated the Royalist threat in the north the Scots could have been forgiven for thinking the crisis was over, but in fact the worst was yet to come, because the English government at Westminster had jumped to quite the opposite conclusion. The defeat, capture and execution of Montrose were of course welcome news in themselves, but the fact that the Scots had notwithstanding patched up a settlement with Charles was held by the English to be an ominous sign of weakness. Failing to appreciate the very real difference between Scots and English notions of kingship, the imminent arrival of Charles was perceived as a direct threat. No matter that the return of the king was to be hedged about by so many restraints as to reduce him to a mere figurehead, the very fact of his being allowed into the country at all confirmed English suspicions that the Scots still acknowledged his authority. It therefore followed, they feared, that sooner or later the Scots would invade England once again and seek to place their king on the throne at Westminster.

Charles himself undoubtedly shared that hope, but the reality was that the immediate Royalist threat had indeed vanished in Montrose's débâcle and that the Scots army, although pitifully small, was firmly behind the government. Indeed it was a touch ironic that only after the English invasion did Royalist sympathies emerge – within the ranks of the new levies raised to oppose it.

Therefore, on 12 June 1650, a bare three weeks after the marquis was hanged and still more than a week before the king landed, Thomas, now Lord Fairfax, and Oliver Cromwell (who had just returned from campaigning in Ireland) were appointed to command a new field army as general and lieutenant-general respectively. Initially Fairfax assumed that this was a precautionary move and that he was only to command in the event of another Scots invasion, but a week later Parliament declared its intention of invading Scotland first. This was too much for Fairfax. Considering the rush to war to be far too precipitate he had sufficient scruple to refuse the charge, but Oliver Cromwell did not and on 26 June was created lord-general in his stead.

A New Army

In the meantime despite the all-too-clear signs of English preparations for war – which included buying up horses in markets on both sides of the border – the Scots government, far from acting aggressively, was still desperately anxious to avoid any moves that could be construed as provocative. In June 1650 the Scots army, which was so exercising the English government, still numbered something in the region of only 2,500 horse and 3,000 foot. This small force was barely adequate for ordinary internal security purposes – the necessity for which had been clearly demonstrated by both Pluscardine's uprising and Montrose's subsequent invasion – and it was not until 25 June, nearly two weeks after the English concentration began, that a full mobilisation of the army was ordered, not to invade England but to defend Scotland.

After nearly twelve years of conflict the original fencible system had effectively collapsed and the government was by now reduced to exercising a very rudimentary rule of thumb in simply demanding a certain number of men to be levied from each sheriffdom. Unfortunately the terrible drain on the available resources of both men and materiel over such a long period meant that ordering the men to be levied out and actually mustering them into service were often two entirely different things.

Musters carried out in July 1649 reveal that the majority of the 'old' regiments were generally only four companies strong and varying wildly in size. On 28 February 1649 for example Viscount Arbuthnott had been commissioned to lead 800 men raised out of Aberdeenshire and the Mearns, but by 31 July his regiment still comprised only a single company of eighty men. A year later Arbuthnott was allotted a further 900 men, but the only recruits who can actually be verified are just thirty out of the ninety men demanded from the burgh of Aberdeen.

Consequently on 21 June 1650, in the immediate run-up to mobilisation, Leslie requested the Estates that 'old troops and regiments may by your new leavyes be completed to 75 each troop, and 108 each regiment of foot, a mixture being better than to keep the new entirely by themselves'. Although the wording is ambiguous he presumably meant that each of the four *companies* in the existing infantry regiments should be made up to 108 men apiece – or 432 in total – and then went on to underline the point by requesting that no new regiments should be formed until the old ones were complete.

To that end on 25 June the Estates duly ordered the levying of some 9,749 foot and 2,882 horse, largely to reinforce existing units, although some new regiments were also authorised. This particular levy had actually been sanctioned the year before, and the failure to implement it at the time should have given pause for thought. Nevertheless a week later the Estates threw all caution to the wind and on 3 July 1650 a second and much larger levy was ordered, which was even more optimistically expected to produce an additional 19,614 foot, forming twenty-one new infantry regiments. Unsurprisingly this second demand for men, following so soon after the first, largely proved to be counter-productive, and once the 'old' regiments had been brought up to strength many of the new ones existed only as cadres.[11]

For obvious reasons there were immediate problems in the southeast. The two regiments ordered to be raised out of Berwickshire, Roxburgh and the other border sheriffdoms simply did not appear at all, largely as a result of the collapse of the civilian administration in the face of the invasion which followed so quickly after. Instead any men actually levied presumably went into the badly depleted ranks of Home of Wedderburn's and Ker of Greenhead's regiments, which had originally been raised in Berwickshire and Teviotdale in 1649. There is similarly little sign of the Haddingtonshire men either, although some of them at least must have formed the garrison of Tantallon Castle. Farther from the border, Lord Balmerino evidently raised some men in Edinburgh for a colour bearing his crest was taken at Dunbar, but otherwise there is no trace of his regiment and his few men almost certainly fought there attached to Colonel Alexander Stewart's Regiment.

To the west matters were even more problematic since opposition to the king was greatest in that area and the levies were consequently reluctant to turn out in his service. As late as August, after the campaign was well under way, some influential officers such as Archibald Strachan were assuring Cromwell that they regarded the king, not the English, as their real enemy.[12] There is no evidence that Douglas of Darroch ever raised any men in Dumfries or that Sir William Carmichael brought out the Lanarkshire levies in accordance with the government's decree. Lord Kirkcudbright certainly raised some men but appears to have mounted them as dragooners, which suggests there were comparatively few of them.[13] Similarly Lord Mauchline and the Earl of Cassillis were commissioned to raise infantry regiments but instead sought and received permission to mount their levies as troopers, on the basis of producing one trooper for each of the three infantrymen originally demanded. Both did indeed lead cavalry regiments at Dunbar, although it seems unlikely that they should have mustered as many as 580 troopers between them.

The levies in Fife, Linlithgow, Stirling and Clackmannan on the other hand were slightly more successful, largely because no fresh recruits were diverted into the two existing regiments from the area – Colin Pitscottie's and James Holburne's. A total of four new regiments were to have been formed, and while they made it to Dunbar they must have been fairly weak for they appear to have been consolidated into just two battalions representing the first and second levies respectively. The apparent failure to muster only about half the men called for was certainly borne out by the experience of Colonel John Lindsay of Edzell, who was commissioned to raise some 1,200 men in Forfarshire but only succeeded in getting about 600, and also in neighbouring Perthshire where once again a notional total of four regiments fought at Dunbar as two.[14]

Farther north time was also very much against the recruiters. There was already a small regiment in Aberdeenshire commanded by the Master of Forbes, which should have been brought up to strength by fresh drafts from the first levy, while Viscount Arbuthnott and John Forbes of Leslie were expected to raise new regiments in the second. Instead all of the levies went into the Master of Forbes' regiment. On the other hand Sir Alexander Sutherland of Duffus, charged with raising a regiment in Moray and Nairn, did not commence his recruiting at all until after Dunbar. Similarly although the Master of Lovat's Regiment marched south to Dunbar it did so with a mere three companies, albeit they were consolidated with the better part of Argyle's Regiment, drawn out of the Highland garrisons.[15]

If levying sufficient men to form an army was difficult, finding suitable officers to command them was even more problematic. Inevitably after a decade of conflict a fair proportion of them had at one time or another marched as king's men or Engagers, or otherwise rendered themselves odious to the Kirk party, and no sooner were the levies brought together than a great purging of the ungodly began.

There had been intermittent purgings before, but now an ominous-sounding Committee for Purging the Army was set up on 21 June. Hostile commentators, the most eloquent of whom was the English Cavalier Sir Edward Walker, charged that between 2 and 5 August as many as 4,000 good soldiers were expelled from the army simply because of their Royalist sympathies. They were then replaced, he said in an eminently quotable turn of phrase, with 'ministers' sons, clerks, and such other sanctified creatures, who hardly ever saw or heard of any sword but that of the spirit'.

This might well have been the pious intention of some of the more extreme adherents of the Kirk, such as Archibald Johnston of Wariston and Colonel Archibald Strachan, who were opposed to the return of the king and even prepared if necessary to enter into secret negotiations with Cromwell. However, in reality a much more modest total of only about eighty officers and men were dismissed, rather than Walker's 4,000, albeit with the (unfulfilled) threat that more would follow at the end of the month. The position is slightly complicated by the fact an unknown number had already been dismissed in the preceding months, and further confused by the fact that those purges were not confined to commissioned officers but included ordinary soldiers and troopers as well.

On the other hand, while there is ample documentary evidence of English Cavaliers and Scots 'Engagers' being dismissed from some regiments, in others their services were retained.[16] Ironically a number of the trophies afterwards taken by the English army at Dunbar also reveal that Leven may actually have been using the Committee for an entirely different purpose from that originally intended by its sponsors.

All Scots infantry companies carried saltire colours in a variety of tinctures, and ordinarily it was customary to place the captain's crest or some other device in the centre, but in 1649, perhaps because the regiments raised in that year were intended to form a standing army, a system of heraldic cadency marks was applied to their colours in order to designate the seniority of each company within the regiment. However most of those 1649 pattern colours captured at Dunbar are in some measure disfigured by the hasty application of numerals indicating a quite different seniority from that apparently designated by the cadency mark. At first sight this might be taken simply as evidence of the original company commanders having been 'purged' and replaced by others, but yet the officers of these particular regiments ought to have been among the most politically reliable and free from the taint of Royalism.

The answer to this seeming paradox is that in the haste to levy new companies and troops in 1650 a great many unsuitable officers were appointed to lead them by the local authorities responsible. Some of the new men may well have been politically suspect, for there is certainly ample evidence of an upsurge in Royalist support, particularly when the king actually visited the army while it was in the Leith lines. On the whole though it is far more likely that, as in the case of the burgh levy from Aberdeen, the local worthies who led them lacked military experience and were simply not up to the job. Leven therefore took advantage of the purges to have them turned out in favour of the veteran officers already serving in the 1649 regiments. The ministers' sons and other 'sanctified creatures' complained of by Walker were merely slotted in at the end of the process to fill the vacancies at the most junior grades created by promoting or transferring the veterans, rather than their actually being given command of regiments or companies as Walker scathingly implies.

In short, notwithstanding an undoubted but relatively brief period of disruption, which must have involved a great many inter-regimental transfers rather than wholesale sackings of experienced officers, the purges were in all likelihood ultimately a positive step. In any case if some of the new men brought into the army were filled with religious zeal, then that was perhaps no bad thing, for as Cromwell himself demonstrated fanaticism and military efficiency are by no means incompatible.

Invasion

By then the English army had already crossed the border at Berwick with 16,354 men on 22 July, and meeting no resistance, got safely through the dangerous defile of Cockburnspath and so arrived in the small town of Dunbar four days later. There Cromwell paused to take stock. Almost as a matter of course the Scots had obeyed 'King Robert's Testament', and as in the days of the Bruce had driven off their animals and burned or hidden anything else that could be of use to the invaders. The English encountered no one but women and children, who claimed that all the men had been taken by the army, but it soon transpired that in reality their husbands and sons were much closer at hand and the road back to the border soon became worryingly infested with bandits and partisans locally known as Moss-troopers. Equally worryingly although fifteen ships, including four men-of-war, had been ordered to support the army, not all of them had yet arrived at Dunbar and consequently the supplies unloaded in that first lift amounted to a mere 'pittance'. It was an ominous sign for the future.

Nevertheless, from Dunbar Cromwell began to push westwards across the coastal plain and next occupied the town of Haddington. At Gladsmuir not far beyond he at last encountered Leven's outpost line, and thereafter Scots soldiers were increasingly in evidence. The English cavalry, under Lambert, were unable to penetrate Leven's cavalry screen but nevertheless the Scots continued to fall back steadily. On 29 July, just beyond Musselburgh and the river Esk, the English army at last uncovered the main body of the Scots army, causing first Lambert and then Cromwell to halt in dismay.

For the first time Cromwell discovered that Leven, instead of meeting him in open battle, had elected to dig his raw army in behind a line of forts and entrenchments stretching all the way from Edinburgh to the Forth, along the present line of Leith Walk.[17] The works were impossible to outflank, and a probe into Holyrood Park encountered stiff resistance.

A Scots outpost there was quickly overrun, but just as quickly recaptured by Sir James Campbell of Lawers, without waiting to don his armour but 'quho doublett alone, mounted hill at St. Leonards chapell, and dange them from ther cannon . . .' A cavalry charge then recovered the guns, but by then Lawers' men were well ensconced on the slopes of the rocky outcrop known as Arthur's Seat and 'from the hedges and rockes played wncessantly with ther musketts'.[18]

Cromwell quickly recognised that there could be absolutely no question of mounting a formal frontal assault on the main position when the professionalism and experience of his outnumbered men would count for much less than in the open field. Nevertheless, encouraged by the Scots' willingness to engage in skirmishing, he rather optimistically tried to tempt Leven to come out and fight after all. He placed his cavalry at Restalrig and his infantry at Jock's Lodge while four warships bombarded Leith, but Leven still refused to rise to the bait. Then to make matters worse, the weather turned bad. The army spent the night in makeshift bivouacs under pouring rain, and next morning 'the ground being very wet, and our provisions scarce' Cromwell disgustedly decided to fall back on Musselburgh 'there to refresh and revictual'.

The withdrawal began at about 10 a.m. on 30 July, and it is a measure of deteriorating morale that discipline broke down almost at once. Cromwell with the infantry simply hurried down the road at their best speed and soon left Lambert and the rearguard dangerously exposed. Recognising the opportunity, Leven (or perhaps Leslie) promptly sent his cavalry in pursuit, one body debouching from Edinburgh's Canongate port and the other from the Leith end of the lines.

Notwithstanding the understandable gloss afterwards placed on the affair in Cromwell's letters and in some later memoirs, there is no doubting that what followed was a severely chastening experience. The Scots who sallied out from Leith were seemingly quickly driven back by Colonel Hacker, but on the Edinburgh road it was a very different matter indeed. Captain William Evanson's troop of Whalley's Regiment, the rearmost unit, 'received the charge; but being overpowered by the enemy, retreated', which was perhaps only to be expected given that they were badly outnumbered. Cromwell's own regiment of horse – the original Ironsides whom he had personally raised and trained in 1643 – then charged forward to their rescue and initially checked the Scots pursuit, but more lancers came up, put in another charge, wounded Captain John Gladman and sent the Ironsides tumbling back in considerable confusion. Next Colonel Whalley counter-charged with four more troops of his regiment and Lambert also brought up his own regiment, but by this time there were cavalrymen scattered all around. Instead of riding down the Scots they simply became sucked into a fierce, whirling mêlée in which the greater weight of the English horses counted for nothing.

In the midst of it all Lambert had his horse 'shot in the neck and head; himself run through the arm with a lance, and run through another part of his body', and in the process was thrown off his horse and taken prisoner. As he was being led off towards Edinburgh however Lieutenant Empson of Cromwell's Regiment charged and rescued him, and shortly the Scots drew off. According to Cromwell the scales were finally turned by Captain Chillenden with the sixth troop of Whalley's Regiment, who 'being in good order, charged them, and put them to the run, pursuing and killing them, even to and within their line'. Cromwell also went on to boast of having 'killed divers of them upon the place, and took some prisoners, without any considerable loss; which indeed did so amaze and quiet them, that we marched off to Muscleborough, but they dar'd not send out a man to trouble us'.[19]

It would perhaps be more accurate to say that having made their point the Scots decided to call it a day and effectively quit while they were ahead. For their part they equally predictably claimed to have killed five colonels and lieutenant-colonels, mortally wounded Lambert and 'above 500'. They too claimed to have returned with 'no grate losse'. Moreover far from marching off triumphantly as he claimed Cromwell and his men eventually arrived at Musselburgh 'so tired and wearied for want of sleep, and so dirty by reason of the weather, that we expected the enemy would make an infall upon us'. Indeed, just by way of rubbing it in, they found that Musselburgh had been occupied and barricaded against them by a large body of partisans – perhaps some of the Haddingtonshire levies who were supposed to have been raised by Angus. Although the rabble were soon chased out again, it was clearly an ominous sign. Worse was to follow. That very night the Scots did indeed proceed to follow up their success by mounting a heavy raid on the English camp.

Some time between 3 a.m. and 4 a.m. on 31 July Major-General Robin Montgomerie attacked out of the darkness with what some observers estimated to be as many as fifteen troops of horse numbering 800 or more picked cavalrymen, belonging to his own, Sir James Halkett's and Gibby Kerr's regiments. According to at least one account Montgomerie was supported by a couple of hundred infantry as well.

Despite the fact that their arrival was nervously anticipated, Montgomerie successfully achieved tactical surprise by posting a number of English Royalists at the head of his column. The familiar accents of these Cavaliers misled the outlying picquets into thinking that the approaching troopers were in fact a friendly patrol – until it was too late. Those picquets were furnished that night by two troops of Colonel Robert Lilburne's Horse, and while an English account states that the Scots were received 'very gallantly' one of Lilburne's cornets was killed in the mêlée and his colours taken. At least however the picquet's doomed fight gave time for their commander, Captain George Watkinson, 'a person of great worth for conduct and valour', to sound the alarm and rouse the infantry. Some of Lambert's Foot managed to get off a volley, and this seemingly was enough to see off Hackett and his men, and as Sir James Balfour sneered: 'Sir Jams Hackett receavid a grate fryte at a skirmishe with the enemey, he should haue secondit the L. Generall, bot turnit and never lowsid a pistoll against the enimey, bot tooke him to the speed of his horsse heels.'[20]

Nevertheless the rest of the Scots successfully laid about them, inflicted a fair few casualties and best of all spread a suitable degree of confusion, fear and despondency, before withdrawing in time-honoured fashion just as quickly as they had come.[21] Their casualties were negligible and they were not pursued, but ironically there was an unrelated skirmish on the way back with the very same English patrol they had impersonated in deceiving Lilburne's unfortunate picquets.

Naturally enough Cromwell, just as he had done the day before, brazenly proclaimed the Scots' departure as a famous victory, and released his handful of prisoners – but then at midnight on 5 August he hastily pulled his army all the way back to Dunbar, where he remained until 12 August. The decision to withdraw so far back was prompted in large part by the rough weather, which prevented any supplies being landed at Musselburgh, and by the fact that having elected to rely on the ships rather than the usual train of wagons Cromwell had great difficulty in bringing supplies forward from Dunbar. Even more importantly, having gambled on good weather and a swift campaign, he had not encumbered his army with tents, and it was now suffering accordingly. The tents were at last landed at Dunbar and issued to the soldiers, but already the foul weather and scarcity of provisions were producing an appallingly high rate of sickness.

Nevertheless, on 11 August Cromwell resolved on another attempt to bring Leven to battle. This time he planned to swing right around to the south and west of Edinburgh, more or less along the line of the present city bypass. In theory it would of course mean temporarily cutting himself off from his base at Dunbar, but as he had no overland supply lines to worry about this was not quite the gamble it might at first appear since his aim was to re-establish contact with the fleet at Queensferry, to the *west* of Edinburgh. On the contrary he would then have successfully interdicted Leven's line of communications to Stirling and the west and might thus force the Scots out into the open, where he wanted them.

At 5 a.m. on the morning of Sunday 13 August Cromwell had two cannon fired as a signal to his ships and marched west again. The move initially took the Scots by surprise, not least because it was the Lord's Day. However his lack of transport meant Cromwell could carry only three days' supplies and instead of pushing blindly into hostile territory he initially contented himself with seizing a strong position on the Braid Hill in the Pentlands. Next day, having established his camp, he sent a letter to his old colleague, David Leslie, urging a peaceful settlement. This produced a meeting of officers from both armies later that day on the sands between Musselburgh and Leith. Although some of the Scots again declared their detestation of the king they were not prepared to change sides. Negotiation having failed and the three days' supplies having been consumed, Cromwell was compelled to fall back again to Musselburgh the next day.

The futility of this rather dot-and-carry mode of campaigning was quickly exposed when Leven, in his absence, duly came out and occupied a strong blocking position on Corstorphine Hill without any molestation. Hurrying back into position on the Braid Hill, Cromwell stormed a minor Scots outpost in a house at Redhall on 26 August, but then decided that Leven's main fighting position was far too strong, and so instead moved farther westwards, still in hopes of cutting the Scots lines of communication with Stirling. However Leven, who was of course operating on interior lines rather predictably forestalled him yet again, and this time blocked his path at the village of Gogar.

Initially the situation looked fairly promising, for the Scots appeared to be standing in the open. Cromwell accordingly prepared to attack, only to have to call the operation off on realising that both of Leven's flanks were secured by boggy ground and that his invitingly open front was not only boggy as well but swept by artillery.[22]

Unwilling to risk a battle under less than favourable conditions, unable to break through to the sea, short of supplies and increasingly concerned about his own line of communications and lack of transport, Cromwell once more fell back first to Musselburgh and then on 31 August pulled out for Dunbar. On the previous night he had convened a council of war, which eventually resolved to retreat there on the rather curious grounds that it would be 'a place for a good magazine', as well as affording shelter for the sick, while they dug in to await reinforcements. Cromwell also rather disingenuously justified the move by expressing the hope that Leven might thereby be tempted to come out and fight. In this at least he was not disappointed for at this point the Scots army suddenly went onto the offensive.

Throughout this period Leven and Leslie had been working hard to improve the efficiency of their raw levies, both by 'exercising' them and by overseeing two successive purges of unsuitable officers. Now they were confident enough to take the army out of its trenches not to pursue but to destroy the English army.

Chapter 10
Curs'd Dunbar

Notwithstanding his oft-expressed hopes that the Scots would come out to fight, Cromwell now showed no inclination at all to stand and face them, but instead hurried straight for Haddington, where once again the rearguard was thrown into disorder as it approached the town. Fortunately however 'the Lord by his providence put a cloud over the moon', and so the rear brigade of horse managed to break contact under cover of the resulting darkness. Nothing daunted, the Scots tried again at midnight. This time the attackers included 'a party of mounted musketeers' – presumably Lord Kirkcudbright's Dragoons. Although other details of the fight are lacking this must have been an altogether much more serious affair for it took an hour's fighting before they were repulsed by Colonel Charles Fairfax's Foot. Just what the English cavalry were doing, or rather not doing, during the battle was not explained.[1]

Next morning Cromwell drew up his exhausted army in order of battle 'into an open field on the south side of Haddington' in the expectation that a full-scale assault was imminent. Whether at this point in time the army was in much condition to withstand that attack is perhaps a moot point, but as the morning wore on Cromwell took the opportunity to send his baggage and sick safely back to the town. Then 'having waited about the space of four hours to see if he would come to us and not finding any inclination in the enemy so to do, we resolved to go, according to our first intendment, to Dunbar'.[2]

Captain John Hodgson recalled the retreat rather less complacently and described how:

> We staid until about ten o'clock, had been at prayer in several regiments, sent away our wagons and carriages towards Dunbar, and not long afterwards marched, a poor, shattered, hungry, discouraged army; and the Scots pursued very close, that our rearguard had much ado to secure our poor weak foot that was not able to march up. We drew near Dunbar towards night and the Scots ready to fall upon our rear: two guns played upon them, and so they drew off and left us that night, having got us unto a pound as they reckoned.[3]

Once again expecting a direct attack since 'the addition of three new regiments added to them,[4] did much heighten their confidence, if not presumption and arrogancy'. Cromwell halted and drew up his army 'in battalia in the town fields, between the Scotch army and the town ready to engage'. The baggage train and the guns were at first secured in the churchyard, but as night came on Cromwell drew the guns out again and placed them in the middle of his lines, no doubt expecting an attack early in the morning.[5]

However, while the English rearguard was being so vigorously hustled by the Scots cavalry, the greater part of Leven's army, instead of following on Cromwell's heels as he supposed, slid eastwards. While Cromwell's men were fighting off the attacks on the camp at Haddington, a Scots infantry brigade had been flung into the defile at Cockburnspath, cutting the Berwick road. Now the bulk of the Scots army secured the adjacent commanding eminence of Doon Hill, overlooking Dunbar and the Berwick road some distance to the south of the town. To all appearances Cromwell was trapped, and a major battle was all but inevitable.

The Armies and the Plans

One of the abiding problems in reconstructing what really happened at Dunbar is that historians have generally accepted without question Oliver Cromwell's greatly magnified claims as to the strength of the Scots army – and his near Biblical numbers of the dead counted and prisoners taken afterwards. In actual fact if all fifteen of the Scots infantry 'regiments' identified in an English intelligence summary were assigned a notional 1,000 men apiece then that might be the justification for Cromwell's exaggerated claim that he was faced by 16,000 foot and 6,000 horse. The highly unreliable account by the English Royalist Sir Edward Walker also evidences a remarkably similar 16,000 foot and 7,000 horse, but notwithstanding the suspicious similarity the total is far too high. As we have already seen David Leslie asked for the older regiments to be recruited up to a strength of 432, while the majority of the new regiments were intended to be 700–900 strong. In the circumstances few of them can have succeeded in raising anything like that number, but allowing for the widespread pairing of units a rough average of 600–700 men per 'battalia' appears to be about right, except in Innes' Brigade, which was very likely weaker. At the very outside therefore there could perhaps have been as many as 10,000 infantry, but probably somewhat fewer, and a more realistic estimate would be about 9,500 infantry.[6]

It should be stressed however that this estimate is largely based on the numbers mustered at the outset of the campaign. There is every reason to suppose that the high levels of wastage attributable to sickness and exposure suffered by the English army applied equally well to the Scots army, and that the numbers actually present and fit to fight on 3 September may have been considerably fewer and that the actual numbers were about even.

Similarly while the English intelligence summary identifies no fewer than nineteen cavalry units, all of them were very considerably smaller than their English counterparts. As we have seen, Scots regiments rarely mustered more than three troops at this period, and some were probably still represented only by a single troop. Nevertheless, assuming an average of three troops per regiment would produce a total of sixty troops. At the outset Leslie asked that each of them should be recruited up to a strength of seventy-five men, which would have produced a total of 4,500 cavalrymen rather than the 6,000–7,000 imagined by Cromwell and Walker. Notwithstanding, there is no reason to suppose that the levying of troopers was any more successful than the levying of infantrymen, and consequently just 3,000–4,000 cavalry is again a much more realistic estimate.

Lacking anything like a morning state setting out the numbers present and fit for duty in each regiment it is equally difficult to be categorical about the actual fighting strength of Cromwell's army at Dunbar. The 16,354 men which he led across the border on 22 July had seemingly sunk to 12,080 by 3 September as a result of sickness and exposure. Some 2,000 of them were sufficiently ill and enfeebled to be evacuated by sea, others had presumably died, but there must still have been upwards of 1,000 sick with the army. Ordinarily of course they would have remained in camp or their quarters during the battle, but if the army was actually trying to break out (as will become apparent) then just about every man still fit to walk or sit in a saddle must have been in the ranks. At any rate Cromwell quite categorically stated afterwards that his army was 'drawn down, as to sound men, to about 7,500 foot and 3,500 horse'.[7]

In examining what these 11,000 men did next, it soon becomes apparent that there are excellent grounds for believing that neither the defeated Scots nor the victorious English were particularly candid.

For the Scots, the widely accepted story is that after having taken up an impregnable position on top of Doon Hill the army's officers were prevailed on by a hideous travelling committee of clerics and politicians to come down off the hill and engage in a vainglorious smiting of the foe rather than tamely awaiting Cromwell's otherwise inevitable surrender. This view of events was certainly widespread on both sides at the time, but takes little account of the military realities of the tactical situation.

When the Scots first flung themselves across Cromwell's line of retreat on 1 September it was only natural that they should secure the dominant heights of Doon Hill. Once they were actually on top of the hill however it will very soon have become apparent to them – if indeed it had not been obvious from the start – that the position suffered significant drawbacks and was in reality no place to fight a battle.

It certainly offered a magnificent view of the coastal plain and the English army far below, and its steep slopes were undoubtedly unassailable, but those advantages counted for nothing if the English were not so accommodating as to attempt such a hopeless assault. It is also questionable whether, lacking heavy artillery, they could have done much to impede any English attempt to force a way straight down the road past the hill. Consequently, as the Reverend Robert Baillie records, the subsequent inquiry into the conduct of David Leslie rightly concluded that he was guilty of 'no maladministration . . . but the removall of the armie from the hill the night before the rowt, which yet was a consequence of the Committee's order, contrare to his mind, to stop the enemie's retreat, and for that end storm Broxmouth House so soon as possible'.[8]

This then is clear enough. The army was ordered to descend the hill not to attack the English, but to more effectually block the Berwick road by seizing Broxmouth House at the point where the road crossed the valley of the Broxburn. Of itself this decision was a perfectly sensible one, but it took time and provoked an immediate response from the English, which in turn led Leslie to take up a false position. The initial move began shortly before sunrise on 2 September, but it was not until about four in the afternoon that the artillery and baggage were finally brought down and secured beside Meikle Pinkerton farm – the length and complexity of the operation once again emphasising the impracticality of the original hill-top position.

In the meantime Cromwell reacted by bringing his army forward from Dunbar and forming a battle line on the north side of the Broxburn. Leslie, no doubt wary of being attacked before all of his men could be brought down and properly deployed, conformed by arranging his own battle line along the southern side. At no time however did he contemplate launching a frontal assault of his own across it. The Broxburn, although neither particularly deep nor broad, for the most part runs through a wide trenchlike ravine and constitutes a significant military obstacle, particularly since the northern or English side of the ravine is rather higher than the southern side and very largely dominates it.

Between the Berwick road and the sea on the other hand it is much easier to cross the stream, and as Baillie notes Leslie had designs on the main crossing point near Broxmouth House. To that end there was some skirmishing during the latter part of the afternoon, since Cromwell was equally alive to its importance, and at one stage a particularly vicious fight took place for possession of a minor crossing point at what is now Brand's Mill:

> On the side of the bank was a poor house which stood in a shelving pass; Lieut.-Gen. Fleetwood and Col. Pride sent 24 foot and 6 horse to secure that pass, that the enemy should not come over. The enemy about four of the clock drew down about two troops of lanciers into this pass to beat off the said party; the six horse gave way; they killed 3 of the foot and took 3, and wounded and drove away the rest, and so they gained the pass, which yet they presently acquitted.[9]

This seemingly pointless skirmish was presumably intended to cover a partial deployment of the Scots army. Although Leslie had by now brought all of his army down off the hill without mishap he rather belatedly realised that, having lined up opposite the English army, it was actually positioned in the wrong place. Accordingly he now tried to extend his right towards the sea, but in this he was only partially successful. Cromwell noted the movement of about two-thirds of the Scots horse from the left flank to reinforce the right, which took place shortly after the skirmish at Brand's Mill, but otherwise Leslie's redeployment was considerably hampered by the very restricted space between the Broxburn and the foot of the hill. Consequently by nightfall on 2 September most of his infantry were still uselessly positioned to the left of the Berwick road with the all but impassable ravine directly to their front.

Nevertheless, notwithstanding the unsatisfactory deployment, Leslie had now very firmly blocked the road and Cromwell knew he was in trouble. Once he was satisfied that Leslie had suspended operations for the night he and his senior officers 'went and supped at Dunbar for refreshment, and presently after, before five of the clock, they took horse and went into the fields, and then called a council of war'.

The battle which followed that council was undoubtedly a stunning victory, and all of those concerned were afterwards at considerable pains to individually claim the credit for both urging the attack and planning its execution. However these claims do not stand up to serious scrutiny and are flatly contradicted by a vital piece of evidence.

There is little doubt that by the evening of 2 September the 'poor, shattered, hungry, discouraged' English army was pretty well at the end of its tether. In the six weeks since crossing the border on 22 July every offensive move had been frustrated by the Scots and every retreat harried by the ever-present lancers. Even the famous Ironsides had found themselves running away at one point. As if that were not enough the weather had been depressingly bad so that the army had suffered constant privation and in consequence may have lost something between 4,000 and 5,000 sick! Captain Hodgson, although not present at the council of war (unless of course he provided its security), memorably recalled that: 'Many of the colonels were for shipping the foot, and the horse to force the passage.' Instead, he claims, his own commanding officer, Major-General Lambert, very properly opposed that notion, pointing out that 'there was no time to ship the foot, for the day would be upon us, and we should lose all our carriages'.[10] What was more the patent inability of the navy and the hired transports to supply the army adequately must have raised considerable doubts as to whether they would be able to lift any appreciable number of the infantry at all. In short, any attempt to evacuate the army by sea would almost certainly result in a rerun of the disaster at Lostwithiel in 1644, when the Earl of Essex's Parliamentarian army had been trapped and forced to surrender to the king himself.

Instead, according to the ever-loyal Hodgson, Lambert forcefully if not inspirationally advocated an all-out assault on the Scots position with the object of turning Leslie's right, pinning the army against the slopes of Doon Hill and then destroying it. This was pretty well what actually happened next morning, and if Hodgson's account is true the plan reflects considerable credit on his commander. Cromwell's version is not inconsistent when he described in his official despatch how:

> The Major-General and myself coming to the Earl of Roxburgh's house (Broxmouth) and
> observing this posture, I told him it did give us an opportunity and advantage to attempt

upon the enemy. To which he immediately replied that he had thought to have said the same thing to me. So that it pleased the Lord to set the same apprehension upon both of our hearts at the same instant. We called for Colonel Monk and showed him the thing . . .[11]

Similarly Monck's biographer, Gumble, attributes the advocacy of the attack to *him*, but on the other hand a one-time professional soldier-turned-hack writer named Fitzpayne Fisher silently and perhaps unwittingly reveals that the council of war almost certainly produced a rather different resolution and that the 'opportunity' sought was not the destruction of the Scots army.[12]

When the English army had flung itself into Dunbar on 1 September the baggage train was secured within the walled churchyard beyond the eastern end of the town. When the resolution was taken to fight at the council of war on the night of 2 September it would have been sensible to have left it there, or even to have sent it into the town itself for greater security.

Yet Fisher's contemporary picture-map of the battle, prepared from eyewitness testimony for a proposed official history of the campaign, shows both the churchyard and the adjacent English camp to be empty. Instead the baggage train is clearly and unambiguously placed within the grounds of Broxmouth House – Cromwell's tactical headquarters and the jumping-off point for the assault!

Ordinarily this would be a most extraordinary place for a seventeenth-century army to place its baggage train, but the fact that Cromwell brought it so far forward indicates that the proposed attack at dawn next morning was not the outcome of a bold resolution to go forward and fight the enemy, as the principal actors and their partisans afterwards claimed. Rather it was a desperate attempt to force open the Berwick road in order that the army could cut its way out of the trap and escape southwards. To that end the baggage train had all too evidently been brought up to the front in order that once the withdrawal commenced it could be passed down the road as soon as possible rather than left to become entangled with the rearguard.

Dawn

First the English army had to secure a passage over the Broxburn itself and there were probably only three places where it was practicable to do so: the narrow 'pass' at Brand's Mill; the main crossing point where the Berwick road led over it; and then farther down on the fairly flat area between Broxmouth House and the sea. For obvious reasons Cromwell planned to pass most of his cavalry across the fairly flat area, but control of the road was essential if he was to get his infantry and that baggage train across.

It was, remembered John Nicoll, 'a drakie nycht full of wind and weit'; or as Walker put it in English: 'very rainy and tempestuous'. Cromwell 'rid all the night before through the several regiments by torchlight, upon a little Scots nag, biting his lip till the blood ran down his chin without his perceiving it, his thoughts being busily employed to be ready for the action now at hand'.[13] There was little wonder he was nervous, for having declined the admittedly risky option of trying to evacuate at least a part of his army by sea he was now gambling everything on reopening the road and escaping overland. If the dawn attack failed, the army even if not actually defeated would have little alternative but to surrender.

For their part the Scots seem to have been aware that something was happening for they remained standing to their arms for much of the night. At 'ten o'clock the enemy did give an alarm to ours. The whole army then being in a readiness they were repulsed.' After it was over the Scots began to settle down, and at about midnight Major-General Holburne gave permission for all but two musketeers in each company to extinguish their slow-match. Ordinarily this would have been a sensible enough precaution which not only prevented waste and ensured that the match could be kept dry within the soldiers' clothing but also meant that the soldiers themselves could try to snatch some sleep. It also once again indicated that, contrary to what is often said, the Scots had no plans to mount an offensive of their own, but were content to sit tight and block the high road to England.

As the soldiers 'made themselves shelter of the corn new-reapt', many of the cavalrymen and officers retired to their tents. Leslie complained two days after the battle that: 'I take God to witness we might as easily have beaten them as we did James Graham at Philiphaugh, if the officers had stayed by their own troops and regiments.' Thus they were quite unprepared when at about four in the morning Cromwell moved forward to secure the crossing points over the Broxburn.

His leading brigade was commanded by John Lambert and comprised Fleetwood's, Lambert's and Whalley's regiments of horse. Immediately behind was another cavalry brigade made up of Lilburne's, Hacker's and Twisleton's regiments, almost certainly commanded by Colonel Robert Lilburne. Assuming Cromwell's estimate of the forces available to him to be correct, the two brigades presumably mustered about 1,500 men apiece. Next came Colonel George Monck's rather weak infantry brigade comprising his own and Malverer's regiments, and the five remaining companies of Colonel George Fenwick's, probably totalling something in the region of about 2,000 men. Cromwell's official report on the battle rather perfunctorily implies that Lieutenant-General Fleetwood was in overall charge of this 'vanguard', although Hodgson rather predictably claims that 'one (of the council) steps up and desires that Colonel

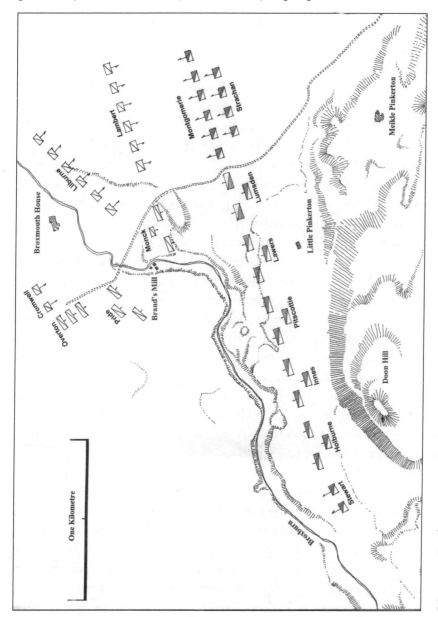

Map 11: *Dunbar 1650: Early morning.*

Lambert might have the conduct of the army that morning, which was granted by the general freely'.

Next came two more infantry brigades. Pride's Brigade was made up of his own regiment, of course, together with the Lord General's, under Major Goffe, and Major-General Lambert's. Behind Pride was Overton's Brigade. His own regiment was not present, but he did have those of Coxe, Daniel and Charles Fairfax. Each of them must have had about 2,500 men. Finally in the rear of all came Cromwell's own regiment of horse acting as a reserve. His official despatch however actually refers to two regiments being in the reserve, which presumably means that his regiment was brigaded with the two companies of Okey's Dragoons already equipped as horse.

This then was the force assigned to destroy the Scots right wing and reopen the Berwick road. As to the rest it would appear that the mounted infantry element of Okey's Dragoons still maintained a picquet line along the edge of the Broxburn, while the artillery was in all probability placed on the high ground above Brand's Mill, where as Lambert allegedly recommended they 'might have fair play at their left wing while we were fighting their right'.

On the other side of the Broxburn information on the Scots dispositions remains scanty, at least as far as the cavalry is concerned. All that can be established with any certainty is that the majority was on the right wing and largely posted between the Berwick road and the seashore. The first line should have been commanded by Major-General Robin Montgomerie, while the second is known to have been led by Colonel Archibald Strachan. Sensibly enough no more than a single brigade remained on the left wing, and as the only unit that can be identified there is Colonel William Stewart's he may well have been the brigade commander. Allowing for this solitary brigade, those cavalry on the right, facing Fleetwood's 'vanguard', may have numbered about 2,500 troopers and as such will have found themselves outnumbered by Fleetwood's 3,000 when the battle began.

As to the Scots infantry, the five brigades can be placed with rather more confidence. As he was the senior infantry commander, Sir James Lumsden's Brigade will have been on the extreme right either beside or astride the Berwick road and, as next in seniority, Major-General James Holburne's Brigade will by convention have stood on the extreme left, while the third Major-General, Colin Pitscottie, had the centre. As to the intervening brigades there is ample evidence that Sir James Campbell of Lawers' Brigade was posted on the right between

Lumsden's and Pitscottie's men, which by a simple process of elimination leaves Colonel John Innes' Brigade standing between Pitscottie's and Holburne's.

Sir James Lumsden's Brigade was at least a fairly strong one, mustering more than 2,000 men at the outset of the campaign. Unfortunately although long-standing custom in all armies placed the brigade on the right it was unique in being entirely made up of new recruits. Lawers' had about the same number, while Pitscottie's had about 1,600, but Innes probably only had something between 1,200 and 1,500, while Holburne must have had another 2,000.

Mustering as many as 9,500 men, they might have had something of an edge over Cromwell's 7,500 had they met head on, although it does need to be stressed once again that this estimate does not allow for wastage. It is entirely possible that far from greatly outnumbering the English the actual numbers present and fit to fight may have been about the same on both sides. In any case any advantage in numbers which might have existed was compromised both by the Scots' faulty dispositions, which prevented more than half the army from coming into action at all, and by the trick of fate that placed the rawest brigade squarely in the path of the English assault column as Fleetwood moved forward at about four in the morning.

At once Lambert's Brigade ran into the Scottish picquet line and quickly drove them back on their supports. There the attack stalled until Monck came up with his brigade and a furious firefight erupted in which the artillery of both sides joined. The semi-official *True Relation* is rather light on detail but nevertheless describes how:

> A party of ours, advancing to gain the wind of the enemy, were discovered by a party of theirs who came to alarm us; but notwithstanding (through the Lord's great mercy), after above an hours dispute at the pass upon the broad way between Dunbar and Berwick, our men obtained their end, possessed the pass, whereby we might with ease come over with our army.

By now the heavy rain had eased and the clouds were breaking up, for Cadwell reported that they fought for a time by moonlight, but it evidently closed in again. After nearly an hour both sides gave over and waited for first light, which came at about 5.30 a.m.

For the Scots it should have been an opportunity to regroup, but as Leslie complained far too many officers were absent. Although he implied that it was regimental officers who were missing, the truth appears to be that they also included many of the brigade commanders and other senior officers. The most notable one, obviously, was the Earl of Leven, who is conspicuously absent from every surviving account of the battle, though at seventy years old he at least had some justification for tucking himself up in a warm bed on a wet and stormy night. Unfortunately it is probably significant that the authorisation to extinguish the musketeers' slow-match was given by Holburne, who was only a brigade commander.

The Crisis

It is also significant that when the fighting resumed Lambert, commanding the cavalry, got safely across the Broxburn after about half an hour. The English cavalry immediately scattered the first line of Scots cavalry and even got in among their tents before being halted and then driven back by a series of Scots counter-attacks led not by Major-General Montgomerie but by Colonel Archibald Strachan.

In the meantime Monck, charging forward again at the head of the vanguard infantry, crashed into Lumsden's Brigade on the right of the Scots infantry. Despite the fact that they must already have been engaged in the firefight when the Broxburn crossings were seized an hour earlier, Lumsden's men were all too evidently unprepared for the onslaught. The musketeers can hardly have still been trying to relight their slow-match, but it is entirely possible that being raw and untried they might have already shot off all their ammunition during the earlier fight. Certainly if Lumsden himself was late in arriving on the scene it would explain an apparent breakdown in command and control. At any rate, whatever the cause, there was no dispute about the result. The brigade disintegrated immediately. Lumsden was badly wounded and captured, and two of his regimental commanders, William Douglas of Kirkness and Lieutenant-Colonel David Wemyss, were killed. A very large number of colours can be identified as having been taken from the brigade, and afterwards Wemyss was the only one of his regiments to continue in service – albeit only fit for garrison duty.

Nevertheless the fight cannot have been entirely one-sided, for Lumsden and his men managed to hold on just long enough for Campbell of Lawers' Brigade to swing around and to completely knock Colonel Monck's Brigade out of the fight. At the same time Colonel Strachan rallied the second line of the Scots cavalry and, catching Lambert while he was still regrouping, likewise flung him back across the Broxburn. Things were looking serious for Cromwell and the breakout must have seemed in jeopardy, but he persevered and as he explained next committed Colonel Thomas Pride's infantry brigade: 'our first foot after they had discharged their duty (being overpowered with the enemy), received some repulse, which they soon recovered. But my own regiment, under the command of Lieutenant-Colonel Goffe, and my major, White, did seasonably come in; and, at push of pike, did repel the stoutest regiment the enemy had there.'[14]

Actually it was not quite so straightforward as that, for in wheeling around to engage Lawers' men Pride's Brigade seems to have come adrift and

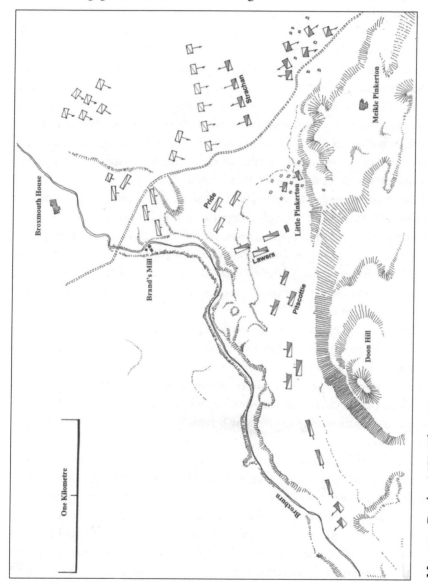

MAP 12: *Dunbar 1650: The crisis.*

consequently engaged piecemeal. The *True Relation* states that: 'The Lord General's regiment of foot charged the enemy with much resolution, and were seconded by Colonel Pride's', but Lambert's Foot scarcely got into the fight at all. According to Hodgson, then a captain in the regiment: 'The General himself comes in the rear of our regiment and commands to incline to the left; that was, to take more ground to be clear of all bodies.' The result was that the regiment came up on to the higher ground by Little Pinkerton and became bogged down in petty skirmishing with 'straggling parties' – presumably the remnants of Lumsden's Brigade.

Behind them meanwhile Lambert next brought Robert Lilburne's cavalry brigade forward from the second line and charged Strachan in front, while Cromwell's own regiment of horse led by Captain Packer, having crossed the Broxburn down by the seashore, charged him in flank. This time the Scots cavalry were knocked out of the fight for good. Some naturally enough fled down the road towards Cockburnspath, while the others swung around the rear of the Scots infantry in order to make for Haddington.

Instead of pursuing, Cromwell and Lambert now halted their victorious troopers and paused long enough to put them in order again and decide what to do next. Traditionally the cavalrymen are said to have sung the 117th Psalm, *Oh Give You Praise Unto the Lord*, while they waited. It must have been at this point rather than on the night before that Cromwell, instead of proceeding with a breakout, took the momentous decision to encompass the total defeat of the Scots army instead.

The constricted nature of the battlefield was probably causing problems for both sides by this time. Monck's Brigade was still out of action, and it was proving difficult for Overton's to get into the fight effectively. The Scots were in a much worse position, hemmed in as they were between the Broxburn and the base of Doon Hill. As the sun rose Cromwell saw and seized his opportunity, pushing his cavalry around the flank of Lawers' position and into the rear of the Scots infantry.

Thus far, although he himself may have been one of the absent officers, Lawers' men had been holding their own, and Gumble, in his well-known *Life of Monck*, describes how: 'Onely Lawers his regiment of Highlanders made a good defence, and the chief officer, a lieutenant colonell, being slain by one of the general's sergeants (the colonel was absent), of the name of the Campbells, they stood to the push of pike and were all cut in pieces'.[15] Actually they must have 'stood' it pretty well, for contradicting the unctuous Gumble, Hodgson related how the Scots 'would not yield though at push of pike and butt-end of musket until a troop of horse charged from one end to another of them, and so left them to the mercy of the foot'.[16]

The destruction of this regiment appeared to an elated Cromwell and his officers to precipitate a total collapse of Scottish resistance. Cadwell for one reported simply that: 'Our horse immediately rallying and our foot advancing charged the enemy, and put them to the run very suddenly, it being near six o'clock of the morning. Which rout the enemy's foot seeing, threw down their arms and fled.'

Retreat

The few surviving Scots accounts – none written by eyewitnesses – are even more laconic, but by analysing the known casualties, captures of colours and some later events it is possible to build up a fairly detailed picture of this last phase of the battle and the long drawn-out agony of the Scots infantry as they struggled to reach safety.

Perhaps one of the more surprising things to emerge is that the 'battalia which stood very stiffly to it' was probably not Campbell of Lawers' Regiment at all, but Sir John Haldane of Gleneagles. Haldane himself certainly died there, together with his lieutenant-colonel, Robert Melvill, and Major John Cockburn, and the regiment was never reconstituted. Yet the other two regiments in the brigade, Lawers' and Valleyfield's, both escaped without serious loss of either men or colours, and with the addition of a new regiment raised in Aberdeenshire by Sir James Wood of Balbegno the brigade was soon fit to take the field again.

Presumably Gleneagles' Regiment stood and fought so hard because it was serving as a rearguard. This in turn indicates that, recognising his right had been well and truly turned, Leslie may already have been trying to withdraw when Cromwell launched the decisive attack. As if by way of confirmation, while Fisher's useful picture-map of the battlefield naturally centres on the fighting around Little Pinkerton, on the Scots army's right he also depicts the attempted retreat not of a mob of fugitives but of formed bodies of Scots infantry marching off to their left.

Significantly, analysis of casualties and captures also suggests exactly the same experience was repeated with Pitscottie's Brigade. If they were to escape, Leslie and Holburne first had to get their men across the Broxburn, and the only practical place to do this was on the far left at what is now Doon bridge. Holburne's and Innes's brigades and perhaps a part of Pitscottie's Brigade may have crossed successfully, but Wedderburn's combined battalion of Borderers was not so lucky. They may simply have thrown down their weapons when the English cavalry caught up, but like Gleneagles' men they more likely went down fighting to give the rest of the brigade time to cross.

Indeed one anonymous Scots account explicitly states that: 'Two regiments of foot fought it out manfully, for they were all killed as they stood (as the enemy confessed).' While it might be natural to assume that the two regiments fought side by side, the evidence clearly indicates that there were actually two quite separate actions.

As we have seen, Gleneagles' men certainly fought and died alone while Lawers' and Valleyfield's regiments escaped. Wedderburn was killed, together with both his son, Lieutenant-Colonel George Home, and Lieutenant-Colonel James Ker, the commander of Greenhead's Regiment. Sir James Douglas of Mouswall and a Major William Menzies appear to have been the only field officers from the combined battalion to escape, and a particularly large number of colours was also taken from the constituent units. Once again however both of the other regiments in the brigade – Pitscottie's and Edzell's – escaped more or less intact.

Having crossed the Broxburn the surviving Scots infantry then marched hard for Haddington, but their retreat was harried all the way by the English cavalry and even some infantry in what must have been a long, drawn-out running battle.

Unsurprisingly, Colonel John Innes' little brigade was badly cut up in the retreat, but although he lost his lieutenant-colonel both his own regiment and the Highland battalion under Lovat survived to be rebuilt again in their old garrisons. Forbes' Regiment on the other hand may have disintegrated, but while it lost all or most of its colours it does not actually seem to have lost many officers or men, which suggests that they broke and ran rather than fought to the last, for it too was afterwards reconstituted. As for Holburne, the evidence suggests that he also got most of his brigade away intact, although Colonel Alexander Stewart was killed and his regiment completely destroyed, losing all its colours – perhaps in another forlorn rearguard action.

As they struggled towards safety some units such as Forbes' may simply have broken up under the pressure, while those that attempted to stand and fight were shot up by the pursuing infantry. Most of the prisoners and the colours were taken during this final stage of the battle, as some regiments threw down their arms and scattered. Some fugitives, according to both Hodgson and Gumble, actually fled towards Dunbar and were taken on the sands at Belhaven, but most held on their course for thirteen terrible kilometres until they reached Haddington. There the pursuit gave over, although Hacker's Regiment followed them a little farther just to make sure.[17]

Characteristically Cromwell boasted at the time of having slain 3,000 Scots 'upon the place or near it' and taking as many as 10,000 prisoners, which rather absurdly exceeds the total number of Scots present at the battle. Balfour on the other hand, while admitting that many of the foot were taken prisoner, noted in his journal that there were '800 or 900 killed'. Walker for his part, commenting that 'not many of them in proportion were either slain or made prisoners', put the number of prisoners at 6,000, of which 1,000 wounded and sick were released, which would in turn suggest no more than about 300 were killed. This is borne out by reports that next day Leslie was falling back on Stirling with an estimated 4,000–5,000 men, at least half of whom must have been formed bodies of infantry.[18]

Meanwhile, with his own army to all intents and purposes undamaged – he only admitted to some 30–40 killed – Cromwell moved swiftly to follow up his victory. On the day after the battle Lambert was sent forward to Edinburgh with a regiment of infantry and all of the cavalry except Hacker's Regiment, which was assigned the job of escorting the prisoners southwards. Having cleared the battlefield and gathered the spoils, which of course included all the Scots guns and baggage, Cromwell followed after with the rest of the army two days later. Edinburgh was surrendered without a fight on 7 September (the castle held out until 23 December), but by that time Leslie had fallen back to Stirling. There Cromwell, intent on finishing him off, followed on 14 September only to realise that he had bitten off more than he could chew.

Hampered by heavy rain and bad roads he marched just ten kilometres that first day, and after sending back two of the heaviest guns only reached Linlithgow the next. From there he marched as far as Falkirk on 16 September, vainly summoned the Scots garrison in Callendar House and struggled on through 'extraordinary wet and stormy' weather to arrive outside Stirling on the following day.

Leslie, understandably shaken by the defeat, had laid down his commission, but like Leven before him was persuaded to take it up again, and as the English approached he threw himself into the task of reconstituting his shattered forces. Three of his five infantry brigades had escaped from Dunbar battered but more or less intact, and to them were added those levies who had either not reached the army in time to fight or who had been left behind as insufficiently trained or equipped. It was very much a scratch force, many were 'green new levied sojours', and Stirling was 'not yet fortified as it should be', but it was enough.

Cromwell duly summoned the town on the morning of 18 September, and when his trumpeter was refused admission ladders were brought up and at one o'clock in the afternoon orders were given to storm the place. The Scots were unimpressed, No one in the English army had the stomach for an assault, and Cromwell was just going through the motions. Even in their incomplete state the defences were too strong for a frontal assault, and the position could not be outflanked. Nor did Cromwell have sufficient heavy guns for a regular siege. On the day after that the English fell back again to Linlithgow and, having established a strong outpost there, Cromwell himself retired all the way back to Edinburgh and commenced a desultory siege of the castle, which would drag on until Christmas.

For the next ten months Linlithgow bridge would effectively serve as the frontier between the English army and the king's army, and thus mark the limit of Cromwell's success. Whatever the actual numbers involved there is no question that the Scots suffered a catastrophic military defeat at Dunbar, but yet at the same time from the English point of view it was an inconclusive and unsatisfactory victory that achieved none of their aims – save of course their own immediate deliverance from impending disaster.

The fact of the matter was that while the Scots army had been beaten it had not been destroyed and, far from neutralising the supposed Royalist threat, Cromwell's victory actually made it a reality. Not only were the Presbyterian fanatics of the Kirk party utterly discredited by the defeat, but also a considerable number of the more vocal ones hurriedly took refuge in Edinburgh Castle rather than accompany the wreck of Leslie's army, and once besieged they were effectively silenced. As for Archibald Strachan, Gibby Kerr and the other Covenanters among the soldiers, instead of falling back with Leslie on Stirling they rode for the west to raise their own army before ultimately being crushed by Lambert. Reports that King Charles variously threw his cap in the air or fell on his knees to give thanks for the victory may be apocryphal, but they certainly reflected a paradoxical mood of optimism among the Royalists.

Chapter 11

The Last Hurrah

Inverkeithing and Worcester

The as-yet-uncrowned king strove from the outset to establish his presence if not his authority, but to all intents and purposes he was at first little more than a prisoner, as emphasised by the assignment of the 'Irish Regiment' to be his lifeguard of foot.[1] Naturally enough he chafed under the restrictions placed on him, and to the horror of many in the Kirk party visited the army while it was in the Leith lines. His all-too-evident popularity on that occasion led directly to that last spasm of purging on 2–5 August, and later that month a request to have the northern levies under Colonel Innes assemble at Stirling was rejected as a too-transparent attempt to assemble an army of his own. The Estates had been unable to prevent the king removing himself from Dunfermline to Perth, but in the quarrelsome aftermath of Dunbar, and perhaps stung by rumours of his alleged delight at the Kirk's humbling, they ordered his household to be purged.

Backed into a corner, Charles agreed to head a coup. Perth was to be infiltrated by his supporters under the Earl of Atholl, and when the commissioners turned up to carry out the purging ordered for 3 October they were instead to be arrested by his loyal horse guards. However, when he confided in them at the very last moment, his English Royalist advisers took fright, protesting at the dangers. As a result the king dithered, first cancelling the uprising and then, when persuaded that everyone was already too deeply committed, he fled eastwards with just a few servants and fetched up in Glen Clova.

Next day wild confusion abounded. Unaware that the Perth coup had been aborted, a Royalist uprising had indeed taken place. A large party under Erskine of Dun was lying just outside the city while Atholl was also assembling some 2,000 men just to the north. Elsewhere other former Engagers and Royalists including John Middleton, the Marquis of Huntly and Lord Ogilvie were all raising men. Hearing of his flight, some of them headed off to join with the king in Glen Clova. For its part the Committee of Estates also sent word after him, professing their surprise and hurt, begging that he return and promising an accommodation. Crucially it was their man, Robin Montgomerie, who caught up with Charles first and persuaded him to return to Perth and to order his supporters to disband. The plain fact of the matter was that, while neither party trusted the other, they were all of them horrified at the prospect of a full-scale civil war in the north while the English were hammering on the gates of Stirling.

Nevertheless, it was still touch and go. At first the Estates were only willing to offer an amnesty to Atholl and his men, and Sir John Brown of Fordell was ordered north with his own and Lord Brechin's Regiment to deal with the others. Instead he got himself badly defeated by Sir David Ogilvie at Newtyle in Forfarshire in the early hours of 21 October 1650. Surprised in their beds four of Brown's men were killed and twenty taken prisoner, which might not have mattered too much had not half of Brechin's Regiment then changed sides and joined the Royalists. From that point on the rising could easily have escalated, but Middleton then had the great good sense to send word to the king promising to obey his orders, while at the same time writing to Leslie and assuring him that he and his colleagues had no wish for a civil war and were willing to fight under his command against the English. In the circumstances there was no alternative but to offer them all the same indemnity already extended to Atholl and to settle the business with a treaty signed at Strathbogie on 4 November.

To all intents and purposes however the 'Start' as it became known was a victory for the Royalists, for thenceforth the king was no longer excluded from governance but sat in on the meetings of the Committee of Estates. What was more, just a month later the balance of power within Scotland changed dramatically.

When Archibald Strachan and Gibby Kerr revived the old Western Association, it was declared that they were to be regarded as a separate force and that Leslie 'should never trouble them with any of his orders'.[2] Thus they stood for a time in simultaneous opposition to both the English invaders and to the king, but encouraged by the positive reception he had received during a brief occupation of Glasgow Cromwell had hopes of winning them over. There is no doubt that there were negotiations to that end with Strachan, and Cromwell might indeed have reached an agreement had he been in a position to move westwards during the northern crisis in October. Instead he was distracted first by a rumoured but probably illusory Scots attempt to recapture Edinburgh, and then by the growing problem of 'Mossers' preying on his tenuous line of communication.

After Dunbar instead of following Leslie to Stirling, many of the scattered fugitives had set up on their own account by forming marauding bands of so-called Moss-troopers,[3] who preyed on stragglers, intercepted messengers and generally made a nuisance of themselves. 'Wat, a tenant of the Earl of Tweeddales' was seemingly the first to come to prominence and equally soon put up against a wall and shot after the taking of Dirleton Castle. But contrary to English hopes his execution failed to solve the problem, and clearing the roads and mopping up the other little fortresses which were sustaining the Mossers took time.

Hamilton

Consequently it was late November before Cromwell and Lambert could again move west with the cavalry. By then the Westlanders had resolved to break off negotiations with the English, and at the beginning of the month they dismissed Archibald Strachan for his strident advocacy of an English alliance. Nevertheless at that point they were still uncommitted. Learning that Robin Montgomerie was coming down from Stirling with a commission to command in the west – or perhaps to fight them if they would not acknowledge his authority – Gibby Kerr decided to bolster the Westlanders' patriotic credentials by launching a heavy raid on what he fondly supposed to be a minor English outpost in the burgh of Hamilton.[4]

In fairness to him the situation there was confused. Having left Edinburgh on the evening of 27 November with eight regiments of horse, intending to force a decision, Cromwell arrived before Bothwell Brig, just short of Hamilton, about noon the next day only to find it barricaded and well defended against him. He spent the afternoon reconnoitring and skirmishing and eventually came to the conclusion that he could neither ford the Clyde nor force the bridge, so he drew back again to Edinburgh.

Both sides reckoned without Lambert, who had been lying down at Peebles with a further four regiments of horse and one of dragoons, when he received Cromwell's orders to rendezvous with him at Hamilton. Setting off later than Cromwell he did not actually arrive at the burgh until some time on 30 November, by which time the latter was well on his way back. Crucially however by virtue of coming from the south he had been able to get over the Clyde much farther upstream – probably at Crossford – thus forcing the Westlanders to abandon their position at the bridge without a fight.

So far so good. Lambert then settled down for the night in Hamilton, while Kerr, now at Rutherglen, held a council of war. Some were apparently all for retiring farther west into Carrick or even Galloway, but with between 2,000–3,000 cavalry present belonging to Halkett's, Kerr's, Kirkcudbright's and Strachan's regiments they eventually resolved to fight.[5] Intending to fall on Lambert at dawn they set off at 10 p.m. that night and *en route* were dismayed to find the wet weather give way to a clear sky, a full moon and a hard frost. In those circumstances Lambert could hardly fail to detect their approach and so they grimly anticipated finding him drawn up to meet them on Hamilton moor.

To their astonishment however there was not even a picquet out there, which immediately gave rise to a nasty suspicion that Lambert might have escaped them. Haste was indicated and at about 2 a.m. on the Sunday morning the 140-strong advance guard under Lieutenant-Colonel William Ralston of Ralston entered the burgh at a hard gallop and promptly ran straight into a large body of English cavalry standing in the broad street leading from the tolbooth to the palace gate. As luck would have it, Lambert was indeed intending to pull out at 3.30 that morning, but he had prematurely pulled in his picquets before his regiments were properly formed up and so was caught totally unawares. Ralston immediately seized his opportunity and in just fifteen minutes, despite being hopelessly outnumbered, he completely rolled up Lambert's whole brigade, scattering the fugitives into houses and closes. Some of the English even contrived to shoot each other up in the confusion, and Lambert himself may have been taken prisoner for a time. At any rate he eventually scrambled 'out at the back entrie of Sarah Jean's Close, then the greatest inn in Hamilton' and proceeded to rally his men by twenties and thirties as they too confusedly tumbled out of the town. Inevitably however Ralston lost a good few of his own men in the process and was probably glad enough to see them go, but Kerr, who ought in the meantime to have been circling around the town to intercept them, left it too late.

By the time he did come forward with the main body at about four o'clock, Lambert was waiting for him, drawn up in 'a great and close body' on the other side of the Cadzow Burn. The stream itself was of no great consequence but it ran through a deep hollow and scrambling up the slope on the far side opened out Kerr's ranks. Baillie says that he then drew back to take another run at it, but it seems more likely that his initial charge bounced off and that he was then counter-charged by Lambert as he rallied his men for a second attempt. In the mêlée that followed both sides seemingly claimed to flank the other, but it was perhaps inevitably Kerr who was sent tumbling back, although he fought hard 'desputing every rig lenth for near two mylles' until he was wounded and taken prisoner. Halkett, who should have supported him, fled, and the gallant Ralston, still mopping up in Hamilton itself, was likewise forced to beat a hasty retreat as soon as daylight revealed he had been left in the lurch.[6]

The scattered remnants of the Westlanders were then pursued by Lambert as far as Paisley and Kilmarnock that day, and afterwards to Ayr. There about 160 of them were finally scattered, and Strachan surrendered himself, with surprising consequences.

Edinburgh

Edinburgh Castle had been under a desultory siege ever since Cromwell's occupation of the city after Dunbar, and thus far he had made little progress. The governor, William Dundas, was content to play a very passive role in the proceedings as first an attempt to mine the Spur and then to reduce it by artillery fire had alike proved ineffective. Of itself this might be ascribed to complacency, but in fact Dundas was a firm adherent of the Kirk party and like all too many of the Westlanders still in two minds as to whether Cromwell or Charles was the lesser evil. There is evidence of his being in clandestine contact with Cromwell's scoutmaster, George Downing, and far from coincidentally Strachan's arrival in Edinburgh with Lambert was immediately followed by a formal summons to the castle on 12 December. Dundas rather curiously declined to return the proper expressions of defiance but instead requested time to consult the Estates. Presumably he wanted to know exactly where they now stood and would fight on in the name of the Estates if that was the will of the Kirk, but might not hold the castle for the king.

The Estates for their part, strengthened rather than weakened by the recent defeat of the Westlanders, responded firmly. The following night, as Sir James Balfour recorded, a Captain Augustine:

> . . . departed from Fife with a party of six-score horse; crossed at Blackness on Friday 13th December; forced Cromwell's guards; killed eighty men to the enemy; put in thirty-six men to Edinburgh Castle, with all sorts of spices and some other things; too thirty-five horses and five prisoners which he sent to Perth the 19th of this instant.

As thus recorded by Balfour the exploit was daring enough, albeit the eighty killed was certainly and exaggeration. Legend also claims that Augustine bluffed his way in by the Bristo Port during the early hours using an English volunteer and then having deposited both men and supplies in the castle burst his way out again by the Netherbow Port.[7]

Whether true or not it did no good, for Dundas, like his colleague Strachan, was by now determined to surrender and after a token bombardment he did so on the evening of 18 December.[8] Insofar as it could and should have held out for much longer the fall of the castle must have seemed just one more blow for the beleaguered Scots, but it actually made very little difference other than to discredit the Kirk party further, and David Leslie's hasty realignment with the Royalists enabled Charles II to be formally crowned at Scone, outside Perth on 1 January 1650.

A month later Cromwell responded by leading his army, or at least eight regiments of foot and nine of horse, westwards from Edinburgh on 4 February with the intention of trying to get around the Stirling position by 'the fords over the river'. Getting across the Forth upstream of Stirling Bridge was possible, but it necessitated a swift and unopposed march through the notorious Flanders Moss. By the time Cromwell had gotten the length of Kilsyth on 6 February the weather had begun to close in, and a 'council of war was called, at which, the difficulties of the design being more fully discovered and the waters found unpassable . . . it was resolved to march for Edinburgh again'.[9]

The most important result of the damp débâcle was that Cromwell himself fell sick with what started off as a bad cold and rapidly turned into something worse, which laid him up for the next two months. This rather discouraged any large-scale operations, but the war still went on at a lower level of intensity. Hume and Tantallon castles were besieged and taken, and the Mossers in the border hills contained, but on the other hand the Scots were fast recovering their strength and confidence. Fresh levies were coming down from the north, and feelers were going out to the west as well.

In early April the Earl of Eglinton and two of his younger sons were betrayed and seized at Dumbarton while heading for Ayrshire with the intention of raising fresh levies of their people, this time in the name of the king. Significantly their capture was followed almost immediately by a retaliatory raid on Linlithgow by the eldest son, Robin Montgomerie. The English forward position there had already been raided a number of times since January, with little success, and the recent capture of Blackness may have given the place a false measure of security. Be that as it may, on 14 April Montgomerie led a large party of horse and dragoons down from Stirling, and:

... taking advantage of an exceeding misty and foggy morning, fell with their horse into Lithgow; they killd only one man, hastned out again: but the major [John Sydenham] with about 30 horse went forth of the town, giving order for the rest to follow. As soon as he was drawn forth, the enemy charged him, and he brake in among them; but his men forsaking him, the enemy pursued both him and them to the town, cutting and hacking them. A fresh party of ours being recollected, the enemy forthwith retreated, and were pursued; in the pursuit our men took 2 or 3 of theirs prisoners, and about 2 or 3 of ours were slain.[10]

This English version of events was more optimistic than accurate, for they were rather more badly beaten than they first admitted and the local commander, Major John Sydenham of Hesilrige's Horse, was fatally wounded. Disturbed by this evidence of increasing activity, Cromwell then essayed another push into the west to try and secure the area once and for all. Glasgow was occupied again, and for a time he appears to have contemplated another attempt to get across the Forth above Stirling. By the end of the month a desperate shortage of supplies forced him back to Edinburgh to rendezvous with a convoy sent up from London, and there exhausted by his exertions he returned to his bed.

All the time Leslie's army was growing stronger, and at the beginning of May Montgomerie took his cavalry brigade into the west. At first it was thought he and Augustine the Mosser were just carrying out another raid and gathering forage, but part of the Hamilton garrison was surprised and taken near Paisley on 19 May. Then, worryingly, instead of pulling back to Stirling Montgomerie pushed on southwards to Kilmarnock, where the garrison fled without waiting for him to come knocking, and then down into Galloway, raising his father's tenants and putting the fear of God into all the English garrisons. The fact of the matter was that Cromwell's men were overstretched and their position in the west tenable only for so long as the local population were at least passively sympathetic. Once patriotism and the age-old loyalties to the Greysteel Eglintons won out over religion and the Kirk, the west was lost. By the end of the month both Dumfries and Hamilton had been abandoned by Cromwell's men, and no attempt was made to intercept Montgomerie and Augustine as they triumphantly returned to Stirling.

Torwood

Buoyed up by this and other minor successes, Charles and Leslie essayed a push southwards to the Torwood at the end of June, taking up a very strong position behind the river Carron, with a line of entrenchments at the foot of the hill and individual redoubts on the slope behind, presumably intended as gun positions. The left or eastern flank of the position was secured both by the boggy Letham Moss and by guns and earthworks in and around the House of Letham itself.[11] At the same time an English garrison was ejected from Callendar House in order that it could be turned into a forward outpost. Charles himself appears to have headed yet another raid towards Kinneil and Linlithgow, which for the first time included some Highland troops.

Cromwell, suspecting both from intelligence reports and Montgomerie's raid into the west, that these were the opening moves in an offensive aimed at carrying the Scots army into England, promptly hurried north to confront it with all of his disposable strength – fourteen regiments of horse, twelve regiments of foot and sixteen guns,[12] reaching Linlithgow on 1 July. To this the Scots very prudently responded by pulling back across the Carron and waiting to see what he would do next.

That turned out to be three days of reconnoitring and skirmishing as Cromwell tried to find a way of getting at the Scots. Initially he focused on the bridge at Larbert, but although a party got across the river somewhere nearby on 2 July they were soon in trouble and had to be extracted by Okey. In the early hours of the following morning the Scots artillery – presumably some of James Wemyss' famous leather guns – having been clandestinely carried forward, opened up on the English camp, causing understandable consternation and forcing Cromwell hastily to draw off to Callendar Muir. There he drew up in expectation of a Scots offensive against him, but finding himself disappointed he fell back to Linlithgow on 5 July. Then, seemingly to avoid the impression of retreating, Cromwell reoccupied Glasgow, where he remained for a week, surveying the Clyde harbours and sending Lambert with three regiments of horse[13] to properly reconnoitre the Forth crossings above Stirling.

Lambert duly got over the river near Cardross and reported that the route over the upper crossings would be practicable and even easy, which might have been promising enough had he not been forced to add the caveat: 'except for the carriages'. In other words it might be possible to outflank the Scots position at Stirling, but unless they were immediately beaten or otherwise uncovered Stirling Bridge it would be difficult to get the artillery across and well nigh impossible to keep the army supplied.

Accordingly, Cromwell once again pulled his men out of Glasgow on 12 July and returned to Linlithgow. During his absence the main body of the Scots army had briefly advanced as far at Kilsyth to cover yet another raid towards Edinburgh, which this time snapped up a hapless draft of reinforcements. All of them were safely back within the Torwood position by the time Cromwell arrived, but having been fired on from Callendar House as he carried out a reconnaissance the general had it stormed on Tuesday 15 July.

Taking no chances the house was subjected to a day-long bombardment. When the governor, Lieutenant-Colonel Galbraith, declined to surrender the place on promise of quarter, a storming party comprising ten files out of each regiment moved forward at dusk: 'They had no quarter that resisted . . . There was 62 killed; and 13 souldiers and 17 countrymen and women who came in for shelter (as they said) were taken prisoners, but afterwards all – except the souldiers – released, and a list of the souldiers sent to the enemy for exchange.'[14]

Predictably enough the Scots retaliated next day with another vicious raid, but then the campaign took an entirely unexpected turn. Back in January, under cover of fog, Colonel George Monck hopefully but quite unsuccessfully attempted a landing at Burntisland on the north shore of the Firth of Forth. It had been a decidedly half-hearted and opportunistic affair seemingly guided by an illusory hope that the port would be betrayed to them. Now, buoyed up by news of the imminent arrival of substantial reinforcements, Cromwell resolved to try again.

Inverkeithing

The obvious place to cross the Firth was by the short route between North and South Queensferry now spanned by the famous railway bridge. Accordingly Colonel Robert Overton was despatched there with 1,600 men and rendezvousing with 500 more from Leith successfully lifted them over very early on the morning of 17 July 1651. As it happens Colonel Harie Barclay was actually in the process of strengthening the defences of Burntisland with some fresh levies, but the Ferry Hills peninsula itself had just a single sconce or earthwork fort with five guns at its southern tip and another twelve guns emplaced at various points along the shore. Although it would hardly have been a dark night at that time of year, Overton's first lift got safely ashore in the Inner Bay, behind the sconce, stormed it out of hand with the loss of six men and then settled down to await events.

At this stage it was only a diversion. Having given time for the word of Overton's landing to spread, Cromwell followed it up with another rush at Leslie's left flank, hoping that the Scots, finding themselves outflanked, would be pulling back to Stirling. Alas for his hopes Leslie was very properly sitting tight, and so, baulked once again, Cromwell decided to reinforce success by despatching Lambert to take over the Queensferry operation.

In the meantime there was a curious lull. Major-General John Leslie, who had superseded Barclay in Inverkeithing, contented himself with sealing off the bridgehead and establishing some kind of picket line on the lower slopes of Castland Hill, with his right anchored on Whinney Hill and his left on the Hill of Selvege, or Muckle Hill, a little to the south and west of Inverkeithing. At least some of his men must have been dug in, for Lambert afterwards reported burying some of the Scots dead in their own trenches, but beyond that all he could do was wait for reinforcements.

It turned out to be a long wait, for James Holburne seemingly did not arrive in Dunfermline until two days later, with his own infantry brigade and Sir John Browne's cavalry.[15] Consequently it all grew rather tense as Lambert afterwards reported:

> Upon Saturday, very early, we came to the water-side, and though I made all possible speed to boat over it, I could not get over more than the foot and my own regiment of horse all that day and the next night: about four in the afternoon on Saturday I discovered the enemy's body advanced as far as Dumfermling, within five miles of us, being, to my judgement, about four thousand.
>
> And that night they encamped there, and, it seems, hearing more forces were come over, got a recruit of five hundred men the next day. All Saturday night we laboured to get over our horse, and before the last came to shore on the Lord's day, the enemy was advanced very near us.[16]

By Sunday morning Lambert had four regiments of foot and three regiments of horse drawn up on the Ferry Hills, still at the very tip of the peninsula, with their backs to the water. The infantry consisted of his own and Colonel William Daniel's regiments, reinforced by four companies of Colonel George Fenwick's, to which had been added Colonel Francis West's Foot and Colonel Edmund Syler's Foot. The cavalry were drawn from his own regiment of horse, Colonel John Okey's former dragoons, and Colonel Leonard Lytcott's Horse. Lambert reckoned he outnumbered the Scots by about 500 men, but the quality of some of his regiments was questionable. His own regiment of foot was certainly a good one, but Daniel's was newly raised and had been left in reserve at Dunbar. Nothing is known of West's Regiment other than it was disbanded a year or two later, while Syler's may actually have been a militia regiment from Lincolnshire.[17]

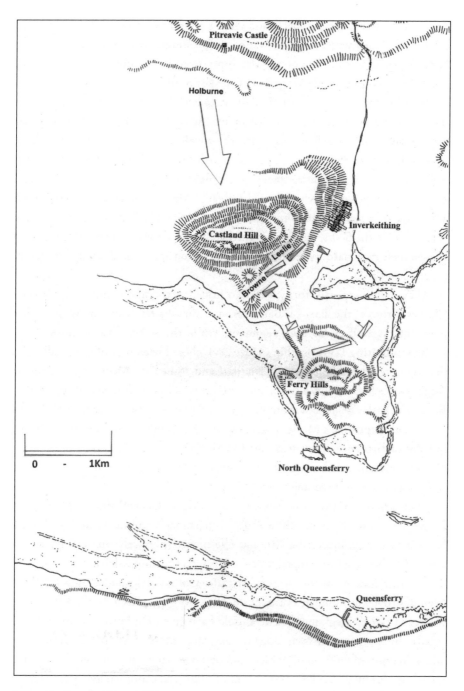

MAP 13: *Inverkeithing 1651.*

As to the cavalry, both Lambert's and Okey's regiments were good veteran units, but Lytcott's men were also newly raised and would perform badly in the coming fight. All in all it is hard to escape the impression that Lambert's army was very much a scratch force pulled together at the last minute.

Nevertheless the arrival of the last of Okey's Horse that morning was the signal for the Scots to begin to withdraw. At this point it would appear that only Browne of Fordell was up with the cavalry, for Lambert describes him, not Holburne, as the commander and makes little reference to Scots infantry in his account of the initial stages of the fighting. Instead Lambert described how Browne 'began to wheel, as if he meant either to march away, or take the advantage of a steep mountain' – obviously Castland Hill. Sensing he might be able to hustle the Scots, Lambert immediately sent forward Okey's Regiment to engage their rearguard, whereupon Browne halted again and drew up his men in order of battle.

They were evidently formed in two brigades, the first comprising Colonel Charles Arnot's, the Earl of Balcarres' and Sir Walter Scott of Whitestede's regiments as well as his own regiment, while the second was a more *ad hoc* formation uniting Lord Brechin's Horse, which had been part of the small force that opposed the initial English landing, and some 200 Moss-troopers under Augustine, who was now a colonel. From subsequent events it would appear that Browne's cavalry brigade was on the right, and that the *ad hoc* brigade of Brechin's Horse and Augustine's Mossers were on the left. Lambert also says that a 'pass', in front of Browne's right, was 'lined by the enemy's musketeers', and as this is his only reference at this stage to Scots infantry they were presumably some of Barclay's men from Inverkeithing.[18]

Somewhere to the rear however was Major-General James Holburne's Brigade. Both his own and the Laird of Buchannan's regiments were still quite large at this time, mustering 646 and 896 men respectively on 18 July, which argues for their having escaped more or less intact from the débâcle at Dunbar.[19] The third regiment in the original brigade, Colonel Alexander Stewart's, had been destroyed at Dunbar, but may since have been replaced by the 610 strong Master of Grey's Regiment.[20] This should have given Holburne a total of 2,152 regular infantry in his own brigade, exclusive of officers. In addition there was a 'recruit of 500 men', which Lambert reported arriving on the Sunday morning; this may have been a regiment of Highland clansmen led by Sir Hector MacLean of Duart.

Secondary sources place Holburne's infantry in the Scots' centre, flanked by the cavalry, but significantly however there is a contemporary complaint in the Fraser Chronicles that: 'Hellish Hoburn came not up, which if he had the Scotch had carried it but doubt.'[21] Taken with Lambert's belief that Browne commanded and also the curious absence of any reference to the Scots infantry in the early stages of the fighting other than Barclay's musketeers in the ditches, this clearly indicates that in fact Holburne had still not arrived on the field when the battle began.

As for the English, Lambert similarly put his greatest strength in his right wing, comprising his own regiment of horse together with two troops apiece of Lytcott's and Okey's regiments. The centre was made up of his four infantry regiments: Lambert's and Daniel's regulars in the front line; and West's and Syler's in reserve. The left wing consisted of only four troops of Okey's and two of Lytcott's Regiment.

Nothing more happened for another hour and a half. At length the stalemate was broken when Lambert received word from Cromwell that reinforcements were marching from Stirling to Browne's assistance. Rather disappointingly, having described his initial movements and deployment in some detail, Lambert then merely states that it was therefore 'resolved we should climb the hill to them, which accordingly we did, and through the Lord's strength, put them to an absolute rout'.[22]

As they came forward, Browne leading the Scots cavalry on the right charged forward and broke some of the English cavalry opposite, but he may have had to put in everything he had to achieve this, and had no reserves to exploit his initial success. The result was that Lytcott counter-attacked with his own reserves and routed the lot, badly wounding and capturing Browne in the process. Similarly on the left Augustine and Brechin were again initially successful, and as the English scoutmaster George Downing relates: 'the Scots with their lances and stoutness of their men gave our horse such charges as did disorder them, and charged quite through the first body'. Once again however they were routed by the reserve led in by Lambert himself, who collected two pistol balls lodged between his armour and his coat, and then very suddenly the battle was won.[23]

As the Scots cavalry scattered, Lambert led his own victorious troopers in pursuit into the valley to the west of the Pinkerton Burn and there ran head on into Holburne's Brigade still tardily making its way towards the battlefield and presumably not yet deployed into a battle line, for Lambert destroyed it utterly. Holburne ran for it and got clean away, only to be cashiered and what was left of his regiment given to Sir James Turner. Grey's Regiment, if it were indeed present, may have been hard hit for there is no mention of it thereafter. Sadly there is no doubting the fate of Buchannan's and Duart's regiments caught on the open hill slopes around Pitreavie Castle. There Duart and his men turned at bay. He himself was killed, but according to legend not before seven of his clansmen had interposed themselves one by one, crying *Fear eile airson Eachainn!* – 'Another for Hector!' – which afterwards became the slogan of the clan. Supposedly all but thirty-five out of 800 [sic] of the Highlanders were killed, though more realistically Sir James Balfour records that the Scots lost about 800 men in *total*, of whom perhaps no more than a hundred were Duart's clansmen.[24]

Afterwards Lambert, claiming to have taken 1,400 prisoners, commented that more were killed than taken because 'divers of them were Highlanders, and had very ill quarter; and indeed I am persuaded few of them escaped without a knock'. It was by any reckoning a quick and decisive victory, which Lambert had won at the cost of 'not above eight men, but divers wounded'. More importantly it secured a proper bridgehead over the Forth, which Cromwell was quick to exploit. Immediately after Lambert's victory, Leslie fell back in some haste to Stirling, seemingly with some notion of dealing with Lambert himself, only to be fixed in the old King's Park position in front of it by Cromwell's own rapid advance. Then while Leslie remained pinned down there more and more English troops were ferried over to join Lambert as fast as they could be shipped.

By 26 July the Lord General reported that 13,000–14,000 men had arrived, and he was ready to resume the offensive. This time, instead of confronting Leslie and the main Scots army head on at Stirling, Cromwell ruthlessly exploited his opportunity by marching on Perth instead, which incontinently surrendered to him on 2 August, just as soon as his engineers drained the wet ditch surrounding its defences.

Shy of fighting in the open ever since Dunbar, David Leslie had made no attempt to engage Cromwell. Instead, with his lines of communication now very firmly cut, he fell in with the king's desperate notion of marching into England in a vain attempt to rally the English Royalists for one last time. On 31 July they set off from Stirling, just 14,000 strong.

Worcester

Colonel Harrison, at Leith, set off after them at once, but Cromwell, although hearing the news at the same time, waited until he had taken Perth and put Overton in charge of the place. Colonel Monck for his part was given a reinforced brigade group and instructed to secure Stirling, and then with the rest Cromwell too took the road to the south. Ahead of him Charles was moving swiftly. He crossed the border near Carlisle on 6 August and just over a week later he was at Warrington, with little to show but worn-out boots, for the North had not risen. At the critical moment, the Earl of Derby, who was to have instigated a pro-Royalist insurrection in Lancashire, lay windbound on the Isle of Man. Not until 15 August did he succeed in getting across and only for his forces to be intercepted and destroyed by Robert Lilburne in a vicious little fight at Wigan ten days later.[25]

By then the Scots army had gotten the length of Worcester and there they stayed, effectively at bay. The city's defences were ordered to be repaired, and on 24 August the king tried to muster the old county militia or *Posse Comitatus*, requiring all men aged between sixteen and sixty to muster on the nearby Pitchcroft Green two days later. Surprisingly enough, as many as 1,000 men were actually rounded up by Lord Talbot and Sir John Packington.

Cromwell however was already closing in. By 27 August he was at Evesham, and the following day Lambert seized the bridge over the Severn at Upton, scattering Edward Massey's cavalry brigade in the process. By now Cromwell may have had as many as 25,000 men at his disposal as against no more than 10,000 Scots infantry and 4,000–5,000 cavalry, and this success allowed him to operate on either or both banks of the river as required. Here the Severn runs due south with the city of Worcester lying on the east bank. Much of the Scots army however was encamped on the west bank, around the suburb of St Johns, and so it was resolved that Major-General Fleetwood would go up the west bank, while Cromwell and Lambert threatened a direct assault on the city from the east. No doubt consciously, the date of the attack was fixed for 3 September, the anniversary of the battle of Dunbar.

At dawn Fleetwood duly pushed forward but did not actually begin his battle until mid-afternoon. His task was complicated from the outset by the fact that the river Teme cut straight across his intended line of advance about a kilometre or so south of Worcester. To all appearances he could only get over the river by Powick bridge, where by another odd coincidence the very first battle of the English Civil War was fought in 1642. This time it was held by two brigades, one of cavalry led by the redoubtable Robin Montgomerie and an infantry one under Colonel George Keith, and they had men, courage and experience enough to keep Fleetwood comfortably in check. Unfortunately the reason for Fleetwood's delay soon became apparent, for a detachment of his men had slowly been making their way forward through the narrow lanes and hedged enclosures on his right to deliver a bridging train to the point where the Teme discharged into the Severn. Only once they were in place did he attack Powick bridge. Under cover of the sound and fury of his battle two bridges were thrown across the Severn and the Teme respectively, enabling Cromwell himself to outflank Montgomerie's position with four regiments of horse and two of foot.

All that stood in Cromwell's path was a single brigade, largely composed of Highlanders, under Colin Pitscottie. Badly outnumbered, Pitscottie soon gave way, and as the main battle line started to withdraw Fleetwood attacked in earnest, capturing Keith, wounding Montgomerie and bundling the whole lot back on their reserve brigade, under the infamous Tam Dalyell of the Binns, at St Johns. Dalyell, a terrifying veteran of the Muscovite service, managed to stabilise the line there, and while he grimly held on among the hedgerows the king himself mounted an enterprising counter-attack on the east side of the river.

The Duke of Hamilton[26] led one party out by the St Martin's Gate to attack the English positions in Perry Wood. Meanwhile the king himself sallied out by the Sidbury Gate with as many foot as he could muster, attacked straight up the London Road, brushing aside the militia and forcing Lambert and Harrison out of their positions on the high ground overlooking the city known as Red Hill. To all appearances he was on the point of winning a notable victory, but his cavalry failed to support him.

Ever since leaving Stirling, David Leslie had been pessimistic and it is very hard to escape the impression he had lost his nerve. He had done very well as a brigade commander at Marston Moor and at Philiphaugh, but he was clearly less happy commanding large bodies of troops, hence his predilection for planting them safely behind field works. Now he was standing on Pitchcroft Green, just to the north of the city and as a cavalryman ought to have seen his opportunity, but Dunbar had destroyed his self-confidence. As Clarendon relates, there was 'no good understanding between the officers of the army. David Leslie appeared dispirited and confounded, gave and revoked his orders, and sometimes contradicted them. He did not love Middleton, and was very jealous that all the officers loved him so well.'[27]

Thus they all stayed exactly where they were while Cromwell broke off his fight at St Johns, recrossed the Severn and restored the situation on the east bank. It took another three hours of fighting before the Essex militia broke into the Worcester defences and Fleetwood took St Johns. With that the battle was effectively won. On the march south Leslie had gloomily commented that 'he well knew that the army, how well soever it looked, would not fight',[28] but they turned out to be made of sterner stuff than their general and fighting continued in the streets all night before the last of the Scots infantry finally surrendered. That last doomed fight allowed the king to make his escape to France by way of the famous oak tree and also gave time for as many as 4,000 cavalry under Leslie and Middleton to break out to the north.

Much good it did them for – both officers were eventually captured by Colonel John Birch at Blackstone Edge.[29] In the end Cromwell claimed an optimistic 3,000 Scots dead, while the English government found itself dealing with some 8,000 prisoners, which it eventually shipped to the American plantations. Nevertheless a surprising number of the cavalry actually made it home to swell the ranks of the Mossers.

At Worcester the war was lost but not quite over. The burgh of Stirling surrendered to Monck on 6 August 1651, and the castle was mortared into submission after a week. Dundee was then stormed and sacked on 1 September, and Aberdeen was occupied without a fight a week later. In the meantime a cavalry raid on Alyth, nineteen kilometres to the northwest of Dundee, had secured what remained of the Committee of Estates, including old Leven, leaving the Scots not only beaten but also leaderless. The last of the field armies, commanded by the Marquis of Huntly and the Earl of Balcarres capitulated on 21 November and 3 December respectively, and it only remained to mop up the last of the Mossers. Augustine disbanded his men in late January or early February,[30] and only with the surrender of the Bass Rock in March and finally Dunottar Castle on 24 May 1652 did the fighting end – at least temporarily.

It was not really the end of the story of course. There was a full-scale revolt in the Highlands led by the indefatigable John Middleton and the Earl of Glencairn in the following year, and a whole series of citadels and forts had to be built, of which only a bastion above Aberdeen harbour now remains. Otherwise the Cromwellian conquest and a political union with England were never seriously challenged. Ironically it would be that same army of occupation, led by George Monck, which would eventually bring about the restoration of King Charles II – and Scotland's independence.

Appendices

Appendices

Appendix 1

The Irish Brigade Under Montrose 1644–1645

The list below is to be found in the Ormonde Papers.[1] The order of the listing presumably reflects the respective regimental seniorities, and would imply that when deployed for battle, McDermott's Regiment, as the most senior, was normally posted on the right, O'Cahan's as second in seniority on the left, and MacColla's/Laghtnan's Regiment in the centre.

List of men gone unto the Isles. Sent by the Lord of Antrim to my Lord Ormonde,
15 Nov. 1644

A list of Collonell James Mac Dermott's regiment, in briefe.
The Collonell's one company consisting of 100 men compleate.
Officers: Lieutenant Sorly Mac Donnell
Ensigne John Mac Heaghin
Sarjants William Mac Keon and Hugh O Kealte

Lieftennant-Collonell Jo. Mac Donnell's company consisting of 100 men compleate.
Officers: Lieftennant Arte Carragh O Guilluir
Ensigne Donnagh O Guilluire
Sarjant Donnagh McGilhany

Sarjeant-Major Swyne's company consisting of 100 men compleate.
Lieftennant – Ensigne – Sarjant –

Captain Twole O Hara's company consisting of 100 men compleate.
Lieftennant James O Hara

Ensigne Bryne O Hara

Sarjeantas Manus O Hara and Christopher Sherlogge.

Captain Hugh O Neal's company consisting of 50 men compleate.

Lieftennant Daniell O Neale

Ensigne Laghlan Mac Keon

Serjeants Eivar O Mullan and Henry O Mulchallin.

Captain John Mac Cleane's company consisting of 50 men compleate.

Lieftennant – Ensigne – Sarjeants

Summa Totius 500 besydes officers.

A breefe note of Collonell [Manus] *O Cahan's regiment:*

Collonnell Cahan's own company consisting of 100 men compleate.

Officers Lieftennant Cnogher O Cahan

Ancient Dualtagh Mac Duffy

Sargeants of the company Owen O Cognoghor and Hugh Mac Cormacke

Lieftennant Collonnell Donnaghe O Cahan's company consisting of 100 men compleate.

Officers Lieftennant Shane O Cahan

Ancient John Cooper

Sarjeants of the company Bryen Oge Mac Cormacke and William Oge Mac Cormacke

Sarjeant-Major Ledwitch his company consisting of 100 men compleate.

Officers Lieftennant James Dease

Ancient Bartholomew Newgent

Sarjeants of the company Tohill Moddirrt Mac Illrey and John That.

Captain Art O Neale's company consisting of 100 men compleate.

Officers Lieftennant Con O Neale

Ancient Bryen O Neale

Serjeants Hugh Oge Lavery and Hary O Muldowne

Captain John Mortimer's company consisting of 50 men compleate.

Officers Patricke O Mallen, Lieftennant

Phelim O Donnelly, Ancient

Daniel Mac Duffy and James O Mulhollan, Sargeants.

Captain Rowry Duffe O Cahan's company consisting of 50 men compleate.

Officers John Mac Guyer, Lieftenant

Donnagh O Cahan, Ancient

Edward Keltey and Terlagh Mac Cana, Serjeant.

In all, 500 besydes officers

A list of Lieftenant-Generall Mac Donnell's regiment.

The said Lieftenant-Generall's owne company consisting of 100 men compleate.

Captain − ,Lieftenant − ,Ensign − ,Sarjeant

Lieftennant-Colonell John Mac Donnell's company consisting of 100 men compleate.

Lieftennant − ,Ensigne − ,Sarjeants

Sarjeant Major Thomas Laghtnan's company consisting of 100 men compleate.

Lieftenant − ,Ensigne − ,Sarjeants

Alexander Mac Coll's company consisting of 100 men compleate.

Lieftenant John Hamilton,

Ensigne − ,Sarjeants

James Mac Donnell's company consisting of 50 men compleate.

Lieftenant − ,Ensigne − ,Serjeants

Captain Henry Mac Henry his company consisting of 50 men compleate.

Lieftenant Congher Mac Henry,

Ensigne Patricke Mac Hughe,

Serjeants Richard Mac Henry and Shane Roe Mac Hugh

Captain Patricke Mac Henry's company consisting of 50 men compleate.

Lieftenant − ,Ensigne − ,Serjeants

Captain Randle Mac Coll Mac Randle Mac Donnell's company consisting of 50 men compleate.

Lieftenant − ,Ensigne − ,Serjeants

Captaine Evar Mac Quillin's company consisting of 50 men compleate.

Lieftenant − ,Ensigne − ,Serjeants

Captain Garrett Mac Quillin's company, 50 men compleate.

Lieftenant − ,Ensigne − ,Serjeants

Captain Donnell Crome Mac Alster's company, 50 men compleate.

Lieftenant Huiston Mac Daniell.

Ensigne − ,Serjeants

Captain William O Shiel's company, 50 men compleate.
Lieftenant – ,Ensigne – ,Serjeants

Captain John Reli's company, 50 men compleate.
Lieftenant – ,Ensigne – ,Serjeants

Captain Donnagh O Cahan's company, 50 men compleate.
Lieftenant – ,Ensigne – ,Serjeants

Captain Manus O Cahan's company, 50 men compleate.
Lieftenant – ,Ensigne – ,Serjeants

Captain Cormucke Oge O Hara his company, 50 men compleate.
Lieftenant – ,Ensigne – ,Serjeants

In all 1030 besides officers.

Appendix 2

News from His Majesty's Army in Scotland

by an Irish Officer in Alexander MacDonnel's Forces

News from His Majesty's Army in Scotland, *to be presented to the Most Honourable the Lord Lieutenant-General of* Ireland; *written at* Inverlochy in Lochaber *the 7th of February, 1644, by an* Irish *officer in* Alexander MacDonnel's *Forces.*[2]

When the Irish forces arrived in Argyle's bounds in Scotland, our General-Major Alexander MacDonnel sent such of his Majesty's commissions and letters to those to whom they were directed; although for the present none was accepted on: which caused our General-Major and those forces to march into *Badenogh*, where they raised the country with them; and from thence to *Castle-Blaire*, in Athol, where the *Lord Marquess of Montrose* came unto and joined them with some other small forces. From thence they marched to *St. Johnston*,[3] where the enemy had gathered together 8000 foot and 800 horse with nine pieces of cannon; his Majesty's army having not so much as one horse: for that day the *Marquess of Montrose* went on foot himself with his target and pike; the *Lord Kilpunt* commanding the bowmen, and our General-Major of the Irish forces commanding his 3 regiments. The armies being drawn up on both sides, they both advanced together, and although the battle continued for some space, we lost not one man on our side, yet still advanced, the enemy being 3 or 4 to one: howsoever God gave us the day; the enemy retreating with their backs towards us, that man might have walked on the dead corps to the town, being two long miles from the place where the battle was pitched. The chase continued from 8 a clock in the morning til 9 at night: all their cannon, arms, munition, colours, drums, tents, baggage, in a word, none of themselves, nor baggage escaped our hands, but their horse and such of the foot as were taken prisoners within the city. This battle to God's glory and our Prince's good was fought the first day of September.

From thence we marched straight to *Aberdeen*, only surprising such as withstood us, with little or no skirmishing until the 13th of the same month. At *Aberdeen* the Covenanters of the North had gathered themselves together to the number of 3,000 foot and 500 horse, with 3 pieces of cannon. We had then about 80 horse. The battle being fairly pitched, it continued for a long space, and the enemy behaved themselves far better than they did at *St. Johnston*. Yet we lost not that day above four, but the enemy were altogether cut off, unless some few that hid themselves in the city. The riches of that town, and the riches they got before, hath made all our soldiers cavaliers. This battle being ended, only our manner of going down to battle, and how each one commanded I omit, till it be drawn and set down in a more ample manner; now tendering only a brevity of our proceedings; for if I should write the whole truth, all that hath been done by our army would be accounted most miraculous; which I protest I will but shew in the least manner I can, leaving the rest to the report of the enemy themselves.

After this battle we marched towards the Highlands again, so far as to *Castle-Blaire*, where I was sent to *Ardamuragh*, with a party to relieve the castle of *Migary* and the castle of *Langhaline*; *Migary Castle* having a leaguer about it, which was raised 2 or 3 days before I could come to them: at which time the *Captain of Clanranald* with all his men joined with the *Glen Coo* men and others who had an inclination to his Majesty's service.[4]

In the meantime while I was interested upon those services, the *M. of Montrose* marched back to the Lowlands, almost the same way that he marched before, til they came to a place called *Fivy* in the shire of *Aberdeen*, where *Argyle* with 16 troops of horse and 3000 foot marched up; and upon a very plain field *Argyle* was most shamefully beaten out of the field, and had it not been for his horse, they had suffered as deeply as the rest; but on their side they lost many of their best horse, and most of all their commanders hurt, and the *Earl Mareschal's* brother killed. After the armies separated the *Lord Marquess* marched again to *Castle-Blaire* in *Athol*; where I met with him again and such of the Highlands as had joined with me. The day of *Fivy* was on Oct. 28.

From *Castle-Blaire* we marched to *Glanurghyes*, called *McCallin McConaghy*, which lands we all burned, and preyed from thence to *Lares*, alias *Lausers*; and burned and preyed all his country from thence to *Aghenbrack's*, whose lands and country were burned and preyed; and so throughout all *Argyle*, we left neither house nor hold unburned, nor corn nor cattle that belonged to the whole name of Campbell. Such of his Majesties friends as lived near them joined with us. We then marched to *Loughaber*, where *Mr Alane* came and joined us, but had few of his men with him. From thence we marched to *Glengarry*, where the *Lord of Glengarry* joined with us. At this place we got intelligence, that *Argyle, Aghenbracke*, and the whole name of Campbell, with all their forces and a great number of Lowlandmen with them, were come to *Inverloughy* in *Loughaber* following us. This caused us to make a countermarch the nearest way over the mountains, till we came within musket-shot of the castle of *Inverloughy*; it then being night so that the enemy stood to their arms all night, the sentries skirmishing together. By this place of *Inverloughy*, the sea comes close to it, and that night *Argyle* embarked himself in his barge, and there lay till the next morning, sending his orders of discipline to *Aghenbracke* and the rest of the officers there, commanding the battle. Which on both sides being pitched and their cannon planted, the fight began; the enemy giving fire upon us on both sides, both with cannon and muskets, to their little avail. For only two regiments of our army, playing with musket shot, advanced till they recovered *Argyle's* standard, and took the standard bearer: at which their whole army broke; which were so hotly pursued both with horse and foot, that little or none of the whole army escaped us, the officers being the first that were cut off. There *Aghenbracke* was killed, with 16 or 17 of the chief Lords of Campbell, their other Lowland commanders (only two Lieutenant-Colonels) all cut off; four others of the name of Campbell taken prisoners, as *Bearbrick*, the young *Laird Carrindel, Inverleeven*, Capt. son of *Enistesinth*, and divers other that got quarter, being men of quality. We lost but two or three that day. This was fought the second of February.

The Scots Army at Dunbar 1650

The majority of the units actually present are identified in an English intelligence summary (BM Harl.6844 fol.123). Probably based on prisoner interrogations this report credits the Scots with having fifteen regiments of foot organised in five brigades.

Leuetenant Gen Lumsdale (Sir James Lumsden)
Maj Gen Hoburn (James Holburne)
Maj Gen Pettscobbie (Colin Pitscottie)
Coll Lawnes (Sir James Campbell of Lawers)
Coll Innis (John Innes)

These commanded Brigades:
Coll Glanagis (Haldane of Gleneagles)
Coll Tallifield (Preston of Valleyfield)
Lord Kilcowberry (Lord Kirkcudbright)
Lord of Egell (Lindsay of Edzell)
Mr Loveit (Master of Lovat)
Lord of Buchannan (Buchannan of Buchannan)
Sir Elex Stuart (Col. Alexander Stewart)
Gen: of the Artillery's Regi: Weams (Lt Col. David Wemyss)
Coll Hume (Home of Wedderburn)
Coll ffreeland (Ruthven of Freeland)

There were in fact elements of as many as twenty-two regiments present and the discrepancy probably arises from the fact that a number of the fifteen 'regiments' which fought in the battle were actually composite formations.

The precise make-up of each of the brigades is not entirely clear and the order of battle below is largely confined to identifying the three major units in each brigade – taking BM Harl.6844 as a starting point. Some of the attributions are necessarily tentative, although the available evidence indicates that so far as possible brigades were organised on a geographical basis: Sir James Lumsden's was from Fife; Sir James Campbell of Lawers' men were all raised in and around Perthshire; Pitscottie's was formed in Forfarshire although most of the regiments actually came from outside the area; Innes's Brigade came down from the north, and Holburne's from Stirling, Linlithgow and Edinburgh.

Infantry
Lieutenant-General Sir James Lumsden's Brigade
General of the Artillery's Regiment
Sir William Douglas of Kirkness' Regiment
Sir James Lumsden's Regiment

Lord Balfour of Burleigh was also nominated to command a regiment in the second levy from Fife and as a colour was taken at Dunbar bearing his crest, his men were presumably consolidated with Kirkness' – the latter is not mentioned in BM Harl.6844. The brigade must have been a fairly strong one, for between 15 and 22 July some 2,700 men should have been mustered for service in Fife. Albeit a proportion of them were put out as horse, which would reduce the theoretical total to some 2,100 men, and even allowing for the usual wastage there must still have been about 2,000 in the ranks at Dunbar.

Sir James Campbell of Lawers' Brigade
Sir James Campbell of Lawers' Regiment
Sir George Preston of Valleyfield's Regiment
Sir John Haldane of Gleneagles' Regiment

In addition to the above BM Harl.6844 mentions a 'Coll ffreeland' who is presumably the Sir Thomas Ruthven of Freeland nominated along with Preston of Valleyfield to command the first levy from Perthshire. A colour was also taken bearing the crest of Lord Coupar, who was similarly nominated together with Haldane of Gleneagles to command the second levy. Presumably in both cases the levies were consolidated into one regiment rather than two, commanded by Valleyfield and Gleneagles respectively. Lawers' own regiment had been 644 strong in six companies the previous summer, far bigger than the other regiments and despite fighting hard at Dunbar still had 413 men in the ranks in June 1651, so a figure of some 600 would not seem unreasonable at Dunbar. The other two regiments probably mustered about 700–800 apiece. All in all therefore the brigade probably had around 2,000 men on the morning of 3 September.

Major-General Colin Pitscottie's Brigade
Major-General Colin Pitscottie's Regiment
Sir David Home of Wedderburn's Regiment
Colonel John Lindsay of Edzell's Regiment

This brigade appears to have been formed in Forfarshire, and in addition to the three named (all identified in BM Harl.6844) must have included two small veteran regiments commanded by Sir Andrew Ker of Greenhead and Sir James Douglas of Mouswall, from Teviotdale and Dumfries respectively, which were also quartered there at the outset of the campaign. It is likely that all three border regiments, which collectively mustered no more than 400 men before the campaign began, were consolidated in a single battalion under Wedderburn, for it seems very unlikely that they should have been able to pick up many recruits. Nevertheless, even if 600 are allowed for Wedderburn's 'battalion', another 600 for Edzell's newly raised regiment and 400 odd for Pitscottie's, the brigade may still have mustered something in the region of only 1,600 men.

Colonel John Innes' Brigade
Colonel John Innes' Regiment
Master of Forbes of Regiment
Master of Lovat's Regiment

Innes' own regiment appears to have had something in the region of 400 men at the outset of the campaign, but a total of 170 of them were ordered to be left behind in various garrisons and thus only 230 marched south to Dunbar. Forbes' Regiment is not mentioned in BM Harl.6844, but was identified by its captured colours. With new levies it should have been at least 400 strong and may well have been bigger. The Master of Lovat's Regiment on the other hand was of itself only about 100 strong, but with the addition of a part of Argyle's

Regiment could have mustered as many as 400 at Dunbar. Consequently the brigade was probably about 1,200 strong or 1,500 at the outside, and therefore the smallest of the five.

Major-General James Holburne
Sir George Buchannan of Buchannan's Regiment
Major-General James Holburne's Regiment
Colonel Alexander Stewart's [Edinburgh] Regiment

Buchannan had been allotted no fewer than 1,124 men in the levying, although it is extremely unlikely that all of them were rounded up, while Holburne should have had at least 430-odd men in his own regiment, but may have had more since he still had about 400 that winter. The same applies to Stewart's Regiment. A colour taken at Dunbar bore the crest of Lord Balmerino, who was nominated to command the second levy from Edinburgh. Presumably his men were added to Colonel Alexander Stewart's Regiment, although neither unit survived. Overall therefore the brigade could well have been 2,000 strong.

* * * *

Not included in the above analysis is 'Lord Kilcowberry', who is presumably Lord Kirkcudbright. He was certainly present at Dunbar, but there is no clue as to which brigade the regiment may have belonged, and indeed his men actually appear to have been dragooners rather than infantrymen.

Cavalry

In contrast to the infantry, no brigade structure was evidenced in the intelligence summary for the eighteen Scots cavalry regiments identified as taking part in the battle, although one certainly existed. While the majority of units had originally been raised in 1649 they had then had a strength of no more than three troops apiece and often fewer. Some comprised just a single independent troop.

Earl of Leven's Regiment
Lieutenant-General David Leslie's Regiment
Major-General Robin Montgomerie's Regiment
Major-General Sir John Browne
Colonel Thomas Craig of Riccarton

Sir Charles Armott's Regiment
Colonel Archibald Strachan's Regiment
Master of Forbes' Regiment
Colonel Walter Scott's Regiment
Sir James Halkett's Regiment
Lord Mauchline's Regiment
Lord Brechin's Regiment
Sir Arthur Erskine of Scotscraig's Regiment
Sir Robert Adair of Kinhilt's Regiment
Colonel William Stewart's Regiment
Earl of Cassillis' Regiment
Colonel Robert Halkett's Regiment
Colonel Gibby Kerr's Regiment

Artillery

The Scots were by no means backward in their use of artillery, but the absence of proper roads effectively confined their heavier guns to castles and other fixed defences while their armies were for the most part accompanied by lighter pack-mounted pieces.

The Scots train of artillery at Dunbar appears to have been captured in its entirety, and the highest estimate offered by those who had the agreeable task of counting them was '32 pieces of ordnance, small, great, and leather guns'. Another account however refers to just nine guns. At first sight the two figures might appear quite incompatible, but presumably Leslie had just nine field guns of conventional style and weight, and twenty-three small-calibre, pack-mounted, leather guns. Most of them were mounted or rather 'bundled' in pairs or even in fours however, and it is not entirely clear whether the reference is to twenty-three 'bundles', or to twenty-three tubes mounted in a variety of combinations. Some of the single-barrelled ones were very light indeed, firing just a half-pound ball and being 'handled like a musket'. These may have been something like the various grenade launchers that were experimented with by a number of European armies in the early eighteenth century, but it is perhaps more likely that they were more akin to the old *hakenbusch* or hook-guns, fired while resting on a collapsible tripod.

Notes

Chapter 1

1 See Marcus Merriman, *The Rough Wooings; Mary Queen of Scots 1542–1551*, East Linton, 2000, for a thorough discussion of this important period.

2 Quoted in C. V. Wedgewood, 'Anglo Scottish relations 1603–40', *Transactions of the Royal Historical Society* (TRHS), 4th Series, vol. xxxii (1950), p. 31.

3 For a full, erudite and eminently readable discussion of the political background and course of events, see David Stevenson, *The Scottish Revolution 1637–1644*, Newton Abbot, 1973.

4 Gordon Donaldson, *Scotland: James V to James VII*, Edinburgh, 1965, p. 219.

5 While attention tends to focus on King James VI's known interest in witchcraft, this aspect of the play is just a thin veneer on its underlying theme of the triumph of the Protestant lords and the crucial assistance given to them by England; with Bothwell scarcely disguised as MacBeth; Mary as Lady MacBeth, and Jamie's father Darnley, supposedly murdered by both, represented by King Duncan.

6 John Spalding, *Memorialls of the Trubles in Scotland 1627–1645*, Spalding Club, 1850–1, vol. 1, p. 34: 'ane brave company of tounes soldiouris, all cled in white satein doubletis, blak veluot breikis, and silk stokingis, with hatis, fedderis, scarfis, bandis, and the rest correspondent. This gallantis had dayntie moscatis, pikis and gilded partisanis and suche like, who gardit his Majestie.'

7 A band was an agreement that bound the signatories to assist and defend each other generally or in a given set of circumstances.

8 Spalding, vol. 1, p. 130.

9 William Barriffe, *Militarie Discipline; or The Young Artilleryman*, 6th edn 1661, p. 42.

10 Spalding, vol. 2, p. 320: 'Vpon Frydday, 16th of Februar Captain Strathauchin marchit out of Abirdene with sex scoir ten soldiouris, capitanes, and commanderis, furneshit out be the said burghe vpone their owne charges and expensis. Ilk soldiour wes furneshit with tua

sarkis, cot, briekis, hoiss and bonet, bandis, and schone; ane suord, ane mvscat, pulder and ball, for so mony; and vtheris sum ane suard, and ane pik, according to the ordour; and ilk soldiour to have sex schillingis ilk day, during the space of 40 dayes, of loan silver. Ilk twelff of thame had ane baggage horss worth fyftie pundis, ane stovp, ane pan, and pot, for thair meat and drink, togidder also with thair hyre or levie or loan money, ilk soldiour estimate to ten dollaris, and in furnishing and all to 100 merks.'

This particular detachment was destined for the Earl Marischal's Regiment, another commanded by Captain McNab which left shortly afterwards was destined for Lord Gordon's. Although Spalding's description of this second detachment is less detailed he does confirm that two muskets were carried for each pike 'according to the ordour'.

11   It should however be noted that these regiments did not actually bear territorial titles as proposed by Professor C. S. Terry, *Papers Relating to the Army of the Solemn League and Covenant*, Scottish History Society, 1917–18, 2 vols – hereafter *Army of the Covenant*. Yester's Regiment was always referred to as such and never as the Linlithgow and Tweeddale Regiment. Only in two cases – the Merse Regiment and the Edinburgh Regiment – were units referred to by anything other than the colonel's name.

12   The companies were supposedly of unequal size reflecting the rank of the officer who commanded. The colonel's own company should have been 200 strong in contrast to the hundred men commanded by an ordinary captain. In practice this distinction was meaningless.

13   While arguably there were some practical advantages to raising new regiments, the primary attraction was the opportunities they presented for the exercise of patronage in the appointment of the new officers required to command them.

14   This was the reality behind the famous New Model Army, which was organised, trained and equipped exactly as its predecessors had been. The only difference was that political manoeuvring ensured that most of those appointed as its officers were Independents rather than Presbyterians.

15   The phrase is lifted from P. Hume Brown's *History of Scotland*, Edinburgh, 1909, and although it does not actually appear in the account of Langside by Melville of Hallhill, which Brown relied upon, it is the most expressive explanation of 'push of pike' that I have ever come across.

16   It was loosely woven and boiled in wine vinegar to aid its burning.

17   This point does require emphasis, for while the different actions painstakingly explained in the drill books appear exceedingly elaborate, once the process has been mastered through practice it can be speeded up considerably and the words of command reduced simply to: 'make ready', 'present' and 'give fire'.

18   The so-called Swedish salvee required the front rank to kneel, the second to stoop and the

third to present between them. Any ranks standing behind them simply formed a reserve. The French salvee was a form of firing by rank, starting with the first and requiring each to swiftly drop to their knees to allow the succeeding rank to fire over their heads. This allowed a greater weight of firepower than the Swedish salvee but for obvious reasons was unpopular with those concerned.

19 Only one cuirassier troop is recorded, raised in the northeast of Scotland in 1639 and equipped with armour sent up from England.

20 Spalding, vol. 1, p. 154.

21 Indeed Sir John Byron explicitly referred to 'pushing' in the cavalry fight at Roundway Down in 1643.

22 And as such were armed with lightweight lances such as half-pikes rather than the heavy 'jousting'-style lances once carried by some cuirassiers.

Chapter 2

1 Spalding, vol. 1, p. 130.

2 The gate in question was not the modern one but was located part way along an outwork known as the Spur, demolished in the eighteenth century to accommodate the present esplanade.

3 Spalding, vol. 1, p. 158.

4 Spalding, vol. 1, p. 136; James Gordon of Rothiemay, *History of Scots Affairs*, Spalding Club, 1841, vol. 2, p. 213.

5 Patrick Gordon of Ruthven, *A Short Abridgement of Britane's Distemper*, Spalding Club, 1844, pp. 15–16.

6 Spalding, vol. 1, p. 150. Headed by a burgh militia officer named William Cuthbert they also took 'one of the toune's cullouris and John Park their drummer with thame'.

7 Strathbogie is a district in northeast Scotland, regarded as the centre of Gordon power – hence the Strathbogie Regiment. Confusingly the name was also applied to what is now the burgh of Huntly, which itself derives its modern name from the marquis, whose principal seat was the adjacent Strathbogie Castle.

8 Gordon of Rothiemay, vol. 2, p. 257.

9 Gordon of Rothiemay, vol. 2, p. 257–8; Gordon of Ruthven, p. 19; Spalding, vol. 1, p. 186.

10 Gordon of Rothiemay, vol. 2, p. 258. Unfortunately it is not clear whether it was the minister or his son who was disguised as a woman.

11 Spalding, vol. 1, p. 195.

12 It is worth noting that the 'o' in Aboyne is silent and that both the village and the man are therefore pronounced Abyne.

13 Calendar State Papers, Domestic, 1639: 49–50, 55, 56.

14 Gordon of Rothiemay, vol. 2, pp. 249–50.

15 Gordon of Rothiemay, vol. 2, p. 270 states that the Aberdeen men 'gott the first place of the foot' – traditionally the right of the line – while convention will have placed the Strathbogie Regiment, as next in seniority, on the left. It will be noted that none of the Aberdeen Militia were encumbered with pikes.

16 'After noone the companies of Dundee, aemulouse of the Aberdeen citizens, desired to be lettne storme the bridge, which Montrose readily yielded too. Two companies fell on, under the commande of one captain Bonner but they found so hotte a welcome from the Aberdeens men that they made a quick retreat; which was seconded with the whooping and hallowing of such as wer looking on who mocked ther poor bravado' (Gordon of Rothiemay, vol. 2, p. 277).

17 Spalding, vol. 1, pp. 210–11. There is a strong suspicion that Spalding himself may have been one of the 'Gallantis' concerned.

18 Robert Baillie, *Letters and Journals*, Bannatyne Club, 1841–2, vol. 1, pp. 186–7.

19 C. S. Terry, *The Life and Campaigns of Alexander Leslie*, London, 1899, pp. 54–6.

20 Terry, *The Life and Campaigns of Alexander Leslie*, pp. 107–8.

21 John Rushworth, *Historical Collections . . . 1618–1649*, London, 1659–1701, p. 1236.

22 Rushworth, p. 1236.

23 The lifeguard was otherwise known at this time as the College of Justice Troop; raised in Edinburgh it appears to have been some 160 strong. Leslie's regiment of horse on the other hand had been raised in Fife (chiefly in Kirkcaldy and Cupar) and was probably around 300 strong.

24 In his otherwise useful reconstruction of the battle, based on admittedly contradictory sources, Terry, *The Life and Campaigns of Alexander Leslie*, suggests that the lifeguard first crossed the ford and were charged by Wilmot's men immediately after the abandonment of the large sconce, and then again charged and were beaten back during the main assault, but the true sequence of events appears to be as described here.

25 For their part the Scots lost just a handful of men; so few in fact that all or most of them were recorded by name: Drummond of Logie; James Mackie and James Ramsay; Thomas Dalying from Edinburgh, and a man named Baxter from Fife. Logie may have been the officer shot at the outset of the battle, while Dalying and Baxter probably served in Leslie's Lifeguard and regiment of horse respectively. See Terry, *The Life and Campaigns of Alexander Leslie*, p. 122.

26 The three regiments in question were those of John Cochrane, Major-General Robert Monro and Lord Sinclair and appear to have survived because they were raised in continental fashion by the officers concerned rather than under the auspices of a particular Committee of War. Sinclair's was particularly ill-disciplined and appears to have been regarded as a penal

battalion. One source (Anon., 'True rehearsall; a little yet true rehearsal of severall passages of affairs, collected by a friend of Doctor Alexander's at Aberdeen', *Transactions of the Royal Historical Society*, vol. 5 (1877) – hereafter 'True rehearsall') went so far as to condemn them as 'adulterers, furnicaters, thieves, murderers, drunkards, Sabbath breakers, who were given up by the minister of every parish'.

Chapter 3

1 Sometimes referred to in early documents as the Levied Regiment or the College of Justice Regiment, this unit had a rather confusing history. Initially command appears to have been conferred upon Lord Sinclair but it is not to be confused with his regiment serving in Ireland. When Leven entered England in January 1644, five companies under Lieutenant-Colonel Sir James Somerville were assigned as the garrison of Morpeth while a detachment left in Berwick under Major Hugh Crawford subsequently became the Marquess of Argyle's Regiment (not to be confused with his Highland regiments) and saw out the war there.

2 Rushworth, vol. 2, p. 315.

3 James Somerville, *Memorie of the Somervills*, Edinburgh, 1815, vol. 2, p. 315.

4 Spalding, vol. 2, p. 320.

5 E. Warburton, *Memoirs of Prince Rupert and the Cavaliers*, London 1849, vol. 2, p. 368.

6 Historical Manuscripts Commission (HMC), 8th Report, vol. 2, p. 60. Fairfax's figure, also confirmed (or copied) by Robert Baillie, presumably does not account for those units that were left outside Newcastle, but will include those drafts that had not yet joined the army when it originally crossed the border.

7 Terry, *The Life and Campaigns of Alexander Leslie*, pp. 181–2. It is frequently stated in secondary sources that the army crossed the border at Coldstream, but that was merely a detachment covering the flank of the army, which crossed dry-shod by the bridge.

8 Since the fifteenth century Newcastle upon Tyne had been both a city and a county in its own right and therefore mustered its Trained Bands independently of the Northumberland and Durham ones.

9 Terry, *The Life and Campaigns of Alexander Leslie*, pp. 187–8. Ammunition returns are found in ibid., p. 1.

10 The date is uncertain, but the location is still remembered as Battle Hill. A party of musketeers attempted to ambush a patrol from the Earl of Eglinton's Horse, but were soundly thrashed, losing a number killed and forty-five taken prisoner – who were exchanged for some Scots stragglers earlier picked up by the garrison.

11 Terry, *The Life and Campaigns of Alexander Leslie*, pp. 192–4. Letter from Edward Bowles to Sir Harry Vane. The Marquis of Newcastle did indeed write it up as such, claiming 200 Scots killed and 150 taken prisoner.

12 As we have seen three companies of the Earl Marischal's Regiment did not leave Aberdeen until 16 February, and it may well be the case that the other four regiments were also under-strength. The troops of horse probably belonged to Colonel Michael Weldon's Regiment – an English Parliamentarian unit which had succeeded in coming north to join the Scots.

13 The respective locations of the armies can be worked out only with a little application. Newcastle's own account mentions Pensher Hill (which is how it is pronounced locally), while there is an unambiguous reference in the Scots army's ordnance papers to thirty axes being issued out while it was at Hamelton Hill. Newcastle's account confirms this not only by complaining how it was necessary to hack through hedges and bushes (hence those axes) but by describing them standing on a 'plain' on the other side of the valley from his own position and oddly enough there was a Plains Farm there. Both armies, it should be emphasised, were on the south side of the river Wear and this fight should not be confused with the later one, variously referred to as Boldon Hill, Bowdon Hill or Hylton, which took place on the north side.

14 Terry, *The Life and Campaigns of Alexander Leslie*, pp. 200–2; C. H. Firth, *Cromwell's Army*, Oxford, 1962, pp. 351–2.

15 In Terry, *The Life and Campaigns of Alexander Leslie*, pp. 168–9.

16 As with the fighting outside Sunderland two weeks earlier there is considerable confusion in both contemporary and secondary sources as to where this battle took place. Boldon is locally pronounced Bowdon, which does not help matters, and it is also sometimes referred to as the battle of Hilton or Hylton. In fact Hylton Castle lies to the south of Boldon Hill in what would have been the Royalist rear area. As it was the home of one of Newcastle's officers, Colonel John Hilton, it is possible that in this case the confusion may have arisen from his having used the house as his headquarters.

17 Or so it may be inferred from the Scots ordnance papers. One of the two cannon recorded as having been 'broken' was in fact recovered from the bed of the river in the nineteenth century and was put on display in Barnes Park – ironically enough on what was the 7 March battlefield.

18 All the extant accounts of the battle are gathered in Terry, *The Life and Campaigns of Alexander Leslie*, pp. 208–11.

19 Quartermaster Somerville, in Historical Manuscripts Commission, 10th Report, appendix pt 1, p. 53.

20 Brigadier Peter Young, *Marston Moor 1644*, Kineton, 1970, pp. 86–7.

21 Stuart Reid, *All the King's Armies; A Military History of the English Civil War*, Staplehurst, 1998, pp. 136–40, n. 11. Gordon himself was not with the army and would eventually change sides. Consequently it was commanded throughout the campaign by Sir James Lumsden.

22 A Fleming of Spanish descent, his real name as revealed by his signature was Bernardo de Gomez.

23 Most of Newcastle's cavalry had left York before the siege began and subsequently joined Rupert's army on its approach march.

24 'Full relation', in C. H. Firth, *Newcastle, Duchess of: The Life of . . . William Cavendish, Duke of Newcastle*, London, 1886, pp. 277 ff.

25 Firth, *Newcastle, Duchess of*.

26 Dudhope himself was fatally wounded and captured, while Lieutenant-Colonel Bryson of Scotscraig's Regiment was killed outright.

27 The Close would not be laid out until 1766, leading to a recent eccentric suggestion that the site of their stand was much farther to the east and away from the Royalist line of retreat in an area then known as the Atterwith Enclosures. However there is no contemporary evidence for fighting in this area, while local tradition is quite firm as to the White Sike area.

28 Cromwell was probably the chief winner, but Sir Thomas Fairfax and his backers made a spirited attempt to give him rather than Balgonie the credit for warning Cromwell of the disaster on the left and for suggesting an immediate counter-attack.

Chapter 4

1 Ludovic Lindsay, 16th Earl of Crawford, had been declared a traitor by the Scots government and stripped of his earldom, which passed to his kinsman, John, Earl of Lindsay. There were thus two Earls of Crawford above ground at one and the same time and for the avoidance of confusion, Ludovic, the sixteenth Earl, continues hereafter to be referred to as Earl of Crawford, while John, the seventeenth Earl, is still styled Earl of Lindsay.

2 Spalding, vol. 2, p. 342 – Gordon of Gight kept the money.

3 Spalding, vol. 2, p. 343.

4 This was the same officer who had commanded the Strathbogie Regiment at the Bridge of Dee in 1639, and more recently he had been serving in the principal English Parliamentarian army under the Earl of Essex!

5 A little confusingly, perhaps, in Scots a gate was a road, while a gateway was a port.

6 It was common at this time for the lower level of town houses to be given over for storage or used as shops or workshops, with the residential accommodation above approached directly from an external stair or 'forestair' at the front.

7 Spalding, vol. 2, pp. 346–7; Gordon of Ruthven, p. 51.

8 Rollo had been serving as captain of Lord Eythin's lifeguard.

9 Sir James Turner, *Memoirs of His Own Life and Times*, ed. by T. Thomson, Bannatyne Club, 1829, pp. 35–8; David Stevenson, *Scottish Covenanters and Irish Confederates*, Belfast, 1981, pp. 153–6.

10 Sir James Balfour, *Historical Works*, Edinburgh, 1825, vol. 3, p. 186. Rutherford was court-martialled and condemned to death but seemingly saved by the intercession of the Earl of Lothian.

11 Terry, *Army of the Covenant*, vol. 1, pp. 108–9, 115, 116, 140 – the gun in question was a 24-pounder. The caveat should of course be added that in time-honoured fashion the panic may also have been a convenient opportunity to write off stores otherwise unaccounted for.

12 Firth (ed.), *Memoirs of the Duke of Newcastle*, p. 38.

13 'List of men gone unto the Isles. Sent by the Lord of Antrim to my Lord Ormonde, 15 Nov. 1644': transcript, in J. Gilbert (ed.), *History of the Irish Confederation and War in Ireland 1641–1649*, Dublin, 1888, vol. 4, p. 54.

14 Spalding, vol. 2, p. 385.

15 'News from His Majesty's Army in Scotland, to be presented to the most Honourable the Lord Lieutenant of Ireland; written at Inverlochy in Lochaber the 7th of February 1644, by an Irish Officer in Alexander MacDonell's Forces', in Thomas Carte, *A Collection of Original Papers*, London, 1739, vol. 1, pp. 73–6. Hereafter 'Irish Officer' although internal evidence clearly indicates it was written by MacColla himself.

16 Frequently referred to as Tippermuir; the battlefield is around the present village of Tibbermore.

17 Gordon of Ruthven, p. 74.

18 Carte, pp. 73–6.

19 James Fraser, *Chronicles of the Frasers; The Wardlaw Manuscript*, Scottish History Society, 1905, p. 286 (6,000 foot, 700 horse); Gordon of Ruthven, p. 73 (6,000 foot, 1,000 horse); Spalding, vol. 2, p. 403 (6,000 foot, 800 horse); George Wishart, *Memoirs of James, Marquis of Montrose, 1639–1650*, London, 1893, pp. 58–9 (6,000 foot, 700 horse). Other than the 8,000 foot and 800 horse optimistically cited by the unknown Irish Officer, the degree of correlation is remarkable and suggests a common source.

20 The eldest son and heir of the Earl of Perth and older brother of the Sir John Drummond serving under Lord Kilpont on the other side of the battlefield!

21 Gordon of Ruthven, p. 74.

22 Wishart, pp. 59–61.

23 Wishart (ibid.) states that the Royalists formed three deep, with the tallest men in the rear rank, the second stooping and the first rank kneeling, 'with orders to discharge all at once'.

24 Duke of Atholl, *Chronicles of the Atholl and Tullibardine Families*, Edinburgh, 1908, vol. 1, appendix contains a detailed census of men and arms in five Atholl parishes in 1638. In summary, out of 451 individuals only a hundred possessed muskets, of whom fifty-six also possessed bows and a further eighty-nine had bows alone. What is equally interesting is

that only 124 men had both sword and buckler (targe), as against 315 with swords alone. As those with both also possessed between them most of the muskets but only eleven of the bows it can be concluded that the remaining 239 'swords' were in fact dirks rather than broadswords. Rather usefully the 451 men surveyed correspond very closely to estimates of the numbers of Athollmen at Tibbermore and this may therefore serve as a very good picture of their armament.

25　Gordon of Ruthven, p. 74 is quite explicit in describing the stone throwing as occurring on this wing rather than all the way along the line as suggested by a hasty reading of Wishart (ibid.), who effectively narrates the battle only from Montrose's viewpoint on the right.

26　M. Napier, *Memorials of Montrose*, Maitland Club, 1848, vol. 2, p. 159.

27　Adding insult to injury this regiment was itself intended to be a replacement for the earlier one serving in England and there reassigned to Sir James Lumsden.

28　Gordon of Ruthven, p. 81; Spalding, vol. 2, pp. 401, 404–5.

29　Astonishingly enough Montrose's summons and the council's response both survive and are reproduced in facsimilie in Spalding, vol. 2, p. 406.

30　One way and another the burgh was fought over too often for a bare reference to the 'battle of Aberdeen' to have any real meaning. Besides lesser raids and skirmishes, there were to be three major fights: in 1639 at the Brig o' Dee; in 1644 at the Craibstane; and in the streets of the burgh in 1646. There had also been an earlier battle at the Craibstane in 1571.

31　Spalding, vol. 2, p. 406. Oddly enough the incident is mentioned only by Spalding, and in the burgh records (ibid. p. 408): 'As thay wer passing by the Fyffe regiment, the drummer was unhappilly killed by some on or uther of the horsemen of our pairtie as wes thoucht.'

32　Gordon of Ruthven, p. 82.

33　Gordon of Ruthven, pp. 81–2.

34　This manoeuvre has caused historians some difficulty in the past. The Irish did not simply open out their files to let the cavalry ride through their ranks, but on the contrary each company closed up tightly, and instead allowed the cavalry pass through the resultant intervals between them.

35　Reconstructing this episode is unduly complicated by a simple error on Wishart's part in transposing Hay and Rollo. Thus in his version of events, Hay is attacked by Lord Lewis Gordon on the right and requires to be reinforced by bringing Rollo across from the left, before requiring all of the Royalist cavalry to then recross the battlefield once again in order to defeat Craigievar on the left. See Wishart, pp. 67–8.

36　Wishart, p. 68.

37　Gordon of Ruthven, p. 83.

38　Spalding, vol. 2, pp. 406–7 – it would appear from the bitterness of his tone that Spalding himself may have been one of those running hard for the town.

39 Spalding, vol. 2, pp. 411–12. In the end, the final death toll according to the burgh council
    was nearly 160 including non-combatants murdered during the three days which followed.
    Royalist losses are unknown; they themselves claimed to have lost just seven men, but
    Wishart alluded to the cannon making 'no small havoc of our men'.

Chapter 5

1 Once inside the town most of the fighting centred around the main road dropping down the
    bridge, which at least until the eighteenth century was called Battle Bank, before memory
    faded and it was corrupted into the present Bottle Bank.
2 Thereby upsetting Callendar and his officers, who complained that despite all their efforts
    they and their men: 'hes not mutche bene taken notice of' by Leven: Terry, *The Life and
    Campaigns of Alexander Leslie*, p. 297.
3 Terry, *The Life and Campaigns of Alexander Leslie*, pp. 294, 299. A minor caveat should
    be added that many of those colliers and keelmen were in fact Scots who had settled
    on Tyneside.
4 Leven to Committee of Both Kingdoms, 7 September 1644: Terry, *The Life and Campaigns of
    Alexander Leslie*, p. 304.
5 The only 'preparation' it had received was a fresh skin of plaster to hinder anyone trying
    to gain a foothold between the stonework – much of which had been plundered from the
    conveniently situated Roman wall.
6 The first was originally commanded by Viscount Dudhope, but after his death at
    Marston Moor it fell to William Baillie. During that battle it had been brigaded with
    Sir Arthur Erskine of Scotscraig's Regiment, otherwise known as the Minister's
    Regiment. This unit certainly took part in the siege of Newcastle and is probably the
    unidentified fifth unit to assault the Newgate. However another possibility might be
    Sir James Lumsden's Regiment, which had been brigaded with Hepburn of Waughton's
    at Marston Moor.
7 The latter three had come south with Callendar and only Livingston's had fought at
    Marston Moor.
8 Terry, *The Life and Campaigns of Alexander Leslie*, pp. 324–35 deals with the storming of the
    city and includes the full text of a number of contemporary narratives.
9 *Mercurius Britannicus* was in fact a pro-Scots newspaper published in London for the express
    purpose of emphasising the considerable Scots contribution to the war effort.
10 At this point the Irish Officer reported to Ormonde that: 'we marched towards the
    Highlands again, so far as to Castle Blaire, where I was sent to Ardamuragh, with a party to
    relieve the castle of Migary and the castle of Langhaline; Migary Castle after having a leaguer
    about it, which was raised 2 or 3 days before I could come to them . . .' from which it can be

concluded that the narrative was written by none other than MacColla, speaking of himself in the third person.

11   Gordon of Ruthven, p. 89.

12   Spalding, vol. 2, p. 426.

13   Wishart, pp. 74–5; Gordon of Ruthven, pp. 90–1. The O'Cahan in question was probably Lieutenant-Colonel Donoghue O'Cahan, for Colonel Manus O'Cahan had been sent back to Ireland with despatches. As the two versions are otherwise contradictory it is likely that both O'Cahan's and Monaltrie's men attacked at the same time.

14   Spalding, vol. 2, p. 426.

15   Spalding, vol. 2, p. 426. Craigievar had been riding with the rebels as a prisoner since his capture at Aberdeen back in September. Argyle responded to this handsome gesture by arranging to have Nathaniel Gordon's excommunication lifted.

16   Gordon of Ruthven, p. 94. Interestingly while this corresponds with the popular image of Highland warriors, the fact Ruthven was so particular in describing these men, 'the strongest and most valiant men amongst the highlanders', clearly suggests they were much more heavily armed than those from Atholl and Huntly's country, who were already serving in the Royalist ranks.

17   Carte, Appendix 2. 'Glanurghyes' is Glenorchy; 'Lares' Lawers; and 'Aghenbrack' Auchinbrec. Oddly enough his narrative makes no specific mention of Inveraray.

18   There is a tolerable degree of uncertainty as to the actual route but it appears the rebels first marched due south up Glen Tarff to Culachy, as though making for Badenoch, but then turned aside and moved parallel to the Great Glen as far as Glen Buck, shielded by the long ridges of Meall a Cholumain and Druim Laragan. Thus far the going is relatively easy, but they then had to cross the gorge of the Calder Burn to reach the head of the glen. By that point they were about 300 metres above sea level and then had another 300 metres to climb to reach the col at Carn na Larach and so pass out on to the windswept Teanga plateau. This was followed by a steep descent into Glen Turret, and after that down Glen Roy to Keppoch. This route was followed in 1980 by an intrepid band of re-enactors drawn from the English Civil War Society and accomplished within the original timetable, albeit in considerably better weather. It has in the past been suggested that they might have swung round by the Corryairack Pass, but while the cavalry may have done so, MacColla (the Irish Officer) categorically states they came by 'the nearest way'.

19   There is some confusion over this officer's name. In describing the battle Ruthven calls him McConeil, while Spalding declares him to be Colonel James McDonnel alias Mc Oneill. The *List of men gone unto the Isles* (see Appendix 1) names him James McDermott. The most likely explanation is that the regiment was commanded by its former Lieutenant-Colonel

John McDonnell. As to O'Cahan's Regiment, Spalding explicitly refers to *Lieutenant-Colonel* O'Cahan.

20 Spalding, vol. 2, p. 444; Gordon of Ruthven, p. 101; J. M. Bulloch, *The House of Gordon (Gordons under Arms)*, Spalding Club, 1903–12, no. 835(a). However Wishart, p. 82, while concurring in an overall total of some 1,500 men, relates that most of Clanranald's and Inchbrackie's people had gone home to secure their plunder.

21 Gordon of Ruthven, p. 101.

22 Napier, vol. 2, p. 176.

23 Napier, vol. 2, p. 177.

24 First published in Cambridge in 1632 and heavily derivative of continental works, it was extremely influential and reprinted during the war.

25 Spalding, vol. 2, pp. 454–5; Gordon of Ruthven, pp. 110–13. The part played by Hurry's infantry in the affair is obscure, but they were more than likely mounted on horseback and posted at the Bridge o' Dee to secure his retreat.

26 Probably the Lieutenant-Colonel John Cockburn who commanded one of the regular battalions at Inverlochy. He had given his parole there not to serve against the Royalists again but can hardly be blamed if they came knocking.

27 Wishart, pp. 93–4.

28 His testimony can be found in Napier, vol. 2, p. 184; ominously it is endorsed *Guilty*.

29 Baillie, vol. 2, p. 418.

30 Gordon of Ruthven, p. 121; Spalding, vol. 2, p. 473.

Chapter 6

1 Gordon of Ruthven, pp. 121–3.

2 Now crowned by the Boath Doo-cot and a not entirely accurate interpretative map of the battlefield.

3 Fraser, p. 295.

4 Wishart, p. 99.

5 *Mercurius Aulicus*, 2 June 1645 (Montrose's own account); Gordon of Ruthven, p. 122; Spalding, vol. 2, p. 473.

6 *Acts of the Parliament of Scotland*, Record Commission, 1835, vol. 6, p. 176.

7 Fraser, p. 294.

8 Balfour, vol. 3, p. 296.

9 Spalding, vol. 2, pp. 463, 473.

10 Fraser, p. 295; Gordon of Ruthven, p. 123. Fraser simply refers to a yellow banner, which has cheerfully been interpreted to mean that Montrose gave MacColla the royal standard – the red lion rampant on a yellow ground – in order to purposefully deceive Hurry as to his

own whereabouts as he prepared his cunning trap, but Fraser conspicuously does not identify it as such. Perhaps significantly a list of Irish colours in a contemporary newsletter, the *True Informer*, which can be linked to the brigade does include a single yellow one bearing an image of the risen Christ.

11 Fraser, p. 296; Sir Thomas Hope, *A Diary of the Public Correspondence etc., 1633–1645*, Bannatyne Club, 1843, p. 220.

12 Gordon of Ruthven, p. 123.

13 Gordon of Ruthven, p. 124.

14 *Mercurius Aulicus*, 2 June 1645.

15 Drummond was subsequently court-martialled at Inverness and shot 'at the post upon the high rodde as yow go to Tomnihurich': Fraser, p. 296.

16 Gordon of Ruthven, pp. 125–6.

17 Fraser, p. 296.

18 Traditionally Montrose is said to have assembled his counter-attack in a hollow to the southwest of the village, but Wishart (ibid.) states that the hollow was 'covered' by the village, i.e., behind it rather than below it, and this is confirmed by Fraser's (ibid.) eyewitness description of the Royalist infantry sweeping round the village. It is possible however that Aboyne's cavalry formed up in what is now known as Montrose's Hollow.

19 Fraser, p. 295; Gordon of Ruthven, p. 126; Spalding, vol. 2, p. 473.

20 All six of them, together with five lieutenants and 200 men were afterwards buried at Cawdor, a Campbell seat, although as the church lies some ten kilometres from the battlefield many of the latter may have been wounded men and fugitives from a variety of other units.

21 The latter three were buried in Auldearn church, along with a Captain Crichton who probably belonged to Findlater's Regiment. A memorial is still set into the wall.

22 Gilbert Gordon of Sallagh, *Continuation of a History of the Earldom of Sutherland by Sir Robert Gordon of Gordonstoun*, Edinburgh, 1813, p. 525; Gordon of Ruthven, pp. 126–7; Spalding, vol. 2, p. 473.

23 They were evidently a hard-bitten crew. In February 1646 the officers complained that they had been in garrison at Inverness since October 1644 and only received a half month's pay in all that time! Indeed the regiment would soldier on under his son, Sir James, to help give Montrose his quietus at Carbisdale five years later – and later survive an even greater débâcle at Dunbar.

24 Baillie, vol. 2, p. 418; Spalding, vol. 2, p. 476.

25 Wishart, p. 108; John Buchan, *Montrose*, London, 1928, p. 255.

26 The ballad was apparently first published in Anon., *The Thistle of Scotland: A Selection of Ancient Ballads*, Aberdeen, 1823:

> We lay at Lesly a' that nicht,
>
> They camped at Asloun
>
> And up we rose afore daylicht,
>
> Tae ding the beggars doun.
>
> Afore we was in battle rank,
>
> We were anent Mill Hill,
>
> I wat fu' weel they garr'd us rue,
>
> We gat fachtin' oor fill.

27 Baillie, vol. 2, p. 419.

28 Fraser, p. 299; Wishart, p. 109.

29 Wishart, p. 109. Anon, 'True rehearsall', p. 61 – the unknown author of the latter mistakenly identifies Kennedy as Cassillis' brother, but picturesquely notes that he was 'ane man of huge stature'.

30 Baillie, vol. 2, p. 419.

31 Fraser, p. 299; Gordon of Ruthven, p. 135; 'True rehearsall', p. 61. William Gordon, *The History of the Ancient, Noble and Illustrious Family of Gordon*, Edinburgh, 1727, p. 469, quotes a now lost portion of Spalding's history to evidence seven dead including Lord Gordon, Mowat of Balquholly and Ogilvy of Milton.

Chapter 7

1 He was the elder but illegitimate son of Sir William Baillie of Lamington. However the Lamington estate went to a younger but legitimate sister, and Baillie was consequently distinguished as Letham, a property he had acquired by marriage.

2 Baillie, vol. 2, p. 417.

3 Baillie, vol. 2, pp. 424–5.

4 Baillie, vol. 2, p. 421. As it is cumbersome to reference each individual line from Baillie's detailed evidence no pagination will be given for subsequent referrals.

5 This was of course the Earl of Lindsay, or rather Earl of Crawford-Lindsay and not to be confused with the Royalist Earl of Crawford, then a prisoner at Edinburgh.

6 Gordon of Ruthven, p. 139. The wearing of shirts over armour in this way was a common practice, especially during night attacks (such affairs being known as *camisadoes*) largely because of the difficulty of telling men apart when both wore the same clothing and spoke the same language.

7 The identity of Argyle's Regiment is unclear; it was most likely what remained of his 'Irish' regiment as it was clearly a regular unit, but there is a possibility that it was the small regiment from the Berwick garrison. As to 'the three that were joyned in one', although only some 300 strong, they must have been a pretty tough bunch for they comprised the remnants

of the Lord Chancellor's, Cassillis' and Glencairn's regiments and their having fought their way out of the disasters at Auldearn and Alford implies a certain hardiness.

8   Gordon of Ruthven, ibid. The 'reide cottes' were Home's.

9   Gordon of Ruthven, p. 145: perhaps not uncoincidentally a hillock by Baillie's start line is identified by the Ordnance Survey as 'Girnal Hill'. As a girnal is a store chest, was this where Baillie's baggage train was parked?

10 David Stevenson (ed.), *Government of Scotland under the Covenanters*, Scottish History Society, 1982, p. 21.

11 Traditionally he was also met at Gladsmuir by a messenger from the Earl of Traquair, telling him that the Royalists were still in Tweeddale, which may be true enough, although it seems unlikely that this news will have come as a surprise.

12 Gordon of Ruthven, p. 158.

13 *Acts of the Parliament of Scotland*, vol. 6, pp. 246–7. The Philiphaugh bounty warrants give a total of 700 men for Coupar's Regiment, yet Leslie is known to have had only 500 musketeers when he went in pursuit of the king. Presumably, to avoid jealousy, the bounty was paid to the whole regiment rather than to the musketeers alone.

14 Gordon of Ruthven, pp. 157–8. Ruthven has Powrie's patrol going out the previous evening, before Amisfield's outpost was surprised, and being 'deceaved' by the country people, but at that point Leslie must still have been on the other side of Galashiels.

15 Gordon of Ruthven, p. 159.

16 Anon. [W. H.], 'A more perfect and particular RELATION OF THE Late great VICTORIE in Scotland', London 25 September 1645.

17 Anon. [W. H.].

18 Wishart, p. 145.

19 Gordon of Ruthven, p. 11; *Extracts from the Council Register of Aberdeen*, vol. 1, p. 578.

20 In a rare moment of comedy the Earl Marischal and the other committee members imprisoned at Pitcaple Castle managed to lock their jailers outside while they were busy skinning an ox, and then held on to the place for twenty-four hours until the Master of Forbes turned up 'in the verie nick of tyme' – account by Alexander Jaffrey, in Spalding, vol. 2, pp. 505–6.

21 *Extracts from the Council Register of Aberdeen*, vol. 2, p. 60.

22 Fraser, pp. 315–16; Gordon of Ruthven, pp. 184–7.

23 Billeting records show that the foot in the burgh on 14 May belonged to Lord Kenmure's and Colonel William Stewart's regiments. These presumably accounted for the bulk of the prisoners.

24 *Extracts from the Council Register of Aberdeen*, vol. 2, p. 63; William Gordon, pp. 511–13; Gordon of Ruthven, pp. 187–8; Spalding, vol. 2, p. 499 (Appendix 16).

Chapter 8

1   National Archives (Kew) SP.41/2.

2   Leslie's Regiment was originally intended to have been commanded by William Stewart, but although a commission was drawn up for the latter on 29 January he declined on the grounds of age and infirmity.

3   David Stevenson, *Revolution and Counter-revolution 1644–1651*, London, 1977, p. 69. Similarly Sir James Campbell of Lawers' Regiment, still grimly holding on to Inverness, flatly refused to give up any of its men to the New Model or to return to Monro's army in Ireland unless their arrears of pay were met.

4   Ironically enough Hamilton had been out of circulation for some time because in 1643 he had gone to the English Royalist capital at Oxford as the Estates' commissioner, only to be denounced as a traitor by Montrose and imprisoned in Pendennis Castle for the duration of the war.

5   See Stevenson, *Revolution and Counter-revolution 1644–1651*, Chapter 3 for a fuller discussion of the political manoeuvrings which led to the signing of the Engagement with the king.

6   This was a purely local revolt which began when Poyer's men refused to disband without their arrears of pay and declared for the king only in hopes that he might pay them instead!

7   Turner, pp. 52–5. Turner was an engaging rogue who cheerfully declared: 'I had swallowed without chewing, in Germanie, a verie dangerous maxime, which all militarie men there too much follow; which was, that so we serve our master honestlie it is no matter which master we serve; so without examination . . . I resolved to go with that ship I first encountered' (ibid., p. 14). That random ship took him to serve in the Scots army at Marston Moor and in 1648 he was given command of Holburne's Regiment when that fanatical Covenanter resigned rather than serve the Engagers.

8   Brother to the more famous (or infamous) Sir John Hurry and sometimes confused with him.

9   George was the nephew and son-in-law of the 'Irish' army's commander, Robert Monro.

10 Brigadier Peter Young, *Edgehill 1642*, Kineton, 1967, p. 22 quotes the dramatist John Lacy, who had been a cavalry officer during the Civil War: 'Rascals, did I not know you at first to be three tattered musketeers, and by plundering a malt mill of three blind horses, you then turned dragooners.'

11 Turner, pp. 66–7.

12 Oliver Cromwell, *The Writings and Speeches of Oliver Cromwell*, ed. by W. C. Abbott and C. D. Crane, Harvard, 1937–47, vol. 1, p. 637.

13 Totals are set out in a contemporary pamphlet 'THREE LETTERS CONCERNING THE SURRENDER OF MANY Scottish Lords . . . Read in both Houses of Parliament the 25 of August 1648', while the colours are pictorially recorded in BM Harl.1460. Although the

latter are unlabelled it is possible to identify them both by heraldic devices and reconciling them with the numbers of ensigns who surrendered from each regiment:

Regiment:

Marquess of Argyle	10 officers, 5 sergeants, no private soldiers; one ensign/colour
Earl of Atholl	9 officers, 5 sergeants, 155 private soldiers; seven colours
William Baillie	5 officers (inc. Baillie), 4 sergeants, 120 private soldiers; three colours
Lord Bargany	6 officers, 6 sergeants, 82 private soldiers; two colours
Lord Carnegie	11 officers, 8 sergeants, 140 private soldiers; five colours
Richard Douglas	10 officers, 7 sergeants, 124 private soldiers; ten colours
Sir James Drummond	8 officers, 2 sergeants, 90 private soldiers; five colours
Earl of Dumfries	8 officers, 4 sergeants, 44 private soldiers; one colour
Fraser's Firelocks	6 officers, 4 sergeants, 150 private soldiers; two colours
Sir John Grey	3 officers, 32 private soldiers; one colour
Duke of Hamilton	17 officers, 19 sergeants, 360 private soldiers; eight colours
Sir Alexander Hamilton	3 officers 5 sergeants, 46 private soldiers; no identified colours
Lord Home	13 officers, 14 sergeants, 250 private soldiers; five colours
George Keith	8 officers, 4 sergeants, 130 private soldiers; five colours (misidentified in 'Three letters' as Lord Riche!)
Earl of Kellie	5 officers, 5 sergeants, 100 private soldiers; three colours
Harry Maule	5 officers, 3 sergeants, 119 private soldiers; four colours
Earl of Roxburgh	3 officers, 3 sergeants, 30 private soldiers; one colour
Earl of Tullibardine	4 officers, 11 sergeants, 116 private soldiers; two colours
James Turner	5 officers, 7 sergeants, 120 private soldiers; three colours
Lord Yester	19 officers, 12 sergeants, 50 private soldiers; eight colours

14 'Sir Philip Musgrave's "Relation" ', in Scottish History Society, *Miscellany II*, Edinburgh, 1904, p. 309.

15 The term supposedly derives from the traditional cry of 'Whiggam' used by western drovers, while those shouting it and by extension all of the Covenanters became known as Whigs.

Chapter 9

1 Again those requiring to know more of the political and diplomatic background to the events described in this chapter are referred to Chapter 4 of Stevenson, *Revolution and Counter-revolution*.

2 *Acts of the Parliament of Scotland*, vol. 6, pt ii, pp. 216–19.

3 Fraser, pp. 338–41. *Acts of the Parliament of Scotland*, vol. 6, pt ii, pp. 394–5.

4   Sir James Balfour (vol. 3, pp. 438–40) has a note that Montrose shipped 1,200 soldiers and officers for two regiments, besides twelve brass guns and the usual warlike stores. It is commented that 'most . . . was destroyed and spoyled', but it is unclear whether it was lost at sea or whether Montrose had been palmed off with useless rubbish. It is also unclear whether this represented all of the soldiers as he apparently only brought some 200 in March or April, or as seems more likely that the 1,200 actually included the Orcadian levies.

5   Wishart, p. 294. Montrose's orders to Hurry: 'part of my company of Guard, with four of my Life regiment, commanded by Lieutenant-Colonel George Drummond, with four other companies of Lieutenant-Colonel Henry Stewart's squadron'.

6   Balfour, vol. 4, p. 9. The 'Irish Troop' is not to be confused with the remnants of Monro's army but was about forty strong and formed in August 1649 from Scots Presbyterian refugees from Ulster. A regiment of foot, four companies strong was also formed from these refugees and later assigned as the king's lifeguard. The identity of Captain Cullace or Collace is unclear.

7   After forming the garrison of Inverness for nearly four years, Lawers' Regiment came south in 1648, but refused to serve under Hamilton. Its movements at that point are obscure, but it may have joined Livingston at Carlisle for a time and afterwards served under Leslie. In February 1649 Lawers was assigned to command the new levies to be raised out of the sheriffdom of Linlithgow, but such men as were raised went into his old regiment rather than forming a new one. Thereafter it appears to have been quartered in Fife before being ordered back up to Inverness. The fact the detachment at Carbisdale was commanded by the quartermaster suggests that this was the only advance party and that the main body of the regiment had not then reached Inverness.

8   While there were doubts as to Lemlair's reliability since he had been 'out' with Pluscardine the year before, there is no evidence to support the popular story that he was actually marching to join Montrose when he accidentally fell in with Strachan and prudently switched sides.

9   Balfour, vol. 4, p. 11. A number of the officers, including Sir John Hurry, were executed, but the majority of the common soldiers were given to Lord Angus and Sir Robert Murray as recruits for their regiments in the French service.

10   A want of any other narrative evidence has compelled reliance upon Gilbert Gordon of Sallagh's *Continuation of a History of the Earldom of Sutherland*. There is no reason to doubt his veracity, but this caveat must be borne in mind.

11   See Appendix 3.

12   Terry, *Life and Campaigns of Alexander Leslie*, p. 474.

13   It might also suggest that the only men willing to come forward were veterans who insisted through long experience on having horses.

14 See Appendix 3.

15 Fraser, ibid.

16 Balfour, vol. 4, p. 89; Sir Edward Walker, *Historical Discourses upon Several Occasions . . .*,
    London, 1705, p. 165.

17 This is not coincidental as the levelled defences served as the foundations for the causeway.

18 Balfour, vol. 4, p. 87.

19 C. S. Terry, 'A true relation of the proceedings of the English army', in C. S. Terry, *The Life
    and Campaigns of Alexander Leslie*, London, 1899, p. 458.

20 Balfour, vol. 3, p. 412.

21 Sir Edward Walker (ibid., p. 163) has a story about Cromwell having to escape in his drawers,
    which if not true certainly ought to be.

22 W. S. Douglas, *Cromwell's Scotch Campaigns*, London, 1898, pp. 81–5. Cromwell rather
    enterprisingly claimed to have killed 'about 80' in the skirmishing before aborting his assault,
    while on the Scots side John Nicoll rather more precisely recorded 'xij of our army hurt, ane
    killed and twa horses'.

Chapter 10

1 Terry, *The Life and Campaigns of Alexander Leslie*, p. 475.

2 Cromwell, vol. 2, pp. 305–14.

3 Sir Henry Slingsby and John Hodgson, *Original Memoirs Written During the Great Civil War;
   Being the Life of Sir Henry Slingsby and Memoirs of Capt. Hodgson*, Edinburgh, 1806, pp. 143–4.

4 Douglas identifies the brigade as Lumsden's Fifers, but in the circumstances it is rather more
   likely to have been Innes' men from the north of Scotland.

5 Terry, *The Life and Campaigns of Alexander Leslie*, p.475.

6 BM Harl.6844. See Appendix 2.

7 Cromwell, vol. 2, pp. 305–14. Five of the seven cavalry regiments belonged to the original
   New Model and John Lambert's had belonged the old Northern Association. Colonel Francis
   Hacker's Regiment on the other hand was only recruited in 1648, though that is not to
   say there were no veterans in the ranks. As to the infantry only three of the eight infantry
   regiments at Dunbar – Colonel Alban Coxe's, the Lord General's and Thomas Pride's –
   were products of the new modelling back in 1645, although Colonel George Monck's was
   formed at the outset of the campaign by combining five companies of Sir Arthur Hesilrige's
   Regiment and five companies of Colonel George Fenwick's. Both parent regiments could
   trace their history under various commanders back to the New Model and beyond. (Oddly
   enough, at the last minute the remaining five companies of Fenwick's Regiment also marched
   north with the army.) Again John Lambert's Foot was also a good regiment which had served
   since 1643 under Colonel John Bright in the old Northern Association, but both Colonel

Charles Fairfax's and John Malverer's regiments were raised as recently as 1648, and while present at the siege of Pontefract in that year they had otherwise seen virtually no action. The last regiment, Colonel William Daniel's, was newly recruited in 1650 and had originally been intended for service in Ireland.

8   Baillie, vol. 3, p. 111.

9   Terry, *The Life and Campaigns of Alexander Leslie*, p. 476.

10   Slingsby and Hodgson, pp. 144–6.

11   Cromwell, vol. 2, pp. 305–14.

12   Fitzpayne Fisher, or Payne Fisher (1615–93), was a sometime professional soldier-turned-artist and poet, who made copies of all the Scots colours captured at Preston and Dunbar and spent some ten months in Scotland in 1653 gathering information on the Dunbar campaign for a proposed Latin verse history. This never materialised, but one concrete result was his well-known picture-map of the battle, now in the Bodleian Library, based on extensive interviews with the participants: *Oxford Dictionary of National Biography*, Oxford, 2009.

13   W. H. D. Longstaffe, *Memoires of the Life of Ambrose Barnes*, Surtees Society, 1866, vol. 1, p. 111. Barnes had the story from a Henry Hudson 'then upon the place'.

14   Cromwell, vol. 2, pp. 305–14.

15   T. Gumble, *The Life of General Monck*, London, 1671, p. 38.

16   Slingsby and Hodgson, p. 147.

17   The writer acknowledges with respect C. H. Firth's seminal 'The Battle of Dunbar', *Transactions of the Royal Historical Society*, no. 14 (1900), pp. 19–52, but obviously begs to differ with his reconstruction.

18   Walker, p. 181.

Chapter 11

1   According to regimental legend the present Scots Guards trace their lineage through this regiment to the Marquess of Argyle's Regiment formed for service in Ulster in 1642. In point of fact no direct connection exists, although a number of officers do appear to have served in the original Ulster army. Its commander, James Wallace of Auchans, was a fanatical Covenanter who later led the insurgents at the battle of Rullion Green in 1666.

2   Baillie, vol. 3, p. 112.

3   The term is sometimes inaccurately applied to the border reivers of the sixteenth century, but the earliest recorded use of the term dates to 1646, and it was applied to landless men hiding in the mosses rather than sallying forth from their family tower houses.

4   Baillie, vol. 3, p. 122; Douglas, p. 170.

5   All but the first were horse and no doubt for the most part lancers. Kirkcudbright's were

originally raised as dragooners, but it is questionable whether they were still serving as mounted infantry.

6   Douglas, pp. 182–5; Somerville, vol. 2, pp. 438–50; Baillie, vol. 3, p. 125.

7   Balfour, vol. 4, pp. 209–10; Douglas, p. 204. Augustine's identity is not entirely certain for he was pretty universally referred to simply as Augustine the Mosser. Balfour calls him 'a heigh Germane being purged out of the armey before Dunbar Drove, bot a stout and resolute young man and lover of the Scotts natione'. He was most likely therefore the Captain Augustine Hoffman who had served in David Leslie's Horse since 1644. Douglas expresses doubts as to the legend of how Augustine broke into and then escaped from Edinburgh, but after three uneventful months the English cannot have been very alert and as he was to prove on a number of occasions Augustine was capable enough of doing it.

8   According to Balfour (ibid.), Augustine's reinforcement were the only soldiers in the garrison to oppose surrender and to take up the customary offer to return to their own lines after the capitulation.

9   Douglas, p. 220.

10 C. H. Firth and Godfrey Davies, *Regimental History of Cromwell's Army*, Oxford, 1940, vol. 1, pp. 240–1.

11 This was of course General Baillie's house and normally referred to as such by English correspondents, although he himself does not figure in the story.

12 Douglas, p. 264. They were rather optimistically said by English newsbooks to total some 19,000 men, while the Scots were estimated at 24,000. Both figures are of course far too high.

13 Lambert's, Robert Lilburne's and Alured's regiments.

14 Douglas, pp. 270–1. Galbraith is referred to as 'Lieut. Gebath' in English sources, but this was clearly a (common) contraction for Lieutenant-Colonel since a post of this size and importance would not have been entrusted to such a junior officer. Galbraith himself was one of those killed.

15 Lambert was for some reason under the impression the Scots were commanded by Sir John Browne of Fordell, but Balfour (vol. 4, p. 313) explicitly names Holburne.

16 Bulstrode Whitelocke, *Memorials of the English Affairs*, Oxford, 1853, vol. 3, pp. 321–3.

17 Information on Lambert's units is drawn from Firth and Davies.

18 When Leslie surrendered Inverkeithing on 29 July his garrison was said to have been 500 strong. Not all of them of course will have been drawn out to fight in the battle and, while many of those who did were obviously killed there, the garrison may also have been swelled afterwards by men from other units. It would not be unreasonable therefore to suggest that some 300 of Barclay's Regiment took part in the battle, allowing for those necessarily left behind to guard the burgh.

19 Edward Furgol, *A Regimental History of the Covenanting Armies*, Edinburgh, 1990, pp. 303, 323.

20 The evidence as to this is uncertain, but Gray's brother Robert was apparently killed at Inverkeithing.

21 Fraser, p. 384: 'Lambert came on, committing the right wing of the horse to Okey, Colonel Lydcot in the left wing and Overton in the reserve. A furious fight began. Okey couragiously charged up the hill, and was a& gallantly charged by the Scotch Lanciers, with great slaughter. The brunt of the battle continued about 3 houres. The Highland foot did great service, and the greatest slaughter was upon them, most justly imputed to command, for hellish Hoborn came not up, which if he had the Scotch had carried it but doubt. There were 2000 slain, and a 1000 taken prisoners. The English had near as great losse, but were double in number; for the Scots were but 4000 in all. Major-General Sir John Brown, Colonel Buchan [Buchannan], Colonel Scot, were taken prisoners; Mcklean and all his regiment were cutt off, standing in their ranks, without help, treacherously; and brave Brown dyed shortly after at Leith.'

22 Whitelocke, ibid.

23 Douglas, p. 282. As Douglas notes, all the English chroniclers seem to have been struck by how suddenly and decisively the battle turned in their favour.

24 Balfour, vol. 4, p. 313.

25 Derby's military commander, Sir Thomas Tyldesley, was killed, and a local tradition holds that Lilburne cried to give his men no quarter. Derby escaped from the field but was afterwards captured and executed.

26 Not of course Duke James, who lost his head after the Preston débâcle, but his younger brother William, previously encountered in these pages as the erstwhile Earl of Lanark.

27 Earl of Clarendon, *History of the Rebellion*, Oxford, 1888, vol. 3, p. 550.

28 Clarendon, vol. 3, p. 540.

29 Effectively that was the end of Leslie, who seems to have had a nervous breakdown, but Middleton although imprisoned for a time in the Tower of London eventually escaped dressed in his wife's clothes.

30 Having done so he is last heard of prudently taking ship for Norway.

Appendices

1   Transcript in Gilbert, vol. 4, p. 54.

2   Carte, vol. 1, pp. 73–6.

3   Perth; or as it was more properly styled St John's town of Perth.

4   As discussed in Chapter 5 it is clear from this passage that the despatch, evidently edited for publication, was originally written by Alasdair MacColla himself.

Bibliography

Primary Sources

Aberdeen Extracts from the Council Register of the Burgh of Aberdeen 1625–1747, Scottish Burgh Records Society, Edinburgh, 1871–72, 2 vols

Acts of the Parliament of Scotland, Record Commission, 1835, vol. 6

Anon. [W. H.], 'A more perfect and particular RELATION OF THE Late great VICTORIE in Scotland', London, 25 September 1645

Anon., 'True rehearsall; a little yet true rehearsal of severall passages of affairs, collected by a friend of Doctor Alexander's at Aberdeen', *Transactions of the Royal Historical Society*, vol. 5 (1877), p. 61

Baillie, Robert, *Letters and Journals*, 3 vols, Bannatyne Club, 1841–2

Balfour, Sir William, *Historical Works*, Edinburgh, 1823–5

Barriffe, William, *Militarie Discipline; or The Young Artilleryman*, 6th edn 1661

Bulloch, J. M., *The House of Gordon (Gordons under Arms)*, Spalding Club, 1903–12, 3 vols

Carte, Thomas, *A Collection of Original Letters and Papers*, London, 1739

Clarendon, Earl of, *History of the Rebellion*, Oxford, 1888, 6 vols

Cromwell, Oliver, *The Writings and Speeches of Oliver Cromwell*, ed. by W. C. Abbott and C. D. Crane, Harvard, 1937–47

Cruso, John, *Militarie Instructions for the Cavallrie*, Cambridge, 1635

Firth, C. H. (ed.), *Newcastle, Duchess of: The Life of . . . William Cavendish, Duke of Newcastle*, London, 1886

Fraser, James, *Chronicles of the Frasers; The Wardlaw Manuscript*, Scottish History Society, Edinburgh, 1905

Gilbert, J. (ed.), *History of the Irish Confederation and War in Ireland 1641–1649*, Dublin, 1888

Gordon, Gilbert, of Sallagh, *Continuation of a History of the Earldom of Sutherland by Sir Robert Gordon of Gordonstoun*, Edinburgh, 1813

Gordon, James, of Rothiemay, *History of Scots Affairs*, 3 vols, Spalding Club, 1841

Gordon, Patrick, of Ruthven, *A Short Abridgement of Britane's Distemper*, Spalding Club, 1844

Gordon, William, *The History on the Ancient, Noble and Illustrious Family of Gordon*, Edinburgh, 1727

Gumble, T., *The Life of General Monck*, London, 1671

Hope, Sir Thomas, *A Diary of the Public Correspondence etc., 1633–1645*, Bannatyne Club, 1843

Longstaffe, W. H. D., *Memoires of the Life of Ambrose Barnes*, Surtees Society, 1866

Napier, M., *Memorials of Montrose*, Maitland Club, 1848

Rushworth, John, *Historical Collections . . . 1618–1649*, London, 1659–1701

Scottish History Society, 'Sir Philip Musgrave's "Relation" ', in *Miscellany II*, Edinburgh, 1904

Slingsby, Sir Henry and Hodgson, John, *Original Memoirs Written During the Great Civil War; Being the Life of Sir Henry Slingsby and Memoirs of Capt. Hodgson*, Edinburgh, 1806

Somerville, James, *Memorie of the Somervills*, Edinburgh, 1815

Spalding, John, *Memorialls of the Trubles in Scotland 1627–1645*, 2 vols, Spalding Club, 1850–1

Terry, C. S., *Papers Relating to the Army of the Solemn League and Covenant*, Scottish History Society, 1917–18, 2 vols

Turner, Sir James, *Memoirs of His Own Life and Times*, ed. by T. Thomson, Bannatyne Club, 1829

Walker, Sir Edward, *Historical Discourses upon Several Occasions . . .*, London, 1705

Whitelocke, Bulstrode, *Memorials of the English Affairs*, Oxford, 1853

Wishart, George, *Memoirs of James, Marquis of Montrose, 1639–1650*, London, 1893

Secondary Sources

Anon., *The Thistle of Scotland: A Selection of Ancient Ballads*, Aberdeen, 1823

Atholl, John, Duke of, *Chronicles of the Atholl and Tullibardine Families*,
　Edinburgh, 1908

Buchan, John, *Montrose*, London, 1928

Cowan, Edward, *Montrose, For Covenant and King*, London, 1977

Donaldson, Gordon, *Scotland: James V to James VII*, Edinburgh, 1965

Douglas, W. S., *Cromwell's Scotch Campaigns*, London, 1898

Eliott, Fitzwilliam, *The Trustworthiness of Border Ballads, Edinburgh* 1906

Firth, C. H., 'The Battle of Dunbar', *Transactions of the Royal Historical Society*,
　vol. 14 (1900), pp. 19–52

Firth, C. H., *Cromwell's Army*, Oxford, 1962

Firth, C. H. and Davies, Godfrey, *Regimental History of Cromwell's Army*,
　Oxford, 1940

Furgol, Edward, *A Regimental History of the Covenanting Armies*,
　Edinburgh, 1990

Hume Brown, P., *History of Scotland*, Edinburgh, 1909

Marren, Peter, *Grampian Battlefields*, Aberdeen, 1990

Merriman, Marcus, *The Rough Wooings; Mary Queen of Scots 1542–1551*,
　East Linton, 2000

Reid, Stuart, *All the King's Armies; A Military History of the English Civil War*,
　Staplehurst, 1998

Reid, Stuart, *The Campaigns of Montrose*, Edinburgh, 1990

Reid, Stuart, *Scots Armies of the English Civil War*, Oxford, 1999

Reid, Stuart, *Scots Colours*, Leigh on Sea, 1990

Stevenson, David, *Alasdair MacColla and the Highland Problem in the 17th Century*,
　Edinburgh, 1980

Stevenson, David (ed.), *Government of Scotland under the Covenanters*, Scottish
　History Society, 1982

Stevenson, David, *Revolution and Counter-revolution in Scotland 1644–1651*,
　London, 1977

Stevenson, David, *Scottish Covenanters and Irish Confederates*, Belfast, 1981

Stevenson, David, *The Scottish Revolution 1637–1644*, Newton Abbot, 1973

Terry, C. S., *The Life and Campaigns of Alexander Leslie*, London, 1899

Warburton, E., *Memoirs of Prince Rupert and the Cavaliers*, London, 1849

Young, Brigadier Peter, *Edgehill 1642*, Kineton, 1967

Young, Brigadier Peter, *Marston Moor 1644*, Kineton, 1970

Young, P. and Holmes, R., *The English Civil War; A Military History of the Three
　Civil Wars*, London, 1974

Index

Aberdeen, 7, 17, 19–20, 23, 53, 63–9, 74, 83, 84, 87, 102, 124, 125, 126, 193, 202
Aboyne, Viscount, *see* Gordon of Aboyne, James
Agnew, Lieut.-Col. James, 121–3
Alford (battle), 104–7
Alyth, 193
Antrim, Earl of, *see* McDonnell, Randall
Appleby, 134
Arbroath, 86
Argyle, Marquess of, *see* Campbell, Archibald
Arnott, Sir Charles, 63
Atholl, Earl of, *see* Murray, John
Augustine the Mosser, *see* Hoffman, Augustine
Auldearn (battle), 89–101

Baillie, William, 47, 49–50, 78, 84–7, 101–3, 104–7, 108, 109–17, 133, 135, 137, 138, 139–40, 223 n. 1
Balcarres, Earl of, *see* Lindsay, Alexander
Balfour of Burleigh, Robert, 63, 111, 112, 205
Balgonie, Lord, *see* Leslie, Alexander
Ballantyne, Lieut.-Col. James, 40
Balvenie, 144–5
Banff, 125
Barclay, Col. Harie, 125, 185
Belasyse, Col. John, 45

Berwick upon Tweed, 29, 35, 37, 119, 120, 131, 142, 213 n. 1
Blackadder, Capt., 122, 125
Blackness Castle, 181, 182
Blair Castle, 59, 77, 78, 84, 101–2, 124, 201, 202
Boldon Hill (battle), 43–4, 214 n. 16
Brig o'Dee (battle), 26–8
Browne of Fordell, Sir John, 178, 186, 188–9
Bruce, Col. Andrew, 42–3
Burntisland, 185
Butler, James, Earl of Ormonde, 197

Callendar House, 184, 185
Campbell, Archibald, Marquess of Argyle, 38–9, 51–2, 56, 62, 74, 76–7, 78–82, 103, 109, 111, 112, 131
Campbell, John, Earl of Loudoun, 141
Campbell, Lieut.-Col. William, 100
Campbell of Auchinbrec, Sir Duncan, 78–82
Campbell of Lawers, Sir James, 154, 168–9, 170, 172–3, 205
Campbell of Lawers, Sir Mungo 92–6, 100
Carbisdale (battle), 146–8
Carlisle, 70, 86, 119, 131, 134, 142, 191

Cavendish, William, Marquis of Newcastle, 36–9, 41, 43–5
Charles I, King of Scots, 2–6, 7, 17, 28–9, 32–3, 34–5, 46, 126–7, 130–1, 142–3, 145, 148–9
Charles II, King of Scots, 176, 177–8, 182, 183–4, 190–3
Charteris of Amisfield, Alexander, 121
Clavering, Sir Robert, 57–8
Cochrane, Col. John, 33
Cockburn, Lieut.-Col. John, 79, 85, 173, 220 n. 26
Cockburnspath, 160
Conway, Viscount, 30–2
Corbridge (battle), 40
Corgarff, 103
Coupar, Lord, 205–6
Crawford, Earl of, *see* Lindsay, Ludovick
Crawford, Major Hugh, 213 n. 1
Crawford, Lawrence, 50
Crichton of Frendraught, 87
Crichton, Lord, 63–4, 65–7
Crieff, 86
Cromwell, Oliver, 46, 48, 49–50, 135–40, 142, 149, 154–5, 156–8, 160–75, 178–9, 182, 183, 184, 185–6, 190–3, 227 n. 21
Cumbernauld Band, 51–2
Cunningham, William, Earl of Glencairn, 132, 193

Dalkeith, 119
Dalyell of the Binns, Col.
    Thomas, 192
Derby, Earl of, *see* Stanley, James
Dirleton Castle, 179
Douglas, Sir William, 32
Douglas, William, Marquis of
    Douglas, 119
Douglas of Kirkness, Col., 170
Douglas of Mouswall, Sir James,
    174, 206
Doune Castle, 86
Downing, George, 181
Drummond, David, Master of
    Madderty, 61
Drummond, George, of Balloch,
    105, 226 n. 5
Drummond, Sir John, 59
Drummond, Lord, 61, 216 n. 20
Drummond, Major, 92, 98, 221
    n. 15
Dudhope, Lord, 215 n. 26
Dudly, Sir Gamaliel, 40
Dumbarton, 17, 18, 182
Dumfries, 56–7
Dunaverty Castle, 130
Dunbar, 157, 158
Dunbar (battle), 160–75
Dunbeath Castle, 145
Dunblane, 129
Dundas, Col. William, 181–2
Dundee, 84–7, 193
Dunoon (massacre), 129
Dunottar Castle, 193
Dunyveg Castle, 120

Edinburgh, 23, 117, 119, 141,
    154–5, 175, 182, 183
Edinburgh Castle, 18, 29, 141,
    175, 181–2
Eglinton, Earl of, *see*
    Montgomerie, Alexander
Elgin, 82, 87, 126
English, Capt. Patrick, 39
Evanson, Capt. William, 155

Fairfax, Ferdinando, Lord, 46
Fairfax, Sir Thomas, 46–50,
    119–20, 131, 149
Farquharson of Inverey, John,
    116, 125
Farquharson of Monaltrie,
    Donald, 21, 24, 55–6, 77, 83
Fisher, Payne, 228 n. 12

Fleetwood, Major-Gen. Charles,
    167, 168, 169, 191–2
Forbes, Major Arthur, 63
Forbes, Lord, 63, 67
Forbes, William, Master of
    Forbes, 124, 206, 223 n. 20
Forbes of Craigievar, Sir William,
    63–4, 67, 77, 219 n. 15
Forbes of Lairgie, John, 67
Forbes of Leslie, Col. John, 152
Forbes of Millbuie, Col. George,
    87
Forfar, 86
Fraser, Lord, 20–1, 63–4, 65–7
Fyvie (battle), 74–6, 202

Galbraith, Lieut.-Col., 185, 229
    n. 14
Gateshead, 70–1
Gladman, Capt. John, 155
Gladsmuir, 120, 121, 154, 223
    n. 11
Glasgow, 111, 117–18, 125, 132,
    178, 183, 184
Glencairn, Earl of, *see*
    Cunningham, William
Glenham, Sir Thomas, 37, 43
Gogar (action), 158
Gordon, George, Lord Gordon,
    59, 63, 82, 85, 91, 98–9, 103,
    105–7
Gordon, George, Marquis of
    Huntly, 17, 18–19, 20, 53–4,
    56, 118, 125–6, 128, 144
Gordon, Lieut. John, 85, 220
    n. 28
Gordon, Lewis, Marquis of
    Huntly, 63–4, 67, 85, 124–5,
    126, 144, 145, 178, 193
Gordon, Nathaniel, 26, 55–6, 65,
    67, 77, 83, 94, 97, 115, 117,
    122–3, 219 n. 15
Gordon of Aboyne, James,
    Viscount Aboyne, 23, 24–8,
    86–7, 98, 105, 108, 110, 115,
    118–19, 124
Gordon of Arradoul, William,
    27, 124
Gordon of Cluny, Sir Alexander,
    19
Gordon of Haddo, Sir John,
    21, 53
Gordon of Littlemill, Capt. John,
    78, 115

Gordon of Rhynie, James, 87
Graham, James, Marquis of
    Montrose, 19, 20, 23, 25–8,
    30, 51–2, 53, 56–9, 83–4,
    102–3, 110, 124–6, 128,
    145, 148
    at Aberdeen 62–69
    at Alford 104–8
    at Auldearn 94–95, 98, 101
    at Carbisdale 146–48, 226 n.
        4–5
    at Dundee 84–87
    at Fyvie 74–76
    at Inverlochy 78–82
    at Kilsyth 110–117
    at Philiphaugh 120–124
    at Tibbermore 59–62
Graham, John, Lord Kilpont, 59,
    62, 65, 201
Graham of Inchbrackie, Patrick,
    59–60, 124
Grant of Freuchie, James, 59,
    74, 82
Grant of Shewglie, Robert, 100
Grey, Col. Edward, 35
Gunn, Col. William, 24–8

Haddington, 154, 159, 175
Haldane of Gleneagles, Col.
    John, 173
Haldane, Archibald, 18
Haldane, Major John, 112–13
Halkerton Wood (skirmish), 84
Halkett of Pitfirrane, Sir James,
    74, 157, 181
Hamilton, Alexander (Sandie),
    14, 18, 43
Hamilton, James, 1st Duke of
    Hamilton, 5, 6, 17, 23–4,
    33, 131, 133–4, 135–8, 140,
    224 n. 4
Hamilton, William, 2nd Duke
    of Hamilton, 111, 117, 141,
    192
Hamilton, Lanarkshire, 179–81,
    183
Harcourt, Sir Simon, 23
Hay, Col. James, 65
Hay of Delgaty, James, 22
Hay of Muriefauld, James, 63
Hay of Yester, James, 8
Hepburn, Major Robert, 73
Hereford (siege), 120
Hexham, 40

Hoffman, Col. Augustine, 181–2, 189, 193, 229 n. 7, 230 n. 30
Holborne, Major-Gen. James, 115, 116, 144, 166, 168–9, 170, 173–4, 186, 188–90, 207
Holyrood Park (action), 154
Home, Lieut.-Col. George, 174
Home, Col. Robert, 102
Home of Wedderburn, Sir David, 174, 206
Hope, Sir Thomas, 32
Huntly, Marquis of, *see* Gordon, George or Gordon, Lewis
Hurry, Sir John, 83–7, 90–101, 102, 103, 108, 110, 145, 147–8, 226 n. 9
Hurry, Col. William, 133, 224 n. 8
Hylton, 214 n. 16

Innes, Col. John, 169, 173–4, 177, 206–7
Inverary, 78
Inverkeithing, 185–90, 229 n. 18
Inverlochy, 78–82, 203
Inverness, 74, 78, 88, 101, 102–3, 125–6, 144
Irvine of Drum, Alexander, 54–6

Jedburgh, 119
Johnston, Col. William, 21–2, 25–7
Johnston of Wariston, Archibald, 152

Keith, Capt. Alexander, 63–4, 77
Keith, Col. George, 137, 191–2
Keith, William, Earl Marischal, 22, 24, 223 n. 20
Keith of Clackriach, James, 63–4
Keith of Ludquharn, Alexander, 22
Keith, Banffshire, 103
Kennedy, Lieut.-Col. John, 107, 115, 223 n. 29
Ker of Greenhead, Sir Andrew, 206
Ker, Lieut.-Col. James, 174
Kerr, Col. Gilbert (Gibby), 144–5, 176, 178, 179–81
Kilmarnock, 183
Kilsyth, 110–17
Kinghorn, Earl of, *see* Lyon, John
Kintore, Aberdeenshire, 124–5

Kintyre, 128
Kirkwall, 145
Knocknanus (battle), 130

Laghtnan, Col. Thomas, 122–3
Lambert, John, 131, 134–5, 154–5, 156, 164, 166, 168, 169, 172, 175, 179–80, 181, 184, 186–90, 191
Lanark, Earl of, *see* Hamilton, William, 2nd Duke of Hamilton
Langdale, Sir Marmaduke, 40, 41, 131, 135–7, 140
Leith, 23, 29, 154, 155, 190
Leslie, Alexander, Earl of Leven, 17, 18, 20, 28, 30, 33, 40–6, 50, 70–3, 119–20, 128–9, 153, 154–5, 158, 170, 193
Leslie, Alexander, Lord Balgonie, 40, 49
Leslie, David, 38–9, 47–50, 70, 119–24, 129–30, 141, 144, 147, 150, 158, 162–76, 182, 183–4, 190, 192–3, 223 n. 11, 239 n. 29
Leslie, Major-Gen. John, 113, 115, 186, 229 n. 18
Leslie, Col. Patrick, 44
Leslie Castle, 104
Leven, Earl of, *see* Leslie, Alexander
Lilburne, Col. Robert, 166, 191, 230 n. 25
Lindsay, Alexander, Earl of Balcarres, 83, 107, 112–13, 117, 193
Lindsay, John, Earl of Lindsay, 102, 103, 108, 110, 112, 116, 215 n. 1
Lindsay, Ludovick, Earl of Crawford, 57, 71, 117, 118–19, 122, 124, 125, 215 n. 1
Linlithgow, 141, 176, 182–3, 184
Livingston, James, Earl of Callendar, 57, 58, 133, 134, 135, 136–8, 139–40, 218 n. 2
Lumsden, Sir James, 41, 44, 47, 49, 168–9, 170, 205, 214 n. 21
Lunsford, Col. Thomas, 31
Lyell, Col. William, 42–3

Lyon, John, Earl of Kinghorn, 19, 20, 23
Lytcott, Col. Leonard, 186, 189
McClellan, Thomas, Lord Kirkcudbright, 207
MacColla, Alasdair, 58–9, 65, 67–8, 74, 78–82, 84–6, 89–91, 92–8, 100, 103, 108, 113, 115, 118, 128–30, 197, 201–3, 218 n. 10, 220 n. 10
McDermott, Col. James, 219 n. 19
MacDonald, Angus, of Glengarry, 105
MacDonald, Col. Keitach, 120
McDonnell, Lieut.-Gen. Alexander, 197–8
McDonnell, Lieut.-Col. John, 219 n. 19
McDonnell, Randall, Earl of Antrim, 53, 56, 128, 197
Mackenzie, Capt. Bernard, 100
Mackenzie, George, Earl of Seaforth, 59, 78, 87, 103
Mackenzie of Pluscardine, Thomas, 144
Maclean of Duart, Hector, 190
Maclean of Treshnish, Ewen, 113
Marley, Sir John, 38–9, 71–3
Marston Moor (battle), 47–50
Massey, Major-Gen. Edward, 191
Mauchline Moor (battle), 132–3
Megray Hill (battle), 24–6
Melvill, Lieut.-Col. Robert, 173
Menzies, Major William, 174
Mercer, Lieut.-Col. James, 40
Methven Wood (skirmish), 108
Michell, Rev. Thomas, 21
Middleton, Major-Gen. John, 27, 124–5, 125–6, 132–3, 138, 140, 144, 145, 178, 193, 230 n. 29
Mingarry Castle, 58
Monck, Col. George, 133, 134, 141, 165, 166, 169, 170, 185, 190–1, 193
Monro, Major-Gen. George, 133, 134, 137–8, 141–2, 224 n. 9
Monro, Major-Gen. Robert, 18, 110
Montgomerie, Alexander, Earl of Eglinton, 47, 182
Montgomerie, Major John, 45, 49

Montgomerie, Robert (Robin), 49, 156, 168, 178, 179, 182–3, 191–2
Montgomery, Lieut.-Col. Hew, 126
Montrose (battle), 55–6
Montrose, Marquis of, *see* Graham, James
Morpeth, 37–8, 57–8
Mortimer, Capt. John, 65, 67–8, 83, 119
Moss-troopers, 179, 181–2, 228 n. 3
Munro, John, of Lemlair, 147–8, 226 n. 8
Murray, James, Earl of Tullibardine, 60–1, 112
Murray, John, Earl of Atholl, 177–8
Murray, Sir John, 100
Musgrave, Sir Philip, 131, 134
Musselburgh, 154, 155, 156–7, 158

Napier, Archibald, Lord Napier, 105, 117
Newark upon Trent, 128, 129
Newburn (battle), 30–2
Newcastle, Marquis of, *see* Cavendish, William
Newcastle upon Tyne, 30–2, 37, 38–9, 70–3
new modelling, 127, 129
Newtyle, 103, 178

O'Cahan, Lieut.-Col. Donoghue, 80, 81, 219 n. 13
O'Cahan, Col. Manus, 77, 122–3, 219 n. 13
Ogilvie, Sir David, 178
Ogilvie, James, Earl of Airlie, 56, 115
Ogilvie, James, Lord Findlater, 100
Ogilvie, Lord, 144, 178
Ogilvie, Sir Thomas, 65, 67, 78, 82
Ogilvie of Banff, Sir George, 21
Ogilvie of Boyne, Walter, 100
Ogilvie of Powrie, Thomas, 121, 223 n. 14
Okey, Col. John, 184
Orkney, 145
Overton, Col. Robert, 168, 185, 190

Paisley, 183
Penrith, 134
Penshaw Hill (battle), 41–2, 213 n. 11, 214 n. 13
Perth, 62, 108, 177, 190
Philiphaugh (battle), 120–4
Pitcaple Castle, 223 n. 20
Pitreavie Castle, 190
Pitscottie, Major-Gen. Colin, 49, 168–9, 173–4, 192, 206
Powick bridge, 191–2
Prat, David, 20
Preston (battle), 135–8
Pride, Col. Thomas, 168, 170–2

Rae, Col. James, 38
Ralston of Ralston, Lieut.-Col. William, 180
Ramsay, Sir James, 74
Redhall, 158
Regiments (English),
  Brandling's Horse, 40
  Bright's Foot, 139
  Cambridge Trained Band, 23
  Coxe's Foot, 168, 227 n. 7
  Earl of Crawford's Horse, 56, 168, 172
  Daniel's Foot, 168, 186, 189, 227 n. 7
  Charles Fairfax's Foot, 159, 168, 227 n. 7
  George Fenwick's Foot, 166, 186, 189, 227 n. 7
  Sir John Fenwick's Horse, 40
  Fleetwood's Horse, 166
  Hacker's Horse, 155, 166, 175, 227 n. 7
  Harcourt's Foot, 23
  Hesilrige's Foot, 227 n. 7
  Hesilrige's Horse, 183
  Kent Trained Band, 23
  Lambert's Foot, 157, 168, 172, 186, 189, 227 n. 7
  Lambert's Horse, 155, 166, 186, 188, 189, 227 n. 7
  Langdale's Horse, 40
  Lilburne's Horse, 156, 166, 172
  Lord General's Foot, 168, 172, 227 n. 7
  Lytcott's Horse, 186, 188, 189
  Malverer's Foot, 166, 227 n. 7
  Monck's Foot, 166, 227 n. 7

Newcastle Trained Band, 38, 71–3
Okey's Dragoons, 168, 186, 188, 189
Pride's Foot, 139, 168, 172, 227 n. 7
Suffolk Trained Band, 23
Syler's Foot, 186, 189
Twisleton's Horse, 166
Weldon's Horse, 214 n. 12
West's Foot, 186, 189
Whalley's Horse, 155, 156, 166
Regiments (Scottish),
  Aberdeen Militia, 20, 24, 25, 26–8, 63–4, 68–9, 83, 211 n. 6, 212 n. 15
  Adair of Kinhilt's Horse, 208
  Earl of Airlie's Horse, 122
  Arbuthnott's Foot, 150
  Marquess of Argyle's Foot, 57, 78, 113–14, 116, 129, 152, 207, 213 n. 1, 223 n. 7, 225 n. 13, 228 n. 1
  Arnott's Horse, 188, 208
  General of the Artillery's Foot, 44, 47, 72, 129, 170, 205, 225 n. 13
  Earl of Atholl's Foot, 225 n. 13
  Augustine's Horse, 188–9, 229 n. 8
  Baillie's Foot, 72, 218 n. 6, 225 n. 13
  Earl of Balcarres' Horse, 8, 83–4, 103, 105, 107, 113, 121, 188
  Balfour of Burleigh's Foot, 205
  Balgonie's Horse, 48, 49
  Balmerino's Foot, 151, 207
  Barclay's Dragoons, 125
  Barclay's Foot, 229 n. 18
  Barclay's Horse, 115, 120, 125
  Bargany's Foot, 225 n. 13
  Brechin's Horse, 178, 188–9, 208
  Browne's Horse, 178, 207
  Browne's Dragoons, 117
  Earl of Buccleugh's Foot, 47, 49, 72
  Buchannan's Foot, 74, 91–2, 188–90, 207
  Earl of Callander's Foot, 102, 104, 107, 142
  Campbell of Ardkinglas' Foot, 129

Regiments (Scottish), (cont.)
Campbell of Lawers' Foot,
74, 91, 92, 93–6, 98–9, 100,
147–8, 172–3, 205–6, 221
n. 20 and n. 23, 224 n. 3, 226
n. 7
Carnegie's Foot, 225 n. 13
Carr's Horse, *see* Kerr's Horse
Earl of Cassillis' Foot, 47, 72,
103, 104, 107, 116, 223 n. 7
Earl of Cassillis' Horse, 151, 208
Lord Chancellor's Foot
(Loudoun's), 32, 44, 47, 49,
72, 87, 91, 98, 100, 223 n. 7
Cochrane's Foot, 212 n. 26
Coupar's Foot, 41, 47, 72, 121,
123, 223 n. 13
Craig of Riccarton's Horse,
208
Cranstoun's Foot, 72
Cullace' Irish Troop, 147, 226
n. 6
Earl of Dalhousie's Horse, 74,
120, 121, 125
Douglas of Cavers' Foot, 225
n. 13
Douglas of Kilhead's Foot, 41,
47, 72
Douglas of Kirkness' Foot, 170,
205
Douglas of Mouswall's Foot,
206
Drummond's Foot, 225 n. 13
Dudhope's (Baillie's) Foot, 47,
49, 218 n. 6
Earl of Dumfries' Foot, 225
n. 13
Earl of Dunfermline's Foot, 47,
72
Earl Marischal's Foot, 36, 41,
72, 209 n. 10, 214 n. 12
Edinburgh Militia, 4, 209 n. 6
Earl of Eglinton's Horse, 45,
49, 213 n. 10
Elcho's Foot, 60, 63–4, 68, 104,
107
Erskine of Scotscraig's Foot, 47,
49, 218 n. 6
Erskine of Scotscraig's Horse,
208
Farquharson of Inverey's Foot,
105, 116
Farquharson of Monaltrie's
Foot, 22, 24–6, 55, 74, 82

Findlater's Foot, 87, 91–2,
100–1, 221 n. 21
Master of Forbes' Foot, 105,
152, 206
Master of Forbes' Horse, 208
Forbes of Craigievar's Horse,
74, 105, 107
Forbes of Leslie's Foot, 206
Forbes of Millbuie's Foot, 87,
125, 126
Fraser of Lovat's Foot, 152,
174, 206–7
Fraser of Philorth's Firelocks,
225 n. 13
Fraser's Dragoons, 16, 36, 40,
44, 50, 121, 125
Earl of Glencairn's Foot, 102,
104, 107, 116, 223 n. 7
Gordon of Monymore's Foot,
89, 91, 94, 105
Lord Gordon's (Lumsden's)
Foot, 38, 47, 209 n. 10, 214
n. 21
Lord Gordon's Horse, 63, 74,
82, 85, 107
Nathaniel Gordon's Horse, 65,
67, 122
Graham of Inchbrackie's Foot,
59–60, 61, 74, 77, 80, 82,
108, 125, 216 n. 24
Grant of Freuchie's Foot, 82, 92
Grant's Company, 26
Sir John Grey's Foot, 225 n. 13
Master of Gray's Foot, 188, 190
Haldane of Gleneagles' Foot,
173, 205
Halkett's Horse, 74, 87, 92,
105, 107, 147, 156–7, 180,
208
Duke of Hamilton's Foot, 225
n. 13
Sir Alexander Hamilton's Foot,
see General of the Artillery's
Foot
Sir Frederick Hamilton's Horse,
74
Hay of Muriefauld's Foot, 64
Hepburn of Waughton's Foot,
38, 47, 72
Holburne's Foot, 129, 151,
188, 207, 224 n. 7
Home of Aytoun's Foot, 72
Home of Wedderburn's Foot,
41, 72–3, 151, 174, 206

Robert Home's Foot, 113–14,
115, 116, 225 n. 13
Hurry's Dragoons, 87, 92
Innes' Foot, 174, 206
Alexander Keith's Horse, 74, 77
George Keith's Foot, 225 n. 13
Keith of Clackriach's Foot, 64
Earl of Kellie's Foot, 225 n. 13
Kenmure's Foot, 125, 223 n. 23
Lord Ker's Foot, 30
Ker of Greenhead's Foot, 151,
174, 206
Kerr's Horse, 147, 156, 180,
208
Kilpont's Foot, 59–60, 65
Kirkcudbright's Dragoons, 151,
159, 180, 207
Kirkcudbright's Horse, 40, 121,
125
Laghtnan's (Irish) Foot, 78,
80, 89, 91, 105, 116, 122,
199–200
Earl of Lanark's Foot, 104, 107
Earl of Lauderdale's Foot, 113,
115, 116
Earl of Loudoun's Foot, *see*
Lord Chancellor's Foot
Ludovick Leslie's Foot, 129,
224 n. 2
David Leslie's Horse, 121, 207
Earl of Leven's Horse, 32, 40
121, 207, 212 n. 23
Lindsay of Edzell's Foot,
151–2, 174, 206
Earl of Lindsay's Foot, 32,
38–9, 44, 47, 49, 113, 115,
116
Earl of Livingston's Foot, 47,
72–3
Earl of Lothian's Foot, 30, 44,
57, 74, 77, 87, 91, 100
Lumsden's Foot, 205, 218 n. 6
MacDonalds of Clanranald, 78
MacDonalds of Glencoe, 78
MacDonalds of Glengarry, 78,
113
MacDonalds of Keppoch, 59
Macleans of Duart, 188–90
MacPhersons of Cluny, 59
Maitland's Foot, 47, 49
Mauchline's Horse, 151, 208
Maule's Foot, 225 n. 13
McDermott's (Irish) Foot, 80,
197–8, 219 n. 19

Regiments (Scottish), (cont.)
Middleton's Horse, 121, 124
Monro's Foot, 212 n. 26
Lord Montgomery's Horse, 121, 124, 125, 207
Robin Montgomerie's Horse, 125, 156
Earl of Moray's Foot, 79, 104, 107, 125
O'Cahan's (Irish) Foot, 65, 80, 105, 116, 122, 198–9, 219 n. 19
Ogilvie's Horse, 65, 67, 78, 82
Oliphant of Gask's Foot, 41
Perth Militia, 60
Pitscottie's Foot, 129, 151, 174, 206
Preston of Valleyfield's Foot, 173, 205
Rae's (Edinburgh) Foot, 38, 47, 72
Ramsay's Horse, 32, 70, 74–6
Earl of Roxburgh's Foot, 225 n. 13
Ruthven of Freeland's Foot, 205–6
Scots Guards, 228 n. 1
Scott's Foot, 129
Scott's Horse, 188, 208
Earl of Seaforth's Levies, 10, 92
Sinclair's Foot, 57, 72, 212 n. 26, 213 n. 1
Alexander Stewart's (Edinburgh) Foot, 151, 174, 207
William Stewart's Foot, 72, 125, 223 n. 23
William Stewart's Horse, 168, 208
Stewarts of Appin, 78
Strachan's Horse, 147, 180, 208
Strathbogie Regiment, 21–2, 25, 26, 28, 74, 82, 85, 100, 105
Earl of Sutherland's Levies, 92, 95

Earl of Tullibardine's Foot, 72, 225 n. 13
Turner's Foot, 224 n. 7, 225 n. 13
Udny's Foot, 64
Wauchope of Niddrie's Foot, 72
Wemyss' Foot, *see* General of the Artillery's Foot
Wood of Balbegno's Foot, 173
Master of Yester's Foot, 8, 44, 47, 72, 225 n. 13
Rhunahoarine Point (battle), 130
Ripon, Treaty of, 33
Rollo, Sir William, 56, 65, 67, 118
Ross, David, of Balnagowan, 147–8
Ross, Major William, 148
Roughe, Lieut.-Col. John, 79
Rutherford, Capt. Thomas, 57, 216 n. 10
Ruthven, Patrick, Lord Ettrick, 29
Ruthven of Freeland, Sir Thomas, 205–6

Scott, James, of Rossie, 60–2
Seaforth, Earl of, *see* Mackenzie, George
Selby (battle), 45
Selkirk, 120–3
Seton, John, of Pitmeddan, 27
Shieldfield Fort (battle), 38–9
Solemn League and Covenant, 35
South Shields Fort (battle), 42–3
Stanley, James, Earl of Derby, 191
Stewart, Col. Alexander, 174
Stewart, Lieut.-Col. Henry, 226 n. 5
Stewart, John, Earl of Traquair, 29, 223 n. 11
Stewart, Col. William, 39, 42–3, 168
Stirling, 57, 110, 117, 125,

141–2, 144, 175–6, 177, 179, 183, 190, 191, 193
Stonehaven, 24–5
Strachan, Col. Archibald, 147–8, 151–2, 168, 170, 172, 176, 178–9, 181
Strathbogie, 21, 76, 77, 102, 124, 211 n. 7
Sunderland, 41, 57–8, 70
Sutherland, Sir Alexander, of Duffus, 152
Sutherland, Earl of, 87, 146
Sydenham, Major John, 183

Tain, 147
Thornhaugh, Col. Francis, 138
Tibbermore (battle), 59–62, 201
Torwood, 183–4
Towie Barclay Castle, 20
Turner, James, 57, 132, 134–5, 136, 138, 139, 140, 190, 224 n. 7
Turriff, 19–22, 77, 124
Tyldesley, Sir Thomas, 140–1, 230 n. 25
Tynemouth Castle, 32, 39, 42, 73

Udny, John, of Udny, 63–4

Van Druschke, Major-Gen. Jonas, 138

Wallace of Auchans, James, 228 n. 1
Watkinson, Capt. George, 156–7
Wemyss, David, Lord Elcho, 60–2, 111–12
Wemyss, Lieut.-Col. David, 170
Wemyss, James, 14, 184
Wentworth, Thomas, Earl of Strafford, 17–18, 31
Western Association, 178–9
Whiggamore Raid, 141
Wigan, 138–9, 191
Winwick (battle), 139–40
Worcester (battle), 191–3